Wakefield Press

AFTER THE FALL

Michael Delahaye is an independent television producer and occasional print journalist. He is a former BBC TV news reporter, correspondent and documentary producer. As a senior media consultant for the Thomson Foundation UK and Internews Network US, he has worked extensively across the former Soviet Union. Since 2004, he has trained journalists for the Al Jazeera Satellite Channel in Qatar, Bosnia and the US.

He is the author of three thrillers commercially published in the UK, US and Japan.

Born and educated in England, a graduate of Van Mildert College, Durham University, he is based in Adelaide, Australia, after many years living in France and the UK.

For more details, please refer to Michael's professional website: www.michaeldelahaye.com

BY THE SAME AUTHOR

The Sale of Lot 236
The Third Day (UK)
On The Third Day (US)
Stalking Horse

AFTER THE FALL

THE BATTLE TO SAVE
INDEPENDENT MEDIA IN THE
POST-SOVIET WORLD

A FOOT-SOLDIER'S STORY

MICHAEL DELAHAYE

Wakefield
Press

Wakefield Press
16 Rose Street
Mile End
South Australia 5031
www.wakefieldpress.com.au

First published 2026

Supported by a grant from the Government of South Australia.

Edited by Roger Zubrinich
Designed and typeset by Debora Souza, Greenhill Publishing
    and Jesse Pollard, Wakefield Press
Author's photo by Andrea Kloeden
Historical maps by Bernard Haseloff

ISBN 978 1 92338 825 3

A catalogue record for this
book is available from the
National Library of Australia

CORIOLE
McLAREN VALE

Wakefield Press thanks
Coriole Vineyards for
continued support

For Rachel,
my daughter and fellow toiler
in the verbal vineyard

+ ———————— +

*First they came for the journalists and I did not speak
out because I was not a journalist. We have no idea what
they did after that.*

– **Arleen Myers Fields'** reworking of Martin Niemöller's quote

CONTENTS

Bering Sea

ARCTIC OCEAN

RUSSIA

ESTONIA
RUSSIA LATVIA
LITHUANIA
BELARUS
MOLDOVA
UKRAINE
Black Sea
GEORGIA
ARMENIA
AZERBAIJAN
Caspian Sea
KAZAKHSTAN
Aral Sea
Lake Baikal
TURKMENISTAN
UZBEKISTAN
TAJIKISTAN
KYRGYZSTAN

The Soviet Union

The Russian Federation

The South Caucasus

AUTHOR'S NOTE

This is not an academic treatise on journalism. Rather, it is first-person reportage – heavy on anecdote, not always chronological and occasionally breaking off to explain an aspect of television journalism to inform the narrative.

Part travelogue, part confessional, it is a story about transition: that of the former Soviet countries from communism to democracy and capitalism, and my own from television reporter/producer to international broadcast consultant.

Although I was working for and paid by the Thomson Foundation UK throughout my many 'tours of duty', I was on most occasions dependent on the facilities and staff of Thomson's American partner, Internews Network US. I should therefore make clear that the views I express here do not necessarily reflect those of either Thomson or Internews.

Any errors are mine alone. The verbal exchanges I quote are mostly from contemporaneous notes, although in some cases I have recreated them from memory.

In the text that follows, I have changed some names. I have indicated this by putting the first mention in inverted commas. I have also, though rarely, changed a person's physical details or location. In all cases, this is to spare individuals reputational damage and/or possible retribution.

Finally, any monetary figures that appear in dollars are US dollars.

M.D. Adelaide, 2026

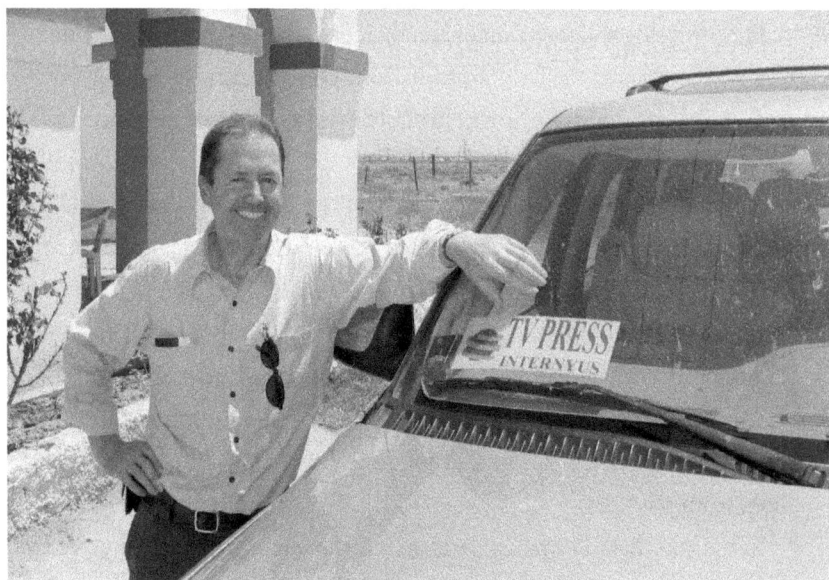

Azerbaijan, early days.

*'You don't realise how much you know. It's just a matter of
unpacking all the knowledge you've acquired over the years.'*

PROLOGUE

I'm sitting in a restaurant in Russia's 'Wild East'. Opposite is my host, whom I'll call 'Sergei'. Between us is a plate of blini, piled with sour cream and caviar.

Sergei is not rich enough to be described as an oligarch or even a mini-garch, but he still qualifies as a product of the era ushered in by President Boris Yeltsin, champion of democracy and promoter of unbridled, let-rip capitalism. In short, Sergei is an archetypal New Russian – a likeable chancer in his smart jacket and Italian shoes, his shirt cuff turned up to reveal a $5000 watch. He also owns a television station with a potential audience of a million viewers. Which is why I've spent the last week doing a 'production and performance' audit in my role as a broadcast consultant funded by the British and American governments. All in the cause of supporting independent journalism in post-Soviet Russia, and beyond.

Glancing through the window to my right, I glimpse Sergei's gleaming top-of-the-range German motor. A question resurfaces which I've been asking myself all week. Where has his money come from? City TV stations like Sergei's tend to be set up by business consortiums, not by individuals. Sure, you can rent a building cheaply enough but you still have to equip it with all the necessary technology – and that costs.

Sergei gives a sheepish grin. 'Actually, I was a bank manager.'

A bank manager making enough to set up a TV station? There is only one scenario I can imagine and in a sense I am right, except that it turns out Sergei robbed his employers in a way so subtle that it left no trace. You could even argue there was no actual loss; that it was indeed 'a victimless crime'.

In 1992, following the collapse of the Soviet Union the previous year, the Bank of Russia gave the national currency a makeover. Part of this involved withdrawing from circulation the old Soviet kopek coins bearing, rather too prominently, the Cyrillic letters CCCP, the initials of the former USSR. Bank managers across the country were duly instructed to exchange them for their equivalent in the new currency. Sergei's branch was chosen as the central collection point for his region.

As numismatists will know, it occasionally happens that the intrinsic value of a coin will exceed its face value because of global fluctuations in metal prices. Sergei realised that this was the case with the higher denomination kopeks he had taken in, containing as they did copper, zinc and, most valuable, nickel.

Whether he electronically transferred to the Bank of Russia's Moscow HQ the equivalent of the coins' face value to cover the fact that they never arrived at the smelter, or whether in the freewheeling climate of Yeltsin's Russia nobody cared so long as the paperwork balanced, the upshot was that he loaded the coins – tens of tons of them – into a small fleet of trucks and had them driven to the Chinese border. After some haggling, he came away with a tidy sum. Enough to start his own television station.

What is remarkable about Sergei's story is less the story itself than the fact that at the time it was regarded as nothing out of the ordinary.

1.

AT THE PUSH OF A BUTTON

Turning points in life come in unexpected ways and many forms. In my case, it was a small flashing red light.

One Saturday evening in April 1998, my wife and I were guests at a dinner party. My mood was less than convivial. For weeks I had been facing something I had never experienced – unemployment. After nearly thirty years working for the BBC, with the occasional break, my latest contract was due to run out in a few days and, despite some half-hearted begging letters, I hadn't got so much as a 'Why don't you drop by for a chat?'.

From the moment I had entered the job market, I had led a charmed life. Something had always turned up or just come my way. Weeks after leaving university, I had blagged my way into a teaching job with the British Institute in Florence despite my entire Italian vocabulary consisting of *per favore* and *grazie*. Two years later, back in the UK, I had got myself on to the BBC's first Graduate News Trainee Scheme before it had even been launched. Then, over the next five years, I had been fast-tracked through the corporation: reporter, presenter, correspondent. It made for an impressive CV.

My confidence – more accurately, my complacency – in my professional worth had been bolstered by the fact that, thanks to my working wife being prepared to take over the bread-winning role in exchange for my becoming a house husband, I had taken time out from the BBC to write three thrillers and get them published.

By the late 1990s, back in the bosom of the corporation, I was senior reporter and deputy editor of the BBC's weekly current affairs slot for London and the south-east of England on an annually renewed rolling contract. Then, abruptly, the rolling stopped. There had been another round of salami cuts and the program that had originally run for nine months of the year was to be reduced to five. Its new editor – a man with whom I'd had an increasingly testy relationship – got evident pleasure from dispensing some tough love. My contract would not be renewed but he would always be open to any one-off program ideas I might wish to offer . . . pause . . . as a freelancer. In a moment of bridge-burning hubris, I told him not to hold his breath.

The future could hardly have looked bleaker.

My mood at that evening's dinner party had not been improved by our host, a successful property developer with whom years earlier I had shared a bachelor flat in London's Notting Hill. With what was no doubt genuine concern, he enquired what I intended to do if nothing came up. And, Heaven knows, he could well sympathise, having had his own ups and downs over the years! It must be so worrying – and not just for me but no less so for Anni, my wife. The mortgage, the school fees, the bills . . . The more I tried to move the conversation on, the longer the empathetic evisceration continued.

If I had felt undervalued when we left home, by the time we returned I was utterly worthless. Opening the front door, I noticed the flashing red light on the Ansafone. I pressed the playback button.

The voice, deep and mellifluous, was familiar – that of Ian Masters, a former BBC continuity announcer whom I had got to know decades earlier when, as a BBC news trainee, I had been seconded to the Manchester newsroom. I had heard from various sources that, after rising through the managerial ranks, he had left the corporation and was now the broadcasting controller of the Thomson Foundation, a non-profit organisation that sent consultants, mostly ex-BBC, around the world to train press, radio and television journalists in what were euphemistically called 'emerging democracies'. I had sent him a letter six months earlier when I sensed the way the wind was blowing, coyly indicating that I might be available if he ever needed my services. There had been an acknowledgement but nothing more.

But now he wanted me to phone him, urgently, on a Saturday evening. It was nearly midnight. Desperation, fuelled by paranoia, told me that if I didn't respond there and then, he would be dialling the next number on the list. If he hadn't already.

He picked up on the third ring. It was good to hear from me. What was I doing at the moment?

'Oh, a number of irons in the fire,' I replied, failing to add, 'all of them cold.'

'But right now?'

'Well, nothing immediately.'

'So you're available.'

'Well, put like that. What did you have in mind?'

'To go to Russia.'

I mentally gulped. 'How long for?'

'A couple of months, maybe more. Depends.' He explained that a Thomson Foundation consultant working there had fallen ill, been medevacked out and a replacement was needed . . . *now*.

'So when are we talking about?'

'As soon as we can get you a visa. Days, not weeks.'

I pointed out that, despite a few decades' experience as a television journalist, I had never acted as a consultant and had not a clue what it entailed.

'Oh, you'll pick it up,' came the airy response. 'You don't realise how much you know. It's just a matter of unpacking all the knowledge you've acquired over the years.'

And so, overnight, at the push of a button just days before the run-out of my BBC contract, I became an 'international broadcast consultant', a foot-soldier in the West's attempt to ensure free, independent media across the former Soviet Union.

+——————+

My starting date, April 1998, was nearly a decade after the fall of the Berlin Wall. In Russia and the fourteen other former Soviet republics, there was one word on everybody's lips: *perekhod*. Transition. From communism to capitalism, from a centralised to a market economy, from totalitarianism to democracy and – the particular focus of what was going to be my activity – from the state-controlled dissemination of information to public service broadcasting, with the many small independent TV stations out in the regions to ensure plurality.

Less than a week after the midnight call I checked in at Heathrow's Terminal 2, bound for Sheremetyevo Airport, Moscow. I felt like a travelling salesman of the 1950s except that, instead of brushes and dishcloths, my bulging case contained a dozen VHS cassettes and a box file of human rights material that included a neatly folded, full-size copy of Magna Carta.

2.

WELCOME TO MOSCOW

There's a lot to be said for going late in life to places you've always known but never visited. The first time only happens once; leaving it to the maturity of middle age sharpens both appreciation and observation. I was thirty-two when I first saw America. On this, my first visit to Russia, I was fifty-two.

Yet I'd known the Russian people all my life because for most of it they were going to kill me. Like all British baby boomers born shortly after the Second World War and into the Cold War, I'd spent my formative years under an imagined cloud, mushroom shaped and lethal; a cloud that any day could become terrifyingly real. Not just any day but possibly in the next *four minutes*; this being the time between the detection of a Soviet nuclear missile and its hitting the UK. The cloud was the leitmotif of my youth. Every morning as I left for school, I would scan the headline of the newspaper wedged into our garden gate, pulse racing, to assess how close we might be to nuclear annihilation.

The closest came one October evening in 1962. A Friday.

As US warships enforced a blockade around Cuba to stop Soviet military supplies joining the nuclear missiles already deployed there, my father stood with his back to the fireplace and, in a barely audible whisper, said, 'This is it.' The fact that he was by nature an unemotional man made his utterance the more chilling. My teenage schoolfriends had arranged a party for the next evening, Saturday. There were no phone calls to discuss a change of plan. We'd be dust.

Decades later when asked to say 'something from the soul' (the soul, I was to discover, featured largely in Russian vocabulary) to a group of Siberian journalists, I started with the words, 'For most of my life, you have been the enemy'. Their reaction was equal and opposite: for most of their lives they had been told to think of me, us in the West, as the enemy.

To an extent, the old clichés are right; irrespective of our nationality we are all the same under the skin. We all have hopes, fears, loves, ambitions and disappointments. But the Russians, I would discover, differed in some key respects. The ones I would work with were more than just intelligent and educated; they were smart. Damned smart. They were also cultured. Communism may have suppressed religion – at least its public observance – but not culture.

Before I went to Moscow a friend had told me you could always tell an American from a Russian in the street: an American would walk along plugged into a Sony Walkman whereas a Russian would be reading a book. Too neat a distinction to be true, I thought, and anyway in the case of the Russian downright dangerous. But then on my second day in Moscow I saw a young woman striding along with an open paperback held out before her like a cowcatcher. To complete the image, she was passing the Lenin Library beneath the seated statue of Fyodor Dostoevsky.

+————+

Moscow was both the city of my preconceptions – and not. All the landmarks were there like pop-up postcards: Red Square, the Lenin Mausoleum, St Basil's Cathedral, the Kremlin, surrounded by the ring of Stalin-era wedding cake skyscrapers. But they were obscured by the clutter of capitalism: garish advertising hoardings, huge video screens promoting such consumer delights as TIDE washing powder. As I walked down iconic Tverskaya Street and looked toward the Kremlin, I had to peer through line after line of commercial bunting stretched across the road. This was the brash new capitalist Russia of Boris Yeltsin and the oligarchs.

Worse, because they were more permanent, were the Disneyesque statues planted in Alexander Garden beneath the Kremlin walls and elsewhere around the city centre; the works of Moscow Mayor Luzhkov's favourite sculptor, Zurab Tsereteli. The most eye-catching, in the sense that there was no avoiding it, was a grotesque 98-metre-high monument to Peter the Great at the point where the Moscow River meets the Vodootvodny Canal. Peter himself, while admittedly physically 'great' in real life (reputedly two metres tall), is as big as the boat on which he is standing.

The more I saw of post-Soviet Moscow, the more I realised that the sinister monochrome austerity I had always found perversely thrilling from countless news reports, documentaries, movies and, not least, le Carré novels, was already history. Perhaps, following the example of the producers of Alan Bennett's television drama *An Englishman Abroad,* I should have gone to Glasgow or Dundee to capture the authentic Moscow of Soviet times. Instead, I devised another, more impressionistic, stratagem: a personal *son et lumière* show.

Late one night I walked down to Red Square. Uncomfortably conscious of the philistine American with his Walkman, I had recorded on to my Sony MiniDisc the Red Army Choir singing the Soviet National Anthem, *Soyuz Nerushimi*; music I had for decades associated with Russia because it was played so often at Olympic medal ceremonies. What I did next was, frankly, a bit weird.

The main buildings were dramatically up lit, but the square itself was deserted. The goose-stepping guards outside the Lenin Mausoleum had been removed years earlier. I stood alone in the middle of the vast cobbled expanse where tanks and missiles were still paraded on significant anniversaries, midway between the Lenin Mausoleum and the GUM department store, facing St Basil's onion-topped cathedral at the far end, and played the anthem through my earphones at full blast.

> *Unbreakable Union of freeborn Republics,*
> *Great Russia has welded forever to stand.*
> *Created in struggle by will of the people,*
> *United and mighty, our Soviet land!*

Standing there with the music filling my skull, acutely conscious of where I stood and all it represented – a place I had never thought I would see, a place that crystalised everything I had feared as a child and adolescent – was probably as close as I will come to an out-of-body experience. Actuality merged with memory, and back again. It was my 'Midnight in Moscow' moment, both exultation and exorcism. Not only is the anthem one of the most stirring ever composed but, like no other, it conveys that Soviet sense of common, collective purpose, of 'all for one and one for all'. It is a hymn to a magnificent idea; an idea that was quickly corrupted and ultimately failed, but no less magnificent for that. Only the French *Marseillaise* and the European Anthem, the *Ode to Joy* from Beethoven's Ninth, can stand comparison.

I had been booked into the Hotel Belgrad on Smolenskaya Square, right opposite one of Stalin's neo-Gothic *vysotki* high-rises, the Ministry of Foreign Affairs. Before I left the UK, a Moscow correspondent during the 1980s had told me, if I ever found myself near the building, to count seven floors up and offer a short prayer of thanks. On that floor had been the office of Eduard Shevardnadze, the Soviet foreign minister who, along with Mikhail Gorbachev, had ended the Cold War. Gorbachev and Ronald Reagan had got the credit but it had been the remarkable partnership between Shevardnadze and US Secretary of State, James Baker, which had delivered the peace.

As would be the pattern over the next six years when working in former Soviet countries, I was using the facilities of Internews Network, the US non-governmental organisation which operated in partnership with my UK employers, the Thomson Foundation. Looked at in business terms, such NGOs (as they were usually abbreviated) were free-standing apexes. Since they were non-profit, their existence depended not on shareholders or investors but on a regular stream of grants from governments and philanthropists. The job of an NGO, its raison d'être, was to channel this 'income' into projects consistent with its stated aims while covering its operating costs. The Thomson Foundation was mostly funded by the British Foreign Office and DfID, the UK Government's Department for International Development, while Internews' work in the former Soviet Union was largely dependent on the U.S. Agency for International Development (USAID).

Internews Russia's office was a couple of kilometres from the Hotel Belgrad – a twenty-minute walk along the Old Arbat.

As I entered the courtyard of number 8 Nikitsky Bulvar, an elaborate two-tone eighteenth century building with rococo swags and pilasters announced itself as DOM ZHURNALISTA – House of the Journalist. (While in the sixth form at school, I had tried to teach myself Russian. If nothing else, the Cyrillic alphabet had stuck.) A couple of old guys sat in a corner of the yard playing chess, a half-empty bottle of vodka between them. I pushed open the heavy front door and was hit by the smell of boiled cabbage from the ground floor canteen. It followed me all the way up the stone staircase and would become comfortingly familiar over the next six years.

The Internews office occupied the top floor. It had low ceilings and little natural light. I would discover later that this was one of the buildings, this very floor allegedly, where the poet Pushkin had conducted one of his many amorous liaisons, although given his priapic reputation, the same might have been said of half the buildings in Moscow.

During my time with the BBC, I must have worked in a dozen newsrooms and production offices, and they all shared the same bland corporate ambiance – grey desks, beige monitors, slatted blinds, acoustic ceiling tiles and industrial-grade flooring. Add to that the ubiquitous strip lights that rendered everything two-dimensional.

By contrast, Internews' Moscow office was a mysterious world of shadow, depth and discovery, the effect enhanced by all the desks, cupboards and bookcases being a glossy black. Around me people spoke both Russian and English, sometimes switching mid-sentence. At the back there was access to a large, improvised roof terrace where in summer you could sit out and shoot the breeze. Most of the photos I have from that time seem to have been taken there, with colleagues invariably holding a cigarette or a beer, or both. Time and again, Russians would quote me the old saw that 'the man who neither smokes nor drinks will die healthy'. As a philosophy of life, it's very Russian with its fate-baiting bravado. (There was the same devil-may-care attitude to seat belts. Try as a risk-averse Westerner to disentangle a belt that had clearly never been used and you'd be accused of doubting the driver's competence: 'Do you wear a parachute on a plane?') It's relevant to add that Russian male life expectancy at the time was 58.

The office atmosphere was refreshingly collegiate, with none of the rivalry and occasional bitchiness of so many other media workplaces I had known. On my first day I had been struck by the opened tins of sweets and biscuits on every other desk which anybody could, and did, dip into as they passed. When I commented on it, I was told they were brought in as gifts by foreign consultants. (Note to self: next visit spend more time in Duty Free.)

The same spirit of generosity was evident out on the streets. A smoker would stop another smoker, a total stranger, and ask not for a light but a cigarette – which would be given without hesitation. In the West we would call it bumming, with an implication of begging on one side, charity on the other. Here it was just a normal interaction. Perhaps, I speculated, it was a hangover from Soviet times when everything belonged to the state and all comrades were equal or, more accurately, equally poor.

That said, such exchanges could also have a commercial element. Instead of hailing a taxi, it was common to flag down any passing car (though generally avoiding Mercs, Audis and BMWs), negotiate a fee within ten seconds . . . and jump in. I tried it myself. Mightily pleased at having survived this rite of passage, I mentioned it casually to a Russian colleague. When I told him how much I'd paid, he snorted. 'You could have hired a stretched limo for that!'

Doubtless aware how foreigners could be taken for a ride, metaphorically as well as literally, Internews offices used to issue visiting consultants with a local information manual that was regularly updated. This covered everything from greetings – shake, hug, kiss and, if the last, how many – to recommended eateries and their prices. There would sometimes also be warnings of situations to avoid which varied according to the country. In some, for example, you could safely use unofficial money changers on the street to convert your per diem dollars; in others you risked being stung by a government agent provocateur.

In Moscow at the time there was one scam that many a hapless Westerner fell for and was doubtless traumatised by. I was targeted only once and, thanks to being forewarned, avoided the consequences. It was an elaborate form of street theatre with its own list of dramatis personae.

Enter, stage left, an unsuspecting Westerner walking along a street, typically one with few people in it. You are that Westerner, the leading actor in this unfolding drama and, though you might not realise it, your clothes, body language and inane grin shout your identity to every local.

You are minding your own business, taking in the surroundings, when you notice a well-dressed individual ahead of you drop something, apparently by accident. Being a public-spirited foreigner, you rush to pick up the item so you can give it back. But it turns out that this isn't just 'something'; it's a tight roll of $100 bills. A thousand dollars' worth? Perhaps two thousand? All the more reason to ensure its return to its rightful owner.

His first reaction is overwhelming gratitude. *How stupid of me! How honest of you!* You may not understand Russian but you get the gist. As he is saying this, he is flicking through the dollar bills. In an instant his demeanour changes and he starts shouting at you and anyone within earshot. Verbal abuse turns to a threat of physical violence.

At this point, seemingly from nowhere, a pair of accomplices appear and forcibly intervene. While one keeps your potential attacker at bay, the other, an English speaker as luck would have it, moves you, by now shaken, to one side. He explains that the man is claiming you peeled off some notes before returning the roll to him. Bad enough. Worse, your new-found friend is sorry to have to tell you but this is a particularly nasty character (possible hints of the Chechen Mafia) and not to be crossed if you value your life. *Trust me, I know what his type are capable of.*

By now a quivering wreck, you'll do anything to extricate yourself from the situation. That you are innocent is beside the point. Your protector, an experienced player of many roles, now morphs into the sympathetic negotiator. He's on your side. Of course, the thug is mistaken in thinking you've taken his money but the only way to appease him is to hand over whatever cash you've got on you. Just empty your wallet. A couple of hundred dollars or its rouble equivalent should do it. And, if you haven't enough, there's one of those new cash dispensers round the corner. It really is your lucky day!

The one time I was targeted, south of the river, I saw the roll of dollars drop and, giving it a wide berth, walked briskly on. Quick to improvise, one of the accomplices scooped it up himself and, catching up with me, waved it in my face with the suggestion, in English, that we should split it. This was evidently an improvisation and I was half-tempted to see how it would play out. Instead, I responded in voluble Italian that I didn't understand a word he was saying and managed to shake him off.

I was starting to get the hang of the place. But just as I was settling into the Internews office, the director, a formidable Armenian woman, reminded me that this was my base, not my workplace. I was awaited 800 kilometres east in Kazan, the capital of Tatarstan, to replace that other consultant who had been taken ill and flown home. There was work to do.

3.

THE MEDIA LANDSCAPE

In 1998 television in Russia was in a state of flux. Put more positively, it was evolving. Its role in society, the part it would play in democracy, while being actively debated, had yet to be defined. To an outsider, particularly one like me brought in to help, the media landscape could be baffling.

There were the national networks: the two Kremlin-supporting 'state' channels, ORT and RTR, and the popular commercial channel, NTV. But out in the provinces there was a plethora of independent stations of all sizes. Some 600 of them, spread like a rash across the map. Now, Russia is big with no fewer than eleven time zones, but 600 regional TV stations? The population at the time, around 148 million, was two-and-a-half times that of the UK's 58 million, yet we in Britain had roughly a dozen independent regional television companies. How on earth did all these Russian stations survive?

No less intriguing was how they had come about in the first place.

Russians, as already noted, are smart. Part of that smartness is ingenuity and resourcefulness, well-honed during the seven decades of working through and around the Soviet system. In the late 1950s, the Soviet leader Nikita Khrushchev pushed through an ambitious, country-wide, housing plan. The result, still to be seen today, was large, characterless estates of what quickly came to be known as *khrushchevki*. These were prefabricated blocks of apartments intended to last no more than twenty-five years. Three to five storeys high, with the architectural élan of a stack of shipping containers, they were the most basic of accommodation and, by Western standards, incredibly cramped. And they had no lifts.

As I soon saw for myself, the two-room apartments would often have to house three generations of a family, with sofas doubling as beds and vice-versa. To save space, the bath was barely four feet long – what we would call a 'hip-bath' – and the kitchen a sink and tap tucked into a corner. The rationale was that when socialism matured into full-blown communism, Soviet man would eat in impressive state canteens, presumably freeing Soviet woman from cooking and dishwashing. More fortunate residents had a balcony that in many cases they would enclose with boards and Perspex to provide another room, if only for storage.

In one respect though, the *khrushchevki* were more technically advanced than their Western tower block counterparts in that each had a large master antenna mounted on the flat roof to pick up terrestrial TV signals. The cable from it was split and would relay the signal, via an internal network, to every television set in every apartment within the building. This was less an example of state munificence – an equivalent of the BBC's role to inform, educate and entertain – than a calculated means of piping propaganda into every Soviet living room. Religion, Karl Marx once observed, was the opium of the people. Television performed a similar role. It was joked that state TV's huge Ostankino transmitter tower in north Moscow, the world's tallest freestanding structure when built in the 1960s, was the hypodermic that inoculated the masses.

As the Soviet Union started to crumble under Mikhail Gorbachev, the words 'an internal network' assumed a new significance.

Entrepreneurial types with a technical bent realised that, in place of state propaganda, there was the possibility of using the egalitarian wiring within their apartment blocks to apply the new capitalist principle of supply and demand. Fortuitously, this coincided with the appearance of video cassette recorder/players (VCRs), both Soviet-made and illegally imported foreign models, together with pirated or smuggled tapes of Western movies, notably Hollywood blockbusters. Once our entrepreneurs had hardwired a VCR into the internal network, it was a simple matter to go knocking on everyone's door and ask if, for a few roubles, they would like to watch the latest iteration of Rambo or, if more to their taste, perhaps a romcom, albeit with a Russian voice-over that, with the original audio turned down, translated the words of all the characters, irrespective of sex, age or emotion, in a single unsynchronised male monotone. (The effect was beyond comical. Instead of meeting Sally, Harry just mumbled to himself for an hour and a half.)

The next step was to improvise a studio requiring nothing more complex than a camcorder and a curtain as a backdrop for the amateur 'continuity announcer', and wire that too into the system. Within no time, our budding entrepreneur had a schedule, an appreciative audience, a regular income stream and, by the most basic of definitions, a cable television network. Transmission might still be within the block, but it required no great initiative to go to the next level: buy a small transmitter (a one kilowatt model was more than adequate) and beam material to the neighbouring blocks. In fact, to the entire estate. With one bound, our station-owner had graduated to a terrestrial broadcaster.[1]

It's hard to convey the ethos of the Yeltsin era. Under Gorbachev and the relaxation that came with *glasnost* (openness) and *perestroika* (restructuring), the population had responded like prisoners serving life terms presented with a half-open door. They had prodded it, at first tentatively, expecting it at any moment to slam shut, and when it didn't, pushed with more force until in disbelief they found themselves outside the cell. With Yeltsin and his program of unfettered capitalism came the realisation that, with no institutional framework to direct and constrain their daily lives, they themselves had to take control. For many, having been conditioned their entire lives by the agencies of a repressive state, the new freedom was profoundly unsettling, inducing a form of anxiety that the psychologist Erich Fromm identified in his 1941 work, *The Fear of Freedom*.[2]

But for others the licence it offered was intoxicating. There was a sense that everything was experimental – democracy and capitalism most of all – and, as the oligarchs would show, ripe for exploitation. The old Soviet state had always been regarded as fair game, summed up in the saying, 'They pretend to pay us and we pretend to work'. But this was a whole new territory, rich in possibilities, and you didn't have to be an oligarch to make what in Soviet times would have been an unimaginable fortune.[3]

So it was that, under Boris Yeltsin, many of the hundreds of independent television stations grew into serious enterprises that no longer operated out of bedrooms in apartment blocks but were now housed in their own dedicated, if often decrepit, premises. Sometimes the only giveaway was a fifteen-metre transmitter sprouting out of the roof.

Gone were the days of collecting payment door-to-door. The challenge now was to find a business model that would generate sufficient income to stay afloat. But that assumed output to a professional standard, preferably including a news element as viewer bait.

Having a nightly news bulletin in the schedule entailed risks. Yes, it pulled in the punters and, additionally, was a handy 'inheritance' tool that induced viewers to stay with the channel beyond the news. In many cities, a game of reverse leapfrog developed as stations strategically started their evening bulletins fifteen minutes ahead of their rivals – sometimes as little as five – to grab and keep the viewership.

But a news service could also put you on the wrong side of the authorities, whether local or national. Politics was news and news was politics. Once you decided to set aside the thirty or forty minutes for a nightly update of the day's events, there was a limit to how editorially selective you could be. If you wanted to keep your audience there would be stories that couldn't be ignored and, no matter how you reported them, one side or the other was likely to take offence . . . and possibly action.

This was where we, the Western media consultants, came in: primarily to improve the quality of the news output but also to help the stations juggle the benefits against the risks.

———

My own visits typically lasted five working days per station, the weekends being for travel between them or return to Moscow. I would invariably have an Internews fixer/interpreter with me and on occasions I would work in tandem with a fellow consultant who would advise the station bosses on budgetary matters. For the stations, it was like a visit from McKinsey & Company, the global consulting firm.

The first day I would spend working out how the station operated, both technically and editorially. Who did what? Who was answerable to whom? How was the newsroom organised (if at all)? What equipment was being used and how? I would often discover, for example, that the camera cassettes, instead of being changed after a maximum of twenty cycles as advised by the makers, had been endlessly recycled for a year or more, with the inevitable dropouts when the image and/or audio would momentarily break up.

Equally revealing would be a request to see that indispensable part of any news operation, the archive. At one station the news editor pointed to a dozen VHS cassettes on a shelf; at another, an armour-plated door swung open to reveal an Aladdin's Cave stacked to the ceiling with cans of highly flammable 35mm nitrate film from the 1930s, the property of the local municipality and a treasure trove for historians if only it could be copied before combusting.

The second day, I would sit in on the morning editorial meeting, assuming there was one, and then shadow a reporter and cameraman out on a story. It could be a revelation. Often I found it was the cameraman who directed not just himself but the story too while the reporter, typically half his age, was reduced to the status of a glove puppet. (This was not always the cameraman's fault. Many 'reporters' were sent out without even the most basic training. One of them in Yaroslavl, north-east of Moscow, confided that the previous week she had been a kindergarten teacher.) In terms of their skills, cameramen of the Soviet era were the equal of their Western counterparts but regrettably, post-collapse, many regarded their specialist knowledge as a black art to be jealously guarded, even if that meant it dying with them. The reason, it became apparent, was the fear that if they passed it on to younger, fitter colleagues, they could put themselves out of a job.

During the remaining days, I would become progressively more proactive, intervening when necessary and, following transmission of the evening bulletin, leading a post-mortem group discussion to go through the reports, one by one: what had worked, what hadn't and, crucially, to check the accuracy and objectivity of the journalism.

The real battle, though, was for hearts and minds, which every consultant faces when parachuted into alien territory.

The first day at a new station, I would be an object of curiosity. The second, the curiosity would turn to suspicion: *Do we have something to learn from this foreigner . . . or something to fear from how he might change our work practices? Or worse.* This was the suspicion which all consultants in all fields elicit: that they have been brought in not to help but to appraise; to inform (in both senses) the bosses who is worth keeping and who to let go. The suspicion was justified. Station managers often asked me for my assessment of individuals. If I thought someone was exceptional, I had no problem saying so, but generally I would politely decline, arguing that bosses knew the strengths and weaknesses of their own people far better than any drop-in outsider. Sub-text: and if they didn't, they *should.*

The third day was make or break; if I hadn't won over the workforce by the end of it, I never would.

The last hour of the last day was reserved for a meeting with the station-owner (or managing director), to present a list of observations and suggestions: in effect, a feedback report. Most bosses were appreciative and took notes but there were occasions when it was clear they knew little about their own news operations and cared even less, the station being a fashion accessory that served a purely reputational purpose. In time, I would devise 'Delahaye's Law': When the station-owner's office is bigger than its newsroom, that station has a problem.

At one station, I asked the owner why he didn't allow his reporters to appear on screen – no pieces-to-camera, no 'reverses' (when, at the end of an interview, the camera swings round to take reaction shots of the reporter that can be dropped into the edit as required). He responded with two words: star fever. Once reporters were recognised in the street, he said, they believed they were the face of the station and demanded more money. The solution was a close-up microphone held by a disembodied hand. It was a variation of the quote frequently misattributed to Stalin: 'No man, no problem'.[4]

The fact that the consultant's final report was delivered in the station-owner's office – often my first sight of it – could provide answers to questions that had been bothering me all week.

Part of my job was to check how the equipment that had been donated by Internews was being used. Arriving at one small station in southern Siberia I noted from the paperwork that, unusually, it had been given not one but two desktop computers: one for reporters to type and print out their scripts and the other, loaded with the necessary software, to manage running-orders, caption generation, autocue and other such operations. Neither computer was anywhere to be seen. The news editor claimed to have no knowledge of them, while the reporters were writing their scripts using torn-off scraps of paper and pencil stubs. After five days of asking and searching, I was no wiser.

Come the afternoon of the last day, I was shown into the owner's well-appointed office to deliver my report. There in pride of place on his desk was one of the Internews computers, complete with screen and keyboard. Inert. Did he find it useful? I asked. His evasive response followed by further questions and further evasion told me all I needed to know. It was desk candy to impress visitors. I doubt it had ever been plugged in.

At the end of my report-back, he told me he had arranged a send-off party that evening for me and my interpreter. Since it was to be held at his house, it would be a chance to meet the family. The hospitality was generous and the atmosphere convivial along with the requisite toasts. Answering a bladder call, I headed off to find the toilet. As I passed the bedroom of his teenage son, I noticed a screen glowing in the dark. At least this one was being used, if only for video games.

Adopting the Western model, the bigger stations located in cities and typically serving a million-plus potential viewers relied on advertising for most of their revenue. Standard practice was to split operations with half the staff in program production and the other half in a backroom, drumming up advertising to finance the broadcasting side and generate a profit. With sometimes half-a-dozen stations in a major city, there was as much competition for advertisers as for viewers and a clear connection between the two. To attract advertisers, a station had to show it had viewers; the more it had, the more it could charge.

Frequently, when I was being shown around a city station, a door would be thrown open to reveal what I came to call the butterfly collection. There would be a large central table surrounded by young women working the phones, offering potential advertisers special deals if they agreed to pay for a campaign over several weeks or months or, when meeting resistance from first-timers, tempting them with free slots for a limited period, sometimes with an offer to produce the adverts for them in-house.

One thing I couldn't understand was why the women were

invariably dressed and made-up as though they would be going on to a nightclub after work. Hence 'the butterfly collection'. Perhaps television was thought to be such a glamorous profession in what, beyond Moscow, was still an essentially grey post-Soviet world that one had, or was expected, to dress accordingly. You may not be on public display like your colleagues in the studio next door but that was no reason not to dress like them and – a spin-off – impress the neighbours with your coveted job in television. My infinitely more perceptive female interpreter suggested a more likely reason: looking 'screen ready' was a way to catch the boss's eye and, with luck, get you before the camera.

For smaller stations in provincial towns with sparser, poorer populations and little chance of generating sufficient revenue from advertising, the best hope of survival was to become a 'mayor's station' – in effect, the communications arm of the local authority. In return, they would be given free or heavily subsidised office space, sometimes along with a contribution to their operating costs and other perks in the mayor's gift. And, crucially, access to a transmitter.

It was a devil's deal or, as the Russians put it, 'the only free cheese is in a mousetrap'. Any editorial independence was illusory. The operators of these stations, being beholden to the mayor and his administration, were expected to cover, uncritically, every press conference trumpeting yet another 'initiative', and, come the next election, they could forget about objective, balanced coverage. It was also not uncommon for mayors to demand access to the airwaves whenever they chose with no need to spell out the 'or else'.

Press conferences were a particular bugbear for consultants, whether the station was a mayor's or not. The standard tactic of those organising the conference, most often the authorities at one level or another, was to contact the newsrooms on the morning of the event, an hour or two before, and demand that they send a reporter and cameraman while giving little or no information other than the time and place. It was 'important', period. The news editor would comply because it filled a slot in the running order and was easy to knock off. As often as not, though, it would turn out to be just another opportunity for a local worthy to burnish his self-image. It was not unusual for three or four press conferences to appear in a single bulletin. They were what in the UK we would call 'stocking fillers'.

For the viewers, press conferences were a total turn-off. Typically, a man in a suit or uniform would be seated at a table flanked by a couple of others either side as they were lobbed easy questions by half-a-dozen journalists going through the motions. It was like watching seals at feeding time. Often, the municipal flag in the corner was more interesting.

Time and again, I would try to persuade news editors to show more journalistic muscle by demanding to know details before agreeing to send a team and, if not convinced of the newsworthiness of the occasion, not sending one at all. It was a battle I seldom won.

This, though, is to look at the situation from a Western perspective. For many who worked in these stations, the editorial straightjacket was not such an imposition compared with what had gone before. Throughout the 70 years of the Soviet Union there had been no such thing as journalism as we know it, let alone objective or balanced journalism. Yes, there had been high-profile dissidents such as Sakharov and Solzhenitsyn, and those equally courageous writers of arguably treasonable samizdat literature who would type out and distribute by hand multiple copies of their work. But journalists? There may well have been newsrooms in Soviet times – for example, that of *VREMYA*, the state broadcaster's evening news bulletin – but any news that came in would be processed through the propaganda machine by the figure in a corner whose job was to check every script and interview against the government line. Any news editor would have to second guess this on-site censor. For the subs beneath him, the most taxing job of the day would be to lightly edit the latest official hand-out. Or not.

Under Gorbachev, the old Soviet order may have passed, but Lenin's view that the function of the press was to serve the Party as 'propagandist, agitator and organiser' still had resonance, if no longer relevance. (That said, I should add that there were many among the new generation of journalists who believed their patriotic duty at a time of transition unprecedented since the October Revolution was to support rather than undermine the authorities.)

+ —————— +

Most challenging for the Western media consultant were those mid-sized stations that fell between the big city stations with their bolt-on advertising departments and the editorially neutered mayors' stations. For these to keep above water, to maintain their financial and editorial independence, revenue could come in many creative forms, as I would discover during my first tour of duty that took in Kazan, Saratov, Syktyvkar, Krasnodar, Biysk, Rybinsk, Nizhny Novgorod and a number of towns along the way. In terms of learning curves, it was to be the north face of the Eiger.

4.

ON THE ROAD

Rybinsk is a city 300 kilometres north of Moscow at the confluence of the rivers Volga and Sheksna. In past centuries, its fisheries provided sturgeon for the tsar's table. On a guided tour of its television station, I had to clamber over a large pile of timber taking up most of the corridor leading to the studio.

'You building a new set?' I asked. The response was oblique and I let it pass.

A couple of days later, I would discover it was payment for some advertising in the form of barter. Looked at from my Western viewpoint, barter was certainly unusual but at least the transaction was overt; you could trip over it. You might even say it was an imaginative solution to a perennial problem: *We're a bit short of the readies this month, Volodya, so here's a load of two-by-four in lieu.*

The Rybinsk station turned out to be illuminating for another reason: the lightbulb moment when I understood the essence of the consultant's job. Up to this point I had a rough idea of what was required but no inkling how to implement it. Looking back, I think I had been suffering from a form of impostor syndrome.

On my second day at the station, during the 9 am meeting, reports came in that the Volga had risen overnight and flooded a dozen or so houses. Cellars had been inundated and, worse, the drains had backed up. This would be bad news in any country but in Russia many householders pick their fruit and vegetables in summer and autumn (often grown on the plots next to their dachas), bag or pickle them and then store the sacks and bottles in the cellar to feed the family through the winter months.

A cameraman and reporter were despatched to what my interpreter described as 'the scene of the slime'. The shots they brought back were predictably affecting. Women wading knee-deep in raw sewage were hauling up sacks of soggy onions, potatoes and carrots from the filthy depths as jars, bottles and other floatables bobbed around them like wartime mines – all the while cursing the local authority for not maintaining the drains or, at the very least, warning householders of the rising water level. It was excellent footage. You could smell it.

As the news editor and reporter discussed how the story should be told, I asked what the response of the local authority had been. The news editor was non-plussed.

'No point asking,' he replied as though swatting away a fly. 'They've never anything to say.'

'Well, perhaps that's part of the story,' I ventured. 'Their failure to communicate. If they had warned the residents, they'd have had time to empty their cellars.'

'They're still not going to talk to us.'

'OK, but again, part of the story. "We asked the mayor's office for a response but they declined." And good, balanced journalism. You've given them the right of reply to the residents' complaints.'

Still the news editor pushed back. His expression said, 'Are you telling me how to do my job?' Answer: 'Well, yes, because that's *my* job.'

'Look,' I persisted, fired by my new-found confidence, 'you've got nothing to lose by calling. It's win-win. It's a story if they won't talk . . . and a story if they do.'

By now, heads were turning in our direction. The news editor crossed to his corner desk, lifted the phone and, unexpectedly, was put through to the mayor himself. No less surprised was the mayor; perhaps because it was the first time he had been asked for his reaction to a news story. To his credit, he responded with a detailed statement. An interview would have been better but, though I may be flattering myself, I left the station feeling that at least I had been instrumental in establishing contact between the two men. And a couple of journalistic principles too – balance and the right of reply. One small step.

——————

From Rybinsk, I moved with my interpreter on to Nizhny Novgorod, the home of the GAZ Automobile Plant, makers of those indestructible civilian tanks, the Volga and the Chaika. The evening of our arrival, our TV station of choice carried a story about a local store selling electrical goods. The only news peg, so far as I could make out, was that the store had recently taken delivery of a range of Western models. As a news item, it was borderline but, like the opening of a new McDonald's in the heart of a former Soviet capital, you could just about make a case that it was an example of transition in action, of East embracing West; in this case, importing it.

At lunchtime the next day I noticed a shiny new microwave in the staff canteen. I'm not in the habit of scrutinising domestic appliances but the sticker, bearing the name of the same local store, was hard to miss. 'A gift,' the reporter assured me when I asked. Another form of barter, like the timber I had seen at the Rybinsk station? Up to a point. Payment for what was clearly an advertisement, fine, but for what purported to be a news report? A wholly different category.

One of my fellow Thomson consultants had told me to expect the accounting practices of some Russian stations to be unorthodox by Western standards. He might have added, by *any* standards.

A fortnight later, interpreter Olga and I found ourselves in a station further south and close to the border with Kazakhstan. I adopted what by now had become my usual practice: standing at the back of the studio gallery and monitoring the evening news bulletin with clipboard in hand and Olga by my side. This was our first evening at the station and the lead story was about the local brick works.

There were bricks as far as the camera could pan. We were given the entire production process – mixing the clay, into moulds, out of moulds, on to conveyor belts, off conveyor belts, into the kiln, out of the kiln . . . stacks of the things, topped off by an interview with a self-satisfied figure I took to be the boss. I asked Olga for the gist of the story.

'Record production figures,' she answered.

'And record sales?' I followed up, my sceptical journalist's hat in place.

'Not clear.'

It sounded suspiciously like one of the old Soviet newsreels announcing yet another bumper harvest or tractor production again exceeding expectations. But, I told myself, I was being the cynical Westerner. For now I would reserve judgement. Look, listen . . . learn.

Two days later, we were again standing at the back of the gallery watching the evening bulletin, and there, this time a little further down the running order, was the brick works. Again. The shots may have been different but frankly I couldn't tell. All I could see was bricks and in the same profusion. It was reminiscent of the Monty

Python spoof travelogue about Venice shown in cinemas as a warm-up for *Life of Brian*. Just as the unsuspecting audience has been lulled into a state of comatose indifference by the clichéd banality of the script, the voice-over intones, '. . . and more fucking gondolas.'

Again, I asked Olga what the story was about.

'They're still doing well,' was her dry response.

'And that's it?'

'That's it.'

I can't remember who in the end explained why the brick factory was getting such extensive coverage but it turned out that they had bought a camera for the station and this – putting non-stories, PR puffs, about them in the news – was the payment.

✦ ⸺ ✦

Hidden adverts like the brick story were one of the curses of post-Soviet television news and, for Western media consultants, top of our hit list.

They were called *jeansa* because, I was told, the first company to benefit from the practice had been a company making jeans. Most independent television stations would, at least in the early days, follow the Western practice of clearly defining commercial breaks between and/or within programs by ring-fencing them from everything around, particularly news, to make clear to the audience that this was paid-for promotional material. And, knowing that, the audience would (one hoped) view them accordingly – interested from their relatively new perspective as consumers but with a healthy dose of suspicion: 'Of course X are going to say their detergent washes whiter; it's their product and they've paid for the airtime!'

How much more effective then if, rather than X saying it themselves, a trusted, supposedly objective journalist said X washes whiter in a news bulletin as a news story. For a television station to connive in such a practice went against every journalistic principle you care to cite. It was the most blatant breach of the contract of credibility between broadcaster and viewer: to tell the truth without fear or favour.

But, as cash-strapped stations discovered, companies were prepared to pay a handsome premium for hidden advertising. One company boss confided to me that, in terms of impact and sales, a hidden advert embedded in the news was worth ten times a regular, ring-fenced commercial slot in the middle of the bulletin.

In March 2002, the *New York Times* claimed the practice was not just widespread but sometimes formalised into period-specific agreements:

> When financing runs dry, stations often strike deals with image-conscious businesses or bureaucrats. For $3,000 to $10,000 a month – sizable sums for the small stations – reporting is for sale. Under these agreements, troubled stations provide positive coverage of factory triumphs, like the production of the millionth aluminum ingot, or a quiet lack of it for less flattering events.[1]

Perhaps we in the West shouldn't be so snooty. So-called advertorials and infomercials can come mighty close to hidden adverts. Yes, they will, or should, indicate that they have been paid for or sponsored but, by getting real journalists to write and/ or present the pieces and closely copying the format of adjacent news items, editors and those journalists are also blurring the line between news and advertising.

Gifts too, like the canteen microwave, can be a grey area. Before leaving the UK, I had a medical check-up and been surprised to find a television set in the surgery's waiting room. My doctor cheerfully admitted that it was 'a gift' from a pharmaceutical company; reward no doubt for his regularly prescribing their product over the cheaper, generic alternative. (Pity he wasn't an 'ologist', or he might have been invited to an all-expenses-paid medical conference in one of the world's more exotic venues.)

A television set in Oxford, a microwave in Nizhny Novgorod. No country has a monopoly on soft corruption.

What the Russian television stations didn't seem to realise was that this was a practice of diminishing returns. Viewers aren't fools. Sitting on their sofas, they soon learnt to spot a puff piece masquerading as news and, the more they came across them, the more their confidence in the truth of the news – of that particular station and the medium generally – was eroded. And this is what happened across the former Soviet Union. Viewers continued to watch the news but, increasingly, they ceased to believe it. It became just another form of entertainment 'inspired by real events'. Sometimes not even that.

No less worrying was that many regional stations encouraged their own reporting staff to set up the hidden adverts as a way of not having to pay them. Instead, the journalists would be paid directly – bribed – by those enterprises seeking such on-screen promotion. For example, the local optician would slip a reporter fifty or a hundred dollars to do a piece about how cheap Chinese-made spectacles sold in the market were ruining people's eyesight (as well as his business, though that wasn't mentioned). It was a form of prostitution with the station boss acting as pimp and, for the consultant, hard to tackle.

At one station I put it directly to the journalists out of earshot of their boss that, as self-respecting professionals, they should refuse to go along with the practice and demand a normal employer-employee relationship with appropriate remuneration. I made clear that I, and more importantly, Internews back in Moscow, would support them. Naively, I had expected their enthusiastic agreement, even gratitude. Instead, they pleaded with me, a couple of them near tears, not to pursue such a line. The station boss would never agree and, if they didn't have the station as an outlet, they and those dependent on their earnings would be destitute and out on the street. Better a job as a compromised journalist than no job at all.

All of which made the training of young regional journalists, most of them in their twenties, worryingly problematic. We, the consultant-trainers, were teaching the theory but they were the ones who were living the reality. As the Director of Internews Russia, Manana Aslamazian, told Radio Free Europe in 2000:

> Young journalists come to our courses and I start talking enthusiastically about 'the journalist's mission', about responsibility and so on. And they reply very calmly and extremely judiciously that such and such is impossible, such and such is forbidden, this will not get through, that will not be broadcast.[2]

The cost-cutting wheezes of station bosses knew no bounds. Cameramen, they realised, would be prepared to work for little or nothing if allowed to take the equipment home at weekends for their personal – or rather, commercial – use to shoot weddings. It was a lucrative business. One cameraman boasted to me he could shoot three weddings a day and then, on top of his fee, charge for extra VHS or DVD copies.

Again, it's easy for a Westerner to condemn such practices. But, given the cynical climate of the times, I doubt that these station-owners saw much wrong with them. This wasn't so much a blurring of the line as an acknowledgement of reality: that news, advertising and PR were one and the same – all part of the market economy.

It was a view seemingly shared by the authorities. According to one aggrieved station-owner, the government's Anti-Trust Ministry, which oversaw advertising, had decided that *any* story that showed a commercial enterprise in a favourable light had to be a paid-for hidden advert, and therefore the broadcaster should be taxed accordingly for every such item aired. As a result, the station-owner told me, he was no longer making a distinction between hidden adverts and genuine news stories. Since he was going to be taxed either way, he was charging up-front for both. This resulted in the absurd situation that a company which, to its reputational detriment, had found itself the subject of a negative story one month – an industrial accident, say, or a labour dispute – could the next month be required to pay for the broadcast of a positive and indisputably newsworthy item such as its taking on more workers to fulfil a substantial export order.

But this was capitalism; this was how it worked. Well, wasn't it? To reverse the old Soviet-era joke: 'Under communism, man exploited man; under capitalism, it was the other way round.'

Democracy brought with it one hugely significant bonus for Russian television stations: elections. And there were plenty of them: local, regional and national; for seats in the State Duma (the national parliament) and for the presidency. Elections could be a lifeline for a regional station. As a news medium, television in the late nineties and early noughties could reach more people than any other if only because, as already mentioned, the old Soviet regime had put a set in everyone's home.

In Russia, strangely, television advertising was less profitable than either print or radio advertising, in contrast to the UK where in the words of media mogul Roy – later Lord – Thomson, it was 'a licence to print money'. Typically, a provincial station would be doing well to get $100 for a one-minute advertising slot in prime time. But, come the elections, the price would increase five-fold. Like shops in the West generating more than half their annual income in the run-up to Christmas, some stations could generate more than half of theirs by selling election slots. Not exactly Super Bowl but, in the context of post-Soviet Russia, not far off.

Again, though, there was the temptation to take money for hidden advertising or, in this case, hidden political promotion. As in the West, a party political broadcast (PPB) in a ring-fenced slot carried less weight with the viewers than a speech or interview on the news. PPBs were a yawn. It followed that candidates preferred to be seen and interviewed as part of an election coverage news story – and many were prepared to pay under the counter for the extra credibility they believed this gave them.

Even when a station refused and insisted on operating above board, there could still be pressure on its editorial independence. No candidate who had paid for a PPB was going to be happy to see an opponent getting a free ride on the station's news bulletin and would, at the very least, demand parity coverage.

As someone who had been trained by the BBC and spent most of his professional life with the corporation, the practice of 'independent' stations providing platforms for election candidates –

shamelessly deciding who they would support before the election and then openly taking money for the service – went against everything I believed in and had practised for the previous twenty-five years.

But this was Russia and, as I was quickly learning, Russia was different. Just *how* different I would discover in early 2003 when I was invited to take part in a public forum in the Siberian city of Novosibirsk.

5.

INTO THE LION'S DEN

Novosibirsk – literally, 'New Siberia' – is the third most populous city in Russia, after Moscow and St Petersburg. During the Second World War it played a vital role in hosting factories relocated from the west of the country because they were deemed vulnerable to the advance of German troops. What little I knew about Novosibirsk I had gleaned from an American friend and colleague, Whit Mason, with whom I had worked in Baku when he had run Internews Network in Azerbaijan. During the closing months of the Gorbachev era Whit took advantage of the relaxed attitude to foreigners. He turned up in Novosibirsk and, along with two colleagues, a fellow American and a Russian, founded an English-language newspaper, the *Siberian Review*. He was twenty-four. The paper carried stories about all aspects of life in Siberia and Russia's Far East, with particular focus on the transition that was taking place at the time from communism to capitalism and democracy.

The Soviet Union's very existence hung in the balance. When it was announced that a pan-Siberian congress was to be held to discuss the future of its biggest element, the Russian Federation – indeed, whether it *had* a future – Whit sent one of his Russian reporters to cover what promised to be a lively, perhaps decisive, debate. On his return, the reporter handed in his copy. It contained not a single quote from a single delegate. When Whit queried the omission, the reporter explained that, rather than attend the conference and do an interview or two, he had written his piece sitting at the bar.

'I didn't need to go into the hall,' he explained. 'I just looked deep into my Russian soul and asked what this issue would mean for me as a Siberian.'

✦ ———— ✦

It was the first week of March when I arrived in Novosibirsk with interpreter Irina. Snow was still thick on the ground, with pavements sheeted by ice as hard and smooth as marble. The temperature, according to Irina, was minus fifteen Celsius. She could tell such things just by looking at the formation of the crystals and was invariably correct to within two degrees. So far as I was concerned, there were only two sorts of cold in Siberia – VC and FC.

We had been booked into the monolithic and curiously monosyllabic Hotel OB. (The Ob, it turned out, was the river that bisected the city.) Like most of Novosibirsk's buildings, it was heated by hot water from the central power station via the municipal grid. Despite this, the windows were so ill-fitting that a previous occupant of my room, possibly attending a boat-builders' convention, had taken a sheet from the bed and, with it, caulked the gap between window and frame to keep out the sub-zero wind.

The forum to which I'd been invited, an 'open discussion' about regional television, was held in what from its size and layout I took to be one of the city's council chambers. The configuration was *High Noon*. On one side were ranged various luminaries from Siberian regional television and, a dozen metres away facing them, were myself, Irina and Alexey Simonov, the president of the Moscow-based Glasnost Defense Foundation, a member of the Helsinki Group and a vocal champion of independent journalism.

The chamber was so cavernous that we each had a microphone built into a panel before us. My role, according to the chairman's opening statement, was 'to represent Western media and explain its values'. *Really?* Sitting next to Alexey, a highly respected public figure with the physical features of an Old Testament prophet, I felt like an emaciated Daniel, suddenly conscious of the enormous weight on my scrawny shoulders. Never in my wildest dreams when working for the BBC had I thought I'd one day find myself in such a position, such a place and bearing such a responsibility: *to represent Western media and explain its values.* Gulp.

I did my best, but it was clear from the stony faces opposite that I could have done better. It wasn't hard to read their thoughts. Here was yet another Western expert come to tell them how to do their business, with precious little knowledge and zilch experience of the broadcasting environment in which they operated.

We got on to the subject of political advertising and, recklessly, I trotted out my misgivings about supposedly independent broadcasters taking money from political candidates for favourable news coverage on their channels to the exclusion of other candidates (which was usually part of the deal). So not even a pretence of balance. I tried to explain that this was as much about perception as about ethics; if the station was seen to be supporting a particular candidate, and known to be taking money from that candidate, there was bound to be an erosive effect on the viewers' perception of its independence which, long after the election, would shade all subsequent political reporting by the station.

Opposite me in a wheelchair sat one of the most powerful men in Siberian television, Yakov London. One of the bravest too, I should add. Five years earlier he had been shot six times in an assassination attempt, allegedly by a rival, but far from being deterred, he had gone on to even deeper involvement in regional broadcasting. Once I had finished, he gave me the full-frontal benefit of his opinion. Unless interpreter Irina was sparing my blushes, he stopped short of calling me a hypocrite . . . just.

Politicians in the West, London observed, had always cozied up to the media and tried to get them on-side, so why object to Russian television stations supporting one candidate over others? One rule for the West, another for the rest. As evidence, he cited Tony Blair's journey halfway across the world in July 1995 to woo Rupert Murdoch at a News Corporation conference on Hayman Island in Australia. Thanks to key support from the Murdoch-owned *Sun* newspaper, it was alleged, New Labour had won the general election two years later.

I should have pointed out that in the UK the rules that applied to print media were different from those applied to broadcasters; that broadcasters were required by law (overseen by Ofcom, the UK's regulator of communication services) to report news 'with due impartiality'. But working through an interpreter and switched microphones doesn't allow for much cut-and-thrust, still less follow-up clarification. Besides, by now Mr London was on a roll. He concluded:

> The [Russian] mass media has passed the stage when they are selling themselves for love and for free, supporting this or that side. Now it's much more honest and open. We take money and say, 'One seat in the State Duma costs so much – say, one

million dollars' . . . So they get the right to sit in the parliament. And we're going to make money on that, like they do, and wherever money is spent, we're going to get our cut. We're a commercial enterprise.

My inclination was to scuttle away as fast as possible after the event but, as a matter of courtesy, I felt I should seek out London and bid him a formal *do svidaniya*. Taking his hand, I expected him to gloat over his knock-out victory. Instead, he gave me a rather sweet smile. I think it was of pity.

At dinner that evening back in the hotel I was grateful for the company of my colleague Alexey Simonov. It had been a punishing day, and not my finest. At the end of the meal, Alexey suggested a toast. This was a day to celebrate! Well, it didn't seem like that to me.

'You don't understand,' he said. 'It's the fifth of March.'

With me still not understanding, he ordered a couple of glasses of Armenian brandy – possibly even a bottle. (It says much about my post-prandial state that I can't now remember which.) We chinked glasses and he explained.

The fifth of March 2003 was the fiftieth anniversary of the death of Stalin. In the months before, he had been formulating what came to be known as 'The Doctors' Plot', a conspiracy theory that a cabal of Jewish doctors treating Soviet leaders were actually intent on killing them. It was to have been the excuse for yet another wave of purges; this one with a clearly antisemitic objective. But Stalin died hours before he could fully activate the plan.

Alexey explained that he was Jewish on his mother's side. In the late 1920s, his maternal grandparents had been exiled to Siberia; then in 1950, his beloved aunt Sofya (his mother's sister) had been sentenced and despatched to an Arctic labour camp where she would spend five years. If Stalin hadn't died, it was very possible that members of the Simonov family, including thirteen-year-old Alexey, would have suffered a similar fate. Or worse. Hence the celebration.

✦ ———— ✦

As many television stations discovered, playing politics was a high-risk game. Once involved with 'the machine', it could crush you between its cogs. Size was more of a liability than a protection. There is no more cautionary tale than that of NTV, a commercial television network launched in 1993.

NTV was part of the influential Media-Most group founded and owned by the oligarch Vladimir Gusinsky. Under the slogan, 'News is Our Profession', the network committed itself to unbiased, uncensored news coverage. But during the presidential elections of 1996, NTV, along with most other broadcasters, took a calculated decision to abandon journalistic balance and promote President Boris Yeltsin's candidacy against the communists to win him a crucial second term. (It was a risk and there are those today who date the public decline of trust in the media from that decision.)

These, so the justification went, were exceptional times. Russia was still emerging from the Soviet era; the fledgling democratic system was still fragile and the country could easily slip back into communism. To prevent that, Yeltsin had to win. The problem was that, second time round, Yeltsin was seen by many, experts and voters alike, as unelectable – a shambling, drunken shadow of the man who had clambered on to a tank outside the Russian parliament to defend democracy at the height of the 1991 attempted coup by communist hardliners. By 1996, he was barely able to stand upright. Only the media, it was reckoned, could get him over the line.

Viewed in these terms, NTV's support was less for Boris Yeltsin personally than for the democratic system he represented. Ultimately, it came down to the lesser of two evils. In order to preserve democracy, the rule of law, due process, human rights, free speech and of course independent media, it was necessary – *temporarily* – to put aside the journalistic notions of objectivity and balance. At times of national emergency when the nation's very existence was at stake, such oxymoronic decisions had to be made. Was it not Churchill who said truth had to be attended by a bodyguard of lies? (In the same vein, Lenin said liberty was so precious it had to be rationed.[1])

And it produced the hoped for outcome. With 54% of the vote in the second round runoff, hardly a ringing endorsement, Yeltsin defeated the communist candidate Gennady Zyuganov in the 1996 election.[2]

But be careful what you wish for . . .

Two years later in September 1998 I happened to be in Saratov on the banks of the Volga in the south-west of the country, working with a local TV station, when I learnt that Igor Malashenko, NTV's General Director and Gusinsky's second-in-command, was in the building. My freelancing instincts kicked in. The independence of the Russian media was a hot topic in the rest of the watching world and here, I realised, was a chance to bag an interview with a major media player in the 1996 election. (I didn't know at the time the extent of Malashenko's involvement; that, despite heading a major news network, he had personally organised Yeltsin's media campaign with Yeltsin's daughter Tatyana – a blatant conflict of interest.[3]) Malashenko spoke English and agreed. I contacted Raymond Snoddy, the media editor of *The Times*, in London. Would he be interested in an article? He would. He ran it across six-columns a few days later with the interview as its centrepiece.[4]

With my recorder running, I asked Malashenko first about NTV's general policy on political involvement. He responded, 'We always advise our partners to be as distanced or detached from political parties as much as they can.'

So far, so predictable. He was of course astute enough to know what was coming next and smoothly made the case for NTV's 'exceptional' support of Yeltsin two years earlier when, yes, their standard advice to others had been jettisoned. But it had been for the greater good and indeed had achieved the desired result: the pro-democracy, pro-capitalism Yeltsin had won and communism had been put back in its box, there to stay with a stake through its heart. What he didn't add was that such seeming altruism coincided with a huge dose of self-interest: if the communists had been returned to power, NTV would have been toast, along with its owner and all the other oligarchs.

What I wanted to know, and get on the record, was what NTV's editorial policy would be in two years' time: the *next* presidential election in 2000. Malashenko's response was cautious. It struck me that, while hoping for the best, he was still hedging his bets: 'I do not think that in the year 2000 the choice is going to be as dramatic or as historical as it was in 1996, when there was still a threat of some return to communism.'

In terms of the communist threat, he was right. Although there was no question of Yeltsin standing again, the assumption was that the winning candidate would be supportive of the freewheeling system that had so benefited Gusinsky and his fellow oligarchs. What neither of us foresaw was that the man standing in 2000 would be Yeltsin's prime minister and, following Yeltsin's resignation, already acting president . . . Vladimir Putin.

Putin was no friend of Gusinsky. In the run-up to the March 2000 election, NTV made devastating fun of him in a puppet show called *Kukly* (similar to the UK's *Spitting Image*) depicting him as an evil gnome. It also ran a hard-hitting investigation into the Second Chechen War that Putin had waged ruthlessly when prime minister and acting president. (Referring to separatist rebels, he was recorded saying, 'If we catch 'em on the can, we'll whack them in the shithouse.'[5])

With the backing of state broadcaster ORT, Putin won the presidency on the first round and immediately set about putting NTV under government control. Gusinsky was arrested, imprisoned and made an offer he couldn't refuse. In return for his freedom, he would sell his Media-Most empire to state-controlled Gazprom-Media at a price determined by them. The message was clear. Mess with the Kremlin and there will be consequences. (As Anne Applebaum has remarked, Gusinsky was no hero: 'Had he not plunged Media-Most into debt, it would have been more difficult for Gazprom to take control.'[6])

Malashenko didn't need his own situation spelt out. He left Russia for the United States and died in Spain in February 2019, seemingly by his own hand. He was 64. Those who saw him in his last days say he was chronically depressed. Even so, there were the inevitable conspiracy theories, as had surrounded the death six years earlier of Boris Berezovsky, another businessman who had fallen foul of Putin.

There's an intriguing 'what if' post-script to Igor Malashenko's life. After he had helped Yeltsin get his second term, Yeltsin offered him the post of chief of staff – head of his presidential administration. Malashenko declined, choosing television over politics. Had he accepted, it is speculated, he would have had Yeltsin's ear and been in a position to thwart the rise of the man whom Yeltsin would anoint as his successor, Vladimir Putin. He might even have become that successor. In an interview in early 2000, the aforementioned Berezovsky, who had been one of Yeltsin's key advisers, revealed that he had recommended Malashenko as prime minister to test his suitability for the top job.[7]

6.

UP COUNTRY IN AZERBAIJAN

Azerbaijan is one of the countries of the South Caucasus, bordering Russia, Georgia, Armenia and Iran. After Russia, it was the second of the former Soviet republics I would work in. Its capital Baku, built on a peninsula jutting out into the Caspian Sea, was a kaleidoscope of impressions where the travel agent's cliché, 'East meets West', hit you at every turn. 'Collided with' would have been more accurate. Oil drilling on a commercial scale started in the 1840s. From the airport, you were driven through a sterile landscape of 'nodding donkeys'. You could smell the stuff. But, 160 years later, the serious extraction was off the coast. You could see the rigs and platforms from the shore, topped by winking lights to warn incoming aircraft.

Baku was, and is, a striking mix of oriental and occidental architecture, an ancient domed *hammam* bathhouse dwarfed by a high-rise glass-and-steel hotel. The central Fountains Square was an oasis of calm; a small-scale Alhambra, and at lunchtime a cool delight to wander around or sit enjoying a chicken *shawarma* wrap.

Azeri culture was bewildering. Officially, this was still the secular state of Soviet times when Moscow had used vodka, its chosen weapon of mass intoxication, to undermine Islam. (During the 1970s, according to my interpreter, it had been sold in bottles which, once opened, couldn't be resealed.) But a sobered Islam was now fighting back with the muezzins again in fine voice five times a day. For an Englishman familiar with the genteel peal of church bells at a civilized hour, it was an exotic jolt to be woken at four-thirty in the morning by the first call to prayer from the surrounding minarets.

But just when you thought you had a handle on the culture, you would be presented in late March with a small basket of grass to celebrate Novruz. No connection with Islam, Novruz is a festival with its origins in neighbouring Iran, tied to the spring equinox and, so far as nature is concerned, the real start of the new year in the Northern Hemisphere. In a further blending, Zoroastrianism is also in the mix.

This would be no hardship posting, I realised. I was working at Internews' Baku training facility, conducting a classroom-based course with professional camera-operators and picture-editors on hand as required. Everything was fresh, fascinating and provided for. And the course participants proved singularly receptive to my ideas on the role of a broadcast journalist in post-Soviet society – scribbling notes, asking questions, gratefully scooping up my every pearl of Western wisdom. (The only jarring note was a comment from an Azerbaijani colleague who, registering my admiring gaze of the roof-top garden on the building opposite, remarked, 'That was where they threw the Armenians off.' If true, this would have been during the conflict over Nagorno-Karabakh in the early 1990s.)

I had no complaints either about the accommodation. Internews had rented for me an entire four-bedroomed apartment on an upper floor in one of the old palace-style buildings in the centre of the city. In the years to come, I would stay in many similar apartments in different cities and different republics. (During one stint in Moscow I found myself in a rented-out apartment belonging, I was told, to Stalin's granddaughter.

The arrangement was a fine example of how a market economy worked in an emerging democracy. Following the collapse of the Soviet Union in 1991, the cannier residents among those who had negotiated the ownership of their homes with their local authority – or, since the old Soviet state no longer existed, acquired them by default or devious means – quickly realised they had a money-making asset when swarms of itinerant Westerners started to appear in their midst. Among them were consultants like me, sent to work in the country for weeks or months and preferring a home from home apartment to an impersonal hotel.

The price that foreign companies, even non-profits like Internews, were prepared to pay for such accommodation was beyond the imaginings of the locals. And, better still, in US dollars. As a result, entire families – maybe three generations – would decant themselves from their own homes to go and stay with relatives, rent out their apartments for weeks at a time and share the proceeds with the family . . . one assumes.

But they didn't take their possessions with them. Moving into a new apartment, I would find every cupboard and drawer had been stuffed to bursting with children's toys and what were very obviously personal possessions (I once came across a set of false-teeth), in much the same way as house-sellers in the West de-clutter the place to create a good impression for prospective buyers.

Arriving, suitcase in hand, at the address I had been given by the Internews office, I was shown round my palatial apartment by a middle-aged woman I took to be the owner. The décor was strikingly 'contemporary'. Every door to every bedroom, all four, had been papered with a life-size poster of a scantily clad woman in a raunchy pose. Tacky would be a fair, and indeed literal, description. A coat of varnish had been applied to the young lovelies which, for whatever technical reason, had failed to dry. I gave it no more thought.

Handing me the keys, the woman asked about my working hours. I told her I would be leaving at 08.30 and back around 16.30. 'Every day?' she enquired. 'Every *working* day,' I stressed. 'And lunch?' 'Oh, the office always provides that,' I replied. She seemed relieved, touchingly so in a maternal way, that I would be getting a proper midday meal.

All went well for the first week, followed by a relaxing weekend. Perhaps too relaxing. On the first day of the second week, I realised on arriving at the Internews office that I had forgotten to bring a video cassette I would be needing in the afternoon. So, skipping lunch, I returned to the apartment . . . to find the front door on the latch.

Inside was the woman who had shown me round a week earlier. My first thought was that she was cleaning the place, though this didn't explain her state of agitation. Then, from the sounds behind the closed bedroom doors, I realised she was not alone. The tacky ladies made sense. But at least my bedroom seemed to be off commercial limits. I retrieved my cassette and, in the immortal words of the *News of the World*, 'made my excuses and left'. Madame's secret was safe with me. In the bright new dawn of free enterprise, I could only applaud the provision of such supply to satisfy manifest demand.

As my assignment neared its end, it was clear that on this, my first stint outside Russia, I had passed muster. In fact, the Internews management were so impressed that they suggested I might stay on and go 'up country' for a few days to check out one of the more problematic regional stations they were supporting. According to a consultant who had visited the station some months earlier, it was under-performing. Her report added: 'There is no sense of urgency or commitment to a deadline'. The reason, she surmised, was 'political fear, lack of electricity and transport problems'.

So, my visit would be a production audit with some on-the-job training bolted on. Five days, with a day for travel either side – how did that sound? It sounded good.

Looking back through my notes on my Azerbaijani period, I came across a photo taken at a lay-by on the way to our destination. I'm leaning nonchalantly against the Internews 4x4. A TV PRESS sticker is prominently displayed on the windscreen. I'm wearing jeans and a light blue chambray shirt, collar open, cuffs turned up, dark glasses stylishly hooked into one breast-pocket, a notebook peeking purposefully out of the other. I'm smiling to camera, more a self-satisfied smirk, every inch the international TV news consultant.

I've a good idea what would have been going through my mind – that leaving the BBC (even if, more accurately, the BBC had left me) was the best thing that had ever happened. Freed from the hamster-wheel of the M25 London ring-road, here I was bestriding the post-Soviet world, a media evangelist preaching the gospel of St John Reith, valued by my new bosses, dispensing my experience and expertise to grateful locals and, no small consideration, being paid far more than I had ever earned at the BBC.

And now – if only in my overheated imagination – I was a man on a mission, being sent up country, playing Charles Marlow in my personal production of Conrad's *Heart of Darkness*. My self-casting was perhaps a tad too close to the truth. Given what was in store, I should have reminded myself of what my fellow consultant David

Seymour often used to murmur in the face of impending disaster, 'And it was all going so well, Mr Michael.' The next five days would turn out to be a case study, condensing in a single station in a single town almost everything that, to various degrees, was afflicting the scores of stations I would see across the former Soviet Union over the next six years.

The town was called Zaqatala. As the driver, interpreter, and I arrived at our accommodation on the outskirts, I noticed from the map that we were closer to Russia and Georgia than to Baku; about twenty kilometres from the respective borders. It would be harder to get any further up country.

✦ —— ✦

The next morning I met the team I would be working with. It was a case of 'I've been sent from head office to help you out' and their nervousness showed they knew it. I had expected, if not a fully staffed and equipped television station, at least a building that resembled one. Instead, there was just a production office, no larger than a normal living-room, housed in part of the commercial premises of the alleged station-owner, a small-time businessman whose main activity was selling satellite dishes.

The team consisted of two women reporters (both English-speakers), one of whom had the title news editor, and two male camera-operators. We sat at a table sipping sweet Azerbaijani tea from small glasses. Over breakfast in the guesthouse, I had run through the list of the equipment Internews had provided and paid for. Looking around now for signs of professional activity, I noticed a $1000 Vinten tripod tucked beneath a desk. Tripods have a hard life but this one looked as though it had never been used. News editor 'Yegana' followed my gaze. 'We don't want to get it dirty,' she responded to my unasked question. Next to it was what I recognised as the case of a Lowel three-piece lighting kit, again in pristine condition with not so much as a scuff mark. 'Too bulky to carry around' was the explanation.

Within a few minutes it became clear that this was not so much a unit that was under-performing as not performing, period. In fact, it hadn't produced a single news story in six months. In fairness, the team hadn't been paid during that time either, because the station-owner took the view that, while he offered them the premises free, together with electricity when the local grid was working, it was Internews' responsibility to support them financially. He saw himself less as a station-owner than as a facilitator. (How Internews supported its affiliated stations I will explain in the next chapter.)

I was becoming more depressed by the minute. News editor Yegana certainly knew how to talk the talk; her aim, she said, was to produce hard-hitting news stories. Well, I wasn't going to argue with that. Yet, though she and her colleagues had known about my visit days, if not weeks, in advance, they hadn't come up with a single idea we could work on.

Referring to the previous consultant's report, I noted they had been researching two stories at the time of her visit; one about Armenians who had fled the town after the latest flare-up in Nagorno-Karabakh, the other about the town's chief executive and his brother finding themselves on opposite sides of the political divide. Both sounded like good human-interest stories. So what had happened? Answer: nothing. Why not? 'Not feasible, too costly, and in the end not really that interesting.'

I was beginning to get the picture. Supressing my impatience, I tried some brainstorming. What were the big issues that most concerned the locals? After all, this was a town with a population of about 30,000. Finally, we came up with a story that sounded feasible – a new law that required taxi drivers to install meters – and yes, there was a lot of discontent for all the reasons one could guess. Top of the list: the cost and the way the meters could be used by the tax authorities to record the drivers' incomes. Brilliant! And no transport problems. All we had to do was find a compliant, and preferably complaining, taxi driver, interview him in his cab as we drove around, and take a few passing-shots and cut-aways. And, with luck, we might get a free ride. Add to that an interview with an official (or a bland statement from a ministry spokesperson), a piece-to-camera by the taxi rank and it was a wrap!

Given the reputation for garrulity of taxi drivers the world over, I felt sure we had a winner. In a mood of mild euphoria, I left the matter for our news editor and crack reporter to research and set up, confident that the next morning we would be out early to do some shooting and interviewing. We may have got off to a rocky start but all would be well from now on.

The next morning I was met by downcast expressions. Despite the team's best efforts, the taxi story had 'fallen down'. No driver was prepared to talk on camera and so there was no access. I was incredulous. It was hardly Watergate. But I was a Westerner, and I couldn't be expected to understand the local sensitivities.

Faced with this latest collapse, I could see the days slipping away. Any story, I now realised, would require my own hands-on involvement, driving it through at every stage or it wouldn't happen. And, being a Westerner who didn't understand, I could at least claim to bring a fresh perspective to the task.

Trying to orient myself the previous afternoon when the team had been busy setting up or, rather, knocking down the taxi story,

I had wandered into the centre of town and, if ever there was a story waiting to be told, there it was before my eyes: a vast pile of crumbling masonry that in Soviet times had been Zaqatala's Tribune. This was the civic dais where, in self-conscious imitation of the march-pasts in Moscow's Red Square, the local communist worthies would line up on significant dates in the Soviet calendar, such as the anniversary of the October Revolution (celebrated on 7 November because of a subsequent change in the dating system).

According to a plaque, the Tribune had been built by Russian craftsmen in 1972 – a good nugget for the script with the possible addition of some archive photos – and, unusually, it was made of marble, not the more common stone or concrete. Many cities and big towns had one. Tbilisi, the capital of neighbouring Georgia, had a corker – not just a dais for its presidium line-up but, looming behind them, a multi-arched structure of sculpted shells soaring thirty metres into the air like the set of a Busby Berkeley spectacular. With characteristic irreverence, the Georgians had dubbed it 'Andropov's Ears'.

And the story? It could be headlined in half a dozen words: 'What to do with the monstrosity?' As it stood – more accurately, lurched – the jagged pile was an urban excrescence and a potentially lethal hazard for any children clambering over it. But who in their right mind would spend public money on restoring such a brutalist monument to a discredited regime? Demolish it then! What? – and provoke cries of 'Desecration!' from all the old unreconstructed communists.

It's worth recording here that there was still more than a whiff of the old regime in the air. The president of Azerbaijan at this time, Heydar Aliyev, had been a KGB officer before being appointed a full member of the Soviet Politburo by General Secretary Yuri Andropov. Come 1991, Aliyev had reinvented himself as a democrat.

In neighbouring Georgia, his counterpart Eduard Shevardnadze, another former member of the Soviet Politburo, had undergone a similarly miraculous conversion and, going a step further, been baptised into the Georgian Orthodox Church. The Vicar of Bray would have found himself in good company.

As for the Tribune, I felt sure there was journalistic gold in its crumbling remains. They offered the prospect of a lively debate on a topical issue, good pictures and the possibility of not just vox pops but even a multi-choice poll of, say, a hundred locals to get a cross-section of public opinion. The choices would be:

1. Restore
2. Remove
3. Leave as is

The team's initial reaction was positive, bordering on enthusiastic. But it wasn't long before the doubts started to stack up. There was an election coming up and the subject could be politically sensitive (Heaven forfend!). And, now that they thought about it, hadn't state TV done something similar about another item of Soviet architecture in another town? (It was amazing how, whatever station I was working with, state TV had just done a similar story.)

True to my new resolve and in the absence of any alternative, I put my foot down. We were going to do the story and, if we failed, it wouldn't be for want of trying. Even if we never shot a foot of tape, this would be a masterclass in research and sourcing.

Zaqatala's administrative authority, our equivalent of a council, was the Executive Committee, generally shortened to Excomm. And the man to talk to was the first deputy. To my Western ears, this all sounded suspiciously Soviet, with its echoes of the Comintern,

Lenin's mechanism for the global spread of communism. As I recall, it too had an Excomm.

Good news! The first deputy wasn't only in but he could see us.

He was warmly welcoming, sitting behind a T-shaped configuration of desks that required visitors to adopt an awkward angle, wedged between the top and the tail. It was the standard layout favoured by all small town office holders, a carry-over from Soviet times and, in its own way, a symbol of how little had changed. Governors, mayors and senior officials loved to be interviewed at them, framed between an impressive range of Soviet-era telephones (some of them even working) and a colourful array of paperweights and desk-flags. Best of all, the arrangement formed an effective barrier, physical and psychological, between themselves and any journalist with the temerity to ask questions.

After briefly explaining via my interpreter my role as an Internews consultant, I left it to Yegana to outline what we had in mind while the interpreter whispered a translation in my ear. I expected her, after laying out the bones of the story, to ask for an on-camera interview with the relevant official – perhaps the first deputy himself. Instead, it became clear she was asking for permission to film in the most public of places in the heart of her own town. So much for freedom of the media. Just as shocking was the tone of craven sycophancy; she wasn't asking, she was begging.

During my time with the BBC, I had always taken the attitude, if only sub-consciously, that as a reporter or producer I was offering people the chance to put their point of view, their side of the story, to the great viewing public. After all, I represented the first and, some would say, the most prestigious public service broadcaster in the world. The status of the BBC aside, one thing I've always tried to drum into those I train is that their ultimate boss is not the head of news in the corner office, certainly not the government, but *the viewer*. The reporter is the viewer's representative on earth, and it is that uniquely privileged role which gives him or her the right to ask penetrating, even impertinent, questions of those in authority.

All great in theory, and impressive when scribbled on a whiteboard beneath, in capital letters, THE ROLE OF THE JOURNALIST IN A FUNCTIONING DEMOCRACY.

But I was being unreasonably tough on Yegana. I should have understood that there was no comparison between our two situations. In this, the real world of post-Soviet, provincial, small town Azerbaijan, Yegana had no power, still less a boss with a corner office. Indeed, on all the available evidence, she didn't even have any viewers to represent, though I was now about to change that.

The first deputy's response was straight out of The Obstructive Bureaucrat's Playbook. Any story involving filming in the centre of town would require a formal letter of request from Internews to the head of Excomm (currently recovering from a heart attack), outlining the nature of the report and itemising the proposed shots.

To be sure that I hadn't misheard, I asked whether he was really saying that without Excomm's permission the team were not allowed to film in the very public centre of their own town. He leaned back and beamed. I had understood perfectly! I didn't need to ask how long such permission might take, still less whether it was likely to be granted.

But the first deputy didn't wish to appear unhelpful. If we wanted to make a report about Zaqatala's magnificent cultural and recreational facilities, by chance there was a folk concert that very evening! He would be happy to give his personal permission there and then.

The scales fell from my eyes. The station's news editor was not

Yegana but the first deputy. The television station's editorial agenda, assuming there was such a thing, was determined by Excomm.

In the end we shot a ho-hum report about a German Government scheme to train local farmers – German trainer standing, sweating in field, local representative of the Ministry of Agriculture sitting behind desk, shots of waving crops . . . more crops waving. A tractor might have crossed the screen at some point but I can't be sure. When it came to the editing, there was not just the usual problem with an intermittent power supply but the discovery that months earlier the editing deck, supplied by Internews, had developed a fault which at any moment could wipe the pictures. Had the fault been reported? It had not.

My visit had been depressing but, putting the best gloss on it, instructive. I could no longer have any illusions about 'free and independent media' and only limited hope of effecting any meaningful change. Reality had dawned.

For all the frustrations, I felt sorry for the hapless team. I had arrived with a bundle of Western preconceptions about the role of objective journalism, holding authority to account, shining a bright light into dark corners and so on. Putting myself in their shoes, living in their community with all the subtle pressures that an oppressive authority can exert and, on top of everything, not even being paid the most basic of retainers, I had to admit that I would have done no better. A harsher critic would have described them as hobby journalists, but in such circumstances, what else could they be?

More painfully, I had to acknowledge my own political naivety. I had assumed that the former Soviet Union was just that: 1922–1991, RIP and Good Riddance. But, like the twitching extremities of a warm corpse, remnants of the old regime were still able to strangle the initiative of any who sought to bury it.

What I had seen in Zaqatala was a microcosm of the media landscape that Internews was seeking to transform. *Perekhod* (*transition* in English), the term most used post-1991, had implied a neat break between past and future, a genuine turning point. There had been no such thing. What Internews was having to manage was not transition but 'legacy', built up over 70 years, deeply embedded and resistant to change. This wasn't just about training journalists and supporting the independent stations employing them; it was about, first, creating an environment in which those stations could operate and, in time, support *themselves*. An environment in which they didn't have to resort to the dubious practices mentioned earlier, such as broadcasting hidden adverts, pimping their own reporters and taking money for blatant political endorsements. The question was, how?

7.

CREATING A MEDIA MARKET

In Soviet times, the republics had been able to look to the Moscow mothership for not just political support but for lucrative commercial markets. It had been a symbiotic relationship. Most of the republics had something to offer which the Russians wanted, particularly foodstuffs.

Take Georgia, which was hit harder than most. Blessed with a climate ranging from humid subtropical in the west to dry continental in the east, it was a rich source of fruit, vegetables, wine and, less obviously, mineral water. Borjomi naturally carbonated water, discovered in the 1820s and closely associated with the Romanov dynasty, was a Russian favourite and, despite the imperial imprimatur, graced Politburo meetings in Moscow throughout the Soviet era.

But post 1991, all the republics had been cast adrift – 'seized their independence' was the alternative wording – and left to their own devices, even though significant proportions of their populations were of Russian origin. General Secretary Mikhail Gorbachev had already dealt a near-lethal blow to Georgia's wine industry, ordering the ploughing up of many of its oldest vineyards in his campaign to fight alcoholism by replacing beer, wine and vodka with soft drinks and spring water, earning him the sarcastic sobriquet, *Mineralny Sekretar*, rather than *Generalny Sekretar*. When both he and the Union went, the former republic found it had bottles but no caps and, in the case of Borjomi, no labels because – an example of Soviet reciprocity – they had been printed in Russia. (Longer term, there would be one unexpected upside for the Georgian wine producers. Because post-independence they hadn't been able to afford pesticides or chemical fertilisers, their soil, whether ploughed up or not, qualified for organic status, enabling them to exploit the Western demand for a whole range of premium-priced, 'certified organic' fruit juices: cranberry, pomegranate, mulberry, blueberry, cherry and, of course, grape.)

Into this dire situation stepped the non-profit media NGOs to help build new structures based on Western principles. Internews' laudable mission statement was/is to 'train journalists, tackle disinformation, and help media outlets become financially sustainable – so that everyone has trustworthy information to make informed decisions and hold power to account'.

Its strategy was to focus on the hundreds of small independent television stations out in the regions. These, it was reckoned, had the best chance of maintaining their independence, even though there would still be a regional governor with the capacity to exert pressure. Often, as already mentioned, these stations were little more than vanity projects established by local businessmen, but some were trying to be serious broadcasters with regular news bulletins and the occasional feature program. Serious, but struggling.

Even when there were potential advertisers to be tapped, there was a lack of knowledge and confidence about how that potential could be turned into revenue. Donning my consultant's hat, I would occasionally expand my journalistic brief to deliver a crash course in capitalism, never mind that my only academic qualification was a degree (second class) in English and Philosophy. Hoping to show the boss of an Azerbaijani television station in the provincial town of Mingechevir the hands-on approach he needed to adopt, I decided to drum up business for him by persuading the owner of the local mini-mart to buy some spot adverts on his channel. Mr Mini-Mart was puzzled by my sales pitch.

'But why? We're a small community. Everyone knows where I am and what I sell.'

I couldn't fault his logic. I tried another tack, hoping to sway him by my familiarity with market terminology.

'But you could increase your customer footfall by advertising weekly specials – for example, cut-price offers on selected items.'

He shrugged, still stubbornly unimpressed. 'But any additional income resulting from greater turnover will be negated by the price markdown and reduced profit on the specials. At the end of the day, what's the point?'

Catching my interpreter nodding in agreement, I had to concede that I lacked the necessary grasp of post-Keynesian economics. Where was J.K. Galbraith when you needed him?

Even in bigger urban centres where there were competing businesses offering the same products or services, station bosses and companies alike often failed to see any connection between advertising and increased revenue; how something that started out as a cost could also be an investment which would produce a dividend. In the view of many, it was a capitalist con, probably to keep advertising agencies in business and therefore money down the drain. They had at least half a point. It has long been accepted lore among manufacturers and service-providers in the West that half of the money spent on advertising is wasted; the trouble is that nobody can say *which* half.

Little wonder that so many independent TV stations, the potential interface between the advertiser and the consumer, couldn't understand how the system was meant to work, still less their part in it. As Victor Muchnik, the editor-in-chief of TV2, a station in Tomsk, Siberia, pointed out, 'There was no advertising market at the time; no one knew how audiences could be monetised – the word "monetisation" itself was still unknown . . . we certainly had no business model.'[1]

What was needed was some form of pump-primer. Internews decided that the answer was to create its own media market. If, as matters currently stood, there was no income to be generated through advertising or just an unwillingness to tap it, then Internews itself would use its funders' resources to pay the stations to provide content (which, incidentally, they could use to fill their own schedules). The more they provided, the more they would earn to sustain themselves. Unconventional? You might well say.

Since there was no commercial relationship between supply and demand, it can be argued that this was an artificial market – a model for a real market which, given time, would replace it. Not capitalism as such; rather, a lesson in capitalism. Like Monopoly, it was a boardgame version to familiarise players with the real thing.

Arguably the most ambitious example was established in the Caucasus, comprising the three former Soviet republics of Georgia, Armenia and Azerbaijan. It was a weekly showcase program called *Perekrestok* – Crossroads. The key to its success, or failure, was that it would be a joint production. Armenia and Azerbaijan were at war over the disputed territory of Nagorno-Karabakh, but Georgia was on reasonable terms with both. The pumping heart of the project was therefore a production centre in the Georgian capital Tbilisi, tasked with packaging regular programs to serve viewers across the three countries.

Over the course of frequent visits to the Caucasus, I would spend many hours with the *Crossroads* production team. The style of the program could best be described as 'news feature' – a mix of video reports, interviews and profiles linked by an in-studio anchor. Its laudable editorial aim was to show the three countries how much they had in common in terms of the post-Soviet challenges they each faced in the areas of education, transport, housing, health care and the like.

Content was provided by the region's many Internews-affiliated (that is, financially supported) independent TV stations across the three former Soviet republics. Sometimes they offered material of their own accord, other times they had to be cajoled or would be directly commissioned. In return, they were paid a small but, in the context of the times, a not insignificant amount: about $60 per video report. Assuming a reasonable turnover of reports, this could generate a modest but regular income, particularly for the smaller outlying stations, and, it was hoped, act as an incentive to provide the most basic of news services for their local populations.

As mentioned earlier, Internews also provided them with the necessary equipment: cameras and accessories, editing gear and computers. Add to that the occasional free-of-charge Western consultant like me to raise professional standards, either working centrally in Tbilisi or on site, and in theory you had the makings of a viable broadcasting network.

But not a genuinely commercial one. The funding for all this – the production centre, the equipment, payments for the reports, fees for the consultants and trainers – came from USAID, with some additional contributions from the European Commission's TACIS program. In other words, the entire operation was underwritten. In that sense, the artificial market was a grown-up version of playing shops.

And the role of the Western consultants? On paper, we were there to raise standards through training, mentoring and general advice, whether it be how to perform a piece-to-camera, structure a video package or lay out a newsroom for maximum efficiency. In two words: best practice. Actually, three words: *Western* best practice. This meant that, while we knew how to do our jobs and how to train others to do them, we were seldom versed in the cultural subtleties and complexities of those we were working with. We were like peripatetic gardeners who, despite their success in planting and propagating in their own part of the world, had little or no knowledge of the climate or soil conditions of the foreign parts they were sent to.

8.

LEARNING THE HARD WAY

'You don't understand our culture. The way we do things is very different from where you come from.'

Playing the culture card was a recurring feature of my six years' work in the post-Soviets. I quickly learnt that, if I didn't challenge it at the first mention, it could thwart every attempt at innovation. In time I developed a counter-spiel which went something like: 'While I respect your culture, you must remember that I have been sent here to show you the way we do things in our part of the world. I cannot do this unless you accept that we too have a culture – and that at times it will be at odds with yours.'

Did it work? Well, I doubt it changed minds, but it did at least remove one layer of resistance. Even so, there is no denying the underlying truth: cultures differ.

Political differences – the systematic way countries organise and administer themselves, whether adopting the communist or capitalist model – are generally clear and they can at least be recognised if not always reconciled. Cultural differences are altogether more opaque. The outsider discovers the traditional 'rules' of a nation, of its customs, behaviour or belief, more often in the breach than the observance. Which is another way of saying, in your efforts to avoid a fall, be prepared for many a *faux pas*. One personal example is gravened on my memory.

I was in Tashkent, the capital of Uzbekistan, a predominantly Muslim country but, as in Azerbaijan, with undercurrents of other religions or, more accurately, superstitions. I've worked in plenty of Muslim countries and thought I had learnt all the necessary lessons, such as not shaking hands with women unless they offer theirs first. It quickly became clear that my Uzbek interpreter, 'Shahzod', was more observant than most. Zealous would not be too strong a word. He refused to wear a seatbelt because, 'if you are blessed, you won't have an accident, and if you are cursed, the seatbelt isn't going to save you'. But predestination was just part of Shahzod's credo. When entering a public toilet, he would put his left foot first (a toilet being a 'dirty' place) and, when leaving, his right, a manoeuvre which involved a well-practised soft-shoe shuffle worthy of Gene Kelly.

Shahzod took particular pride in his parenting skills. He told me that to ensure his two-year-old son grew up to be a good Muslim, he would point to a cloud and assure the terrified toddler that Allah was watching his every move. I wasn't surprised when he told me he had been questioned by State Security about the extent of his beliefs. (Where were Save the Children?)

We took our lunch break in the canteen. Attached to the wall at one end was a basin for handwashing. One day, there was no towel, a fact I noticed only after wetting my hands. Making light of the inconvenience, I playfully flicked a few drops at a fellow diner. The effect was electrifying. Everyone froze, a few gasped, while the man himself reacted as though I'd thrown a pan of boiling oil over him. Though he affected to brush off the incident, he remained visibly shaken throughout the meal. I felt terrible but puzzled.

My action, Shahzod later explained to me, had been to put a curse on the man. It was a variation on giving someone the evil eye. It was nothing to do with Islam but part of a bundle of superstitions going back millennia, their origins lost in the mists of antiquity. But still part of the local culture, and, as I had inadvertently demonstrated, powerfully so.

And that's the problem with culture; sometimes there's just no knowing.

Take the simple act of smiling. In the West, we do it all the time, usually to reassure others of our good intentions. Or, when approaching a hotel reception desk, in the hope of eliciting a similarly positive response from the person behind it. A room with a sea view, or what my late friend Martin Young used to call 'an upgreed'? Try that in a hotel beyond Moscow or St Petersburg in the Russia of the late 1990s and you'd likely be mistaken for an escaped inmate from the local psychiatric unit. Only idiots smiled for no reason.

Worse, the grimly unresponsive expression of the receptionist on the ground floor would be repeated on every floor above because each had its own concierge, with her own desk at the end of the corridor – a legacy from Soviet times when these *etazhnitsi* were widely assumed to be engaged in surveillance for the KGB. Their primary job after The Fall was a humiliating demotion: to ensure that guests didn't check out with the hangers in the wardrobe or the batteries from the TV's remote control. The presence of both had to be confirmed before you were allowed to leave, and of one thing you could be sure: there would be no parting smile.

There was the very rare exception. When working abroad, I always take two items to enable me to wash my 'smalls' in the hotel washbasin: one of those elastic clotheslines with a sucker on each end that stick to bathroom tiles and an airtight Tupperware box of detergent, measuring 10 x 10 x 5 centimetres and clearly marked DETERGENT lest an over-zealous customs official mistake it for cocaine.

Staying in a hotel in the Urals, I was surprised to be getting more attention from my floor-concierge than was customary. Rather than checking my wardrobe and remote, she would regularly, mystifyingly, enquire about my comfort. Was everything OK? Was there anything I needed? Only on the last day did the reason emerge. She had spotted my Tupperware box and instantly understood its true purpose: to keep food fresh. I can only assume that at the time such a technically advanced culinary accessory was unknown in this corner of the Russian Federation. Would I be needing it after my departure? she wondered. I tipped out the remaining detergent and presented her with the much-coveted plastic box. In return, I got the broadest of smiles and a *Spasibo bolshoe* as heartfelt as if I'd given her a Fabergé egg. It seemed a small sacrifice for such a significant advance in Anglo–Russian relations.

By the time I was sent to Siberia (literally), I had learnt not to smile without reason and, still less, to grin. But sometimes you can't win.

I was invited by the manager of the TV station I was working with to join a group touring a local school. Informed that the other members would be education officials from around the region and not wishing to disrupt or slow the tour, I explained to Olga my interpreter that, rather than her translating as we went along, I would keep any questions until we were alone again. By now, I had also learnt to blend by not wearing anything that would mark me out as a foreigner. And of course, no smiling or grinning. I'd have been a credit to a funeral cortege.

As we moved from classroom to classroom, I was aware that all eyes were fixed on me – teachers' and children's alike. For whatever reason, despite all the measures I had taken to be unobtrusive, despite embedding myself in the group, I stood out.

The tour over, I asked Olga whether the head teacher leading the tour had indicated my presence, although by now I could recognise my name in Russian. She assured me he had not.

'Then why were they all looking at me?' I asked.

She pointed to the corners of my eyes. 'You're the only one round here with laughter lines!'

+————+

Back in Azerbaijan, eighteen months after my ill-fated trip up country, my failure to recognise cultural sensitivities would derail an entire training course.

I had been asked back to Baku to conduct a human rights course funded by UNICEF, the United Nations Children's Fund. It not only had a title, *Children & Women in Vision*, it even came with a hefty lever-arch file that turned out to be a complete, officially sanctioned, instruction manual. Every step of the way, page after page, had been itemised, from start to finish.

The trainer, it stipulated, should open the course by walking across desks and tables as he talked. (Yes, you read correctly.) He would then ask one of the participants to repeat what he had just said. The participant's inability to respond, having been distracted by the bizarre behaviour, would make the point that television was essentially a *visual* medium where the word was subordinate to the image. Call me boringly conventional but I decided that, if only in consideration of health and safety, I would stay grounded.

The file came with a video cassette. On it had been recorded half a dozen selected broadcast reports from around the world which served to illustrate the points made in the manual. To be screened as required. Surprisingly, the trainer could choose which to show.

There were thirteen participants – eight television journalists (men and women) and five camera-operators (all male), most of them from regional stations but three from the state broadcaster, Azerbaijan Television. Although on a training course, these were not trainees in the strict sense of the word. All were employed full-time; one of the journalists had been twenty-eight years in the job – a couple more than I had.

With every detail of the training so assiduously pre-packaged, my judgement – my cultural sensitivity, if you like – was less acute than it should have been. Looking through the list of recorded reports, I seized upon one about female circumcision, aka genital mutilation, in Burkina Faso. This was about more than 'children and women in vision'; it was about one of the most egregious breaches of their human rights. And, as it happened, very topical. Here, I thought, was the perfect subject to really open discussion about the clash between rights and tradition, a way of tackling head-on the specious old argument: 'This is part of our culture, something we've been practising for centuries – so none of your business'.

I had already run the tape through to check there were no visuals that might give offence – no genitalia, no blood, no action shots of the grisly procedure. The closest the report came to graphic realism was a shot of a rusty razorblade in the immobile hand of a female circumciser and a close-up of a printed leaflet with a rudimentary line-drawing being used by a health worker to persuade a group of women not to let their daughters be circumcised. I was satisfied there was nothing to cause discomfort or embarrassment. Besides, I reminded myself, these were mature working journalists, operating in a part of the world all too familiar with conflict and violence, sent by their bosses to hone their skills on the reporting of human rights. Anyway, why was I worrying? The video had been sanctioned by UNICEF itself.

After introducing the subject of female genital mutilation in general terms, I slotted the cassette into the machine and pushed PLAY. I wasn't aware of any uneasiness in the room but most of the time I was looking at the screen. At the end of it, I asked for reactions, in the hope of kick-starting the discussion. Silence. So I did my best to lay out what I saw as the main points from a human rights perspective, throwing out such questions as, 'Why did the practice come about and what was its purpose?' (Answer: it was an initiative by men to keep their wives faithful by denying them sexual satisfaction.) Followed by, 'Can it be described as culture or as tradition, and therefore acceptable?'

A couple of participants mumbled their guarded views but it was like wading through molasses. It was one of those moments familiar to all trainers. You're the stand-up whose every joke is falling flat; every attempt to get the punters on side is failing and inside you're dying.

In desperation, I thought of an angle they might connect with – the fact that in their own Islamic culture circumcision was also both customary and strongly encouraged . . . not for women but for *men*. Was that not genital mutilation by any definition one cared to mention? Right here in Azerbaijan. Nor was the Islamic world alone. In the West, in my own home of the UK, male circumcision had frequently been practised for health reasons. So, circumcision was a far wider issue than . . .

One of the male participants shot out of his seat. This was not a fit subject for discussion, he declared. Not now and not here. Whether he added 'in front of women', I can't recall but the implication was clear. The room seemed suddenly full of nodding heads and low-level murmuring. My interpreter stared at his feet. It was a moment of excruciating embarrassment.

Despairingly but vainly, I tried to argue that this was what *real* journalism was about – tackling the subjects that society avoided, the taboos that normalised abuse and protected the abusers. And, in case anyone had forgotten, this was a course about women and children and the human rights to which they were entitled! What I really wanted to say was, 'Why the hell are you here? If you're going to be so bloody sensitive, why did you go into journalism in the first place?'

Instead, I declared an early break and shuffled my notes. Perhaps the M25 hadn't been so bad after all.

With hindsight, I shouldn't have been so surprised by the reaction, by how great a bar a nation's culture, whether religious or secular, can be to its journalistic development. I conducted several longer courses in Baku over the next couple of years, including a series of courses, each lasting six weeks and incorporating the production of actual news bulletins, put out by one of the local TV stations. Over that sort of period, you have a chance to spot, and help develop, the 'naturals' – those participants at total ease before the camera while still commanding authority, those with the ability to 'break through the screen'. I singled out one of them in my end-of-course report and made a note to monitor her future career – in the hope, if I'm honest, of some reflected glory as a talent-spotter. Months later I learnt she had left television. She had got married and her husband didn't want other men ogling her on the screen. Hers wasn't the only such case. If not the husband who objected, it would be his family who equated television with voyeurism at best, prostitution at worst. (Years later when working in the Middle East I was struck by how often female anchors were equated with low level immorality, not themselves but as unwitting inciters. More than once I was asked why so many men got up before dawn to watch television news. The answer: in the hope of catching the anchor in her nightdress. A joke, but possibly reflecting popular perceptions.)

+ ———————— +

Azerbaijan turned out to be a particularly rich source of cultural misunderstanding. On another course, a refreshingly feisty female participant (a pity she hadn't been on the UNICEF course!) suggested making a report about 'male impatience' – which I took to be a coded term for its most extreme form, domestic violence. Some five minutes into a group discussion on the subject I realised that my interpreter had slurred his vowels and she was actually suggesting a report on male *impotence*. Having already admitted that 'impatience' was a major failing of mine that caused my wife frequent fury, I tried to backtrack to salvage whatever remained of my reputation.

My interpreter saw no need to correct or clarify. Here was payback for all those times I had bawled him out over his habitual lateness.

9.

THE 'C' WORD

In April 2004 I had a memorable dinner with a senior American lawyer in the capital city of one of the resource-rich former Soviet republics. We were both there working as consultants in our respective fields. He and some other members of the ABA – the American Bar Association – had been called in to do an audit of the country's judicial system and make recommendations for how it could be brought up to 'Western democratic standards' in the expectation, so it was assumed, that the host country would act upon them.

The restaurant was open-air, set in a walled rectangle like a Victorian kitchen garden with a huge screen erected at one end showing, God knows why, looped episodes of *Mr Bean*. The humour being essentially visual, it needed no sound. Nobody took the slightest notice.

After ordering, my dinner companion confessed to being still in a state of shock at the end of this, his team's first working day. Sure, they had expected things to be bad – the country was rated among the bottom ten in the latest corruption survey by Transparency International – but they had assumed it would be a matter of changing attitudes through training and mentoring rather than changing personnel.

What he and his team had found was that the judges in the country had bought their positions. Every single one of them. The going price, they were told, was $100,000. How, they had asked, had the figure been arrived at? The answer: a judge could assume, on average, an income through bribes of roughly $10,000 a month. So, allowing for fluctuation, the initial outlay would be recouped well within a year, and with dollars to spare. All of this presumably in addition to his state salary.

My new American friend was exasperated. 'How do you tackle such a situation,' he asked rhetorically, 'except by sacking every sitting judge and starting over?' Which wasn't going to happen.

One often heard such stories but generally second-hand and unsourced. But this was a top American lawyer who had been given direct, privileged access to the host government's legal system.

I wasn't as shocked as perhaps I should have been. I already had first-hand experience of corruption and the scars on my back to show for it. A couple of years earlier, I had been part of an ambitious eighteen-month project in Bangladesh funded by a British charity. My role was to recruit and build a team of indigenous TV journalists and, acting as executive producer, manage the production of a dozen half-hour PSBs – public service broadcasts – for transmission on the national TV channel. One of the stipulations of the project (purely for the sake of appearances) was that we, the UK team, had to work with a Bangladeshi NGO as our 'local facilitator'. Ill-advisedly, before I came on board, the charity had given the NGO, up front, a large tranche of the very generous budget.

Arriving in Bangladesh, I asked the director of the NGO for the tender details regarding the camera crews, studio and other facilities I would be needing. His response was that everything had already been taken care of. When I demanded rather than asked, he declared that such things were none of my business; the budget was a gift from the people of the UK to the people of Bangladesh and they – that is, he – would decide how it should be spent. I later discovered that there had been no tendering process and we were paying up to three times the market rate for our camera crews. Even the video cassettes were half the price at the nearest retail outlet.

It didn't get any better. Although it was part of their job, the Bangladeshi Government employees acting as our specialist advisers required a sweetener – cash in an envelope – to attend round-table discussions. Without it, I was assured, they wouldn't come.

A few months into the project, waiting to check in at Heathrow for my regular shuttle flight back to Dhaka, I got chatting with a middle-aged British-nationalised Bangladeshi woman who turned out to be a city councillor in Leicester. She asked what I was doing in Bangladesh. When I told her, she was appalled.

'You shouldn't be there. I know you think you're doing good but they'll fleece you.'

'But you,' I responded, 'you're originally from Bangladesh . . .'

'Exactly.'

Six months into the project and with the NGO asking for another tranche of the budget, I realised there was no hope of the financial accountability we owed the charity and its donors back in the UK. In desperation, I sought out a contact at the British Council. 'How,' I asked, 'can we complete the project in such an environment?' He gave a sardonic gurgle.

'What did you expect? This is Bangladesh!'

We staggered on for a few more months before pulling the plug with half the budget spent and not a single program made.

Broadly speaking, corruption in post-Soviet society fell into two categories: top down and bottom up, although such were the permutations that they generally met somewhere in the middle.

The 'buy-a-judgeship' scheme was a classic top-down model, requiring those immediately below the judges, the lawyers who prosecuted and defended, together with the bureaucrats who ran the courts, to connive with the corruption and in many cases act as intermediaries – as handlers to distance their Honours from the grubby transactions in return, one assumes, for a cut. If the going price for a judgeship was known within the ranks to be $100,000, one had to ask not only how it was collected and by whom, but to whom and how many was it distributed?

Below the judiciary there would be those responsible for enforcing the law, the police and public prosecution service (PPS). Well, if judges and lawyers were going to take bribes to finesse verdicts, dismiss cases and adjust sentences, why shouldn't they exercise the same 'discretion' when it came to deciding whether to charge suspected offenders in the first place – and with what offences?

And from the police and PPS into the prisons, including those handling remand cases. More than once in post-Soviet countries, I heard stories of prisoners on remand being threatened with sharing a cell with a tuberculoid inmate unless their families paid for more salubrious accommodation.

Not that corruption arrived with the collapse of communism. It was more in the nature of a legacy from *l'ancien régime*. The old Soviet ruling class, the *nomenklatura* – or *priviligentsia* as it was sarcastically known – was riddled with cronyism: I scratch your back, comrade . . . you scratch mine.

Power, by definition, means you are able to help others, typically by bending or bypassing the rules. This means you can ask favours in return, whether it's the best table in a restaurant, planning consent for your three-storey holiday home in a national park or the removal of an over-zealous bureaucrat in the taxation department. We tend to think of corruption as involving financial transactions: wodges of notes in brown envelopes. But it's not always so. Far harder to detect, let alone prove, is the centuries-old quid pro quo: those reciprocated favours spread over a period of months or even years. As the British–American journalist Susan Crosland once observed, 'What most corrupts is not money but friendship.' Or there's the British politician Enoch Powell's response when asked who 'The Establishment' were. 'You're asking the wrong question. You keep looking for the copper wire. You should be looking for the electricity.' In other words, it's not the individuals; it's their relationships.[1]

<hr />

The Republic of Georgia tried harder than most of the former-Soviets to tackle corruption, long before The Fall. There is a story which over half a century has probably grown in the telling. It's about Eduard Shevardnadze's first Cabinet meeting after he became leader of the Georgian Communist Party in 1972.

Opening with a short speech, he said he expected those in his new government to serve the Georgian people rather than look to their own advancement or enrichment. Noting nods on all sides, he asked – seemingly as a vote of confidence – that those who agreed should raise their left hands. Slightly mystified by the specificity of the hand, they nevertheless complied. The new leader then did a circuit of the table amassing an impressive haul of Rolexes and Cartiers, the proceeds of which, he declared, would be donated to help their less fortunate fellow citizens as a first step in pursuing the agreed agenda.

It's one of those stories which has never been confirmed or denied, though, as George W. Bush would doubtless say, it has an air of 'truthiness'.[2] One would like to believe it. It might also explain why a number of post-Soviet politicians, Vladimir Putin among them, wear their watches on their right wrists despite being right-handed. Following the collapse of the Soviet Union, Shevardnadze was asked back in 1992 to lead the new democratic state of Georgia. Once again there were the laudable declarations of a crackdown but by the time he was ousted in 2003 by the Rose Revolution, there was no discernible improvement despite his decade in power. In that year's corruption perception index compiled by Transparency International, Georgia was rated joint 124th (with its neighbour, Azerbaijan) out of 133 countries.

My first visit to Georgia, one of a dozen, was at the end of 1998 when Shevardnadze had been leader for six years and already survived at least two assassination attempts. You could tell when his motorcade was passing because the TV sets would be blacked out by the jamming devices designed to thwart bombers using remotely controlled detonators.

Corruption was not just rife but shamelessly on show. Within days of my arrival in the capital Tbilisi, I was struck by the number of spot checks the traffic police were carrying out, whistling and waving down motorists on the suspicion of an irregularity, whether regarding the quality of the driving or the vehicle. Minibuses seemed to be a favourite. I saw it every day and most often at the same intersection on my way to work. On the superficial level, it was an impressive display of law enforcement but why, I naively wondered, this focus on traffic offences when, by all accounts, there was more than enough serious crime to be tackled in and beyond the capital?

I also noticed that there was something ritualistic about it – a choreographed *pas de deux* between driver and officer. Drivers would pull in as required but, even before being questioned, many would have a low denomination banknote held out the window between index and middle finger. Note duly removed, they would be waved back into the traffic, often without a word being exchanged. Corruption, I worked out, even had its own going rates: two lari (just over a dollar) for a token stop-and-go; five lari (just under three dollars) if threatened with a fine.

Most of the officers, it was clear, didn't even pretend to suspect a breach of regulations. It was extortion in plain sight and, no less surprising to my Western eyes, the populace was seemingly going along with it. I assumed that if a driver refused to pay, an offence would be found – a balding tyre, broken indicator, whatever. But it was very seldom that I saw a driver arguing the point. Usually they just paid up with, at most, a resigned shrug.

One morning when being driven to an appointment by one of Internews' drivers, I noticed a stash of notes behind the sun-visor which he would hand out as if it were a regular road toll. Didn't he resent this highway robbery? I asked. He gave a hollow laugh.

'You're looking at it through the eyes of a Westerner,' he said. 'Like everyone else in the public sector, the police have had their salaries either cut or paid so intermittently that it amounts to the same thing. They're meant to be getting about fifty dollars a month – already a pittance – but many of them won't have been paid for months. Like the rest of us, they've families to support – parents, brothers, sisters, cousins, in-laws too . . . most, if not all, unemployed. So this is how we pay for our public services – *directly*: individual member of the public to individual service-provider. If you were to add up what I pay in shakedowns a month, it probably wouldn't be much different, proportionally, to what you pay in your Western taxes for your law enforcement.'

'And it doesn't piss you off?' I asked, incredulous.

He smiled. 'Sometimes – particularly at New Year and Christmas, when they expect an extra dollop.' (In the Georgian Orthodox calendar, New Year precedes Christmas, which falls a week later, on 7 January.)

In some ways the most surprising aspect was that most Georgians I spoke to blamed not the police but the politicians who after so many years, before and after The Fall, had failed to excise the cancer of corruption.

I became so intrigued by the issue that at a 9 am editorial meeting with the journalists I was working alongside I wondered aloud whether we could shoot a news item about it. To my surprise and their credit, a reporter and producer persuaded a couple of the police to talk on screen, backs to camera. What my driver had told me was borne out – they disliked what they were doing. It wasn't just unprofessional; it was as demeaning as sitting with a begging bowl on the pavement. But they were the only ones in their extended families of up to maybe a dozen members who still had a job. Needs must.

But something else emerged. The corruption didn't stop with them. In return for being assigned a profitable patch, they would have to hand part of their takings to their immediate superior and so on up the line, ending presumably at a desk in the ministry itself. If one were looking for a classic example of 'bottom up' corruption, here it was.

And the same applied, in a less overt form, to other so-called public servants. State bureaucrats, the dispensers of essential documents such as certificates, licences, passports, visas, *anything* that required an official stamp, had a unique power across the post-Soviet world. The bribery could be quite subtle. Not an outright refusal to process unless money were handed over. Rather, a choice: 'Do you want to wait the "normal" processing time – perhaps months (implication, possibly forever) – or would you rather ensure your application is closer to the top of the pile and have the document in a week or two?' Of course their superiors knew what was going on and, in return for a cut, would turn a blind eye. And, again, so on up the ladder.

Occasionally, the transactions were less subtle. Flying out of Tbilisi airport at the end of one trip, I was required by a young customs official to show the dollars I was carrying even though I had declared them on the standard exit document. I opened my wallet and fanned out half a dozen $20 notes, at which point he delicately tugged at the corner of one of them and asked, 'Can I?' I was half inclined to reward his cheek but, wondering how much he had already acquired by the same tactic, I adopted a suitably shocked expression and gave a decisive, 'No, you can't.'

Even teachers and doctors weren't exempt. Usually, it was put in terms of gifts but both sides understood the nature of the transaction; this was not 'in appreciation of' but 'in payment for' their services. Whilst it was financially painful for the givers, it could be equally shaming – a moral pain, if you like – for the recipients, many of whom prided themselves on their high ethical standards and, back when they had been members of the Soviet elite, could never have imagined they would find themselves in such a humiliating situation.

This, I came to understand, is how an entire society becomes corrupted, top to bottom and back up again – some no doubt willingly, even enthusiastically, but most drawn in out of sheer desperation. For those of us who have never experienced the sudden, total collapse of a state and its institutions – everything that makes society work and daily life manageable – it is all too easy to judge. There but for the grace of God . . .

This was brought home to me by an incident one winter in Tbilisi when I took to task a member of the Internews support staff who arrived half an hour late for a morning meeting. I later discovered from a mutual colleague that a week earlier his mother had broken a leg after slipping on an icy pavement and, because she lived alone, had been moved into her son's already cramped apartment. Every morning he had been out before dawn to do the rounds of the street corner vendors of kerosene (typically sold in recycled cola bottles) to accumulate enough to keep his mother warm for the next eight hours. I meanwhile had been dithering before the guesthouse breakfast bar, debating whether to have the muesli or the fruit salad. I felt awful but when I apologised, he replied without a trace of resentment, 'You had no means of knowing and I didn't tell you.' True, but nor had I thought to ask.

Coincidentally, back in the UK, *my* 85-year-old mother, who for some years had been confined to an armchair following a stroke, was being kept in her own well-heated home by a daily succession of helpers provided, and paid for, by Hampshire Social Services.

In any society there will be rogues who take advantage of whatever system is current, who see social breakdown as an opportunity to be exploited, just as in wartime Britain there were the spivs who operated a black market to circumvent government-imposed rationing, exploiting not a broken society but, more shamefully, an existential threat to the nation.

But for every rogue there will be scores of decent citizens who, faced with the choice between their children eating or starving, between warmth and cold, between education and ignorance, on occasions literally between life and death, will tear up the social contract and put family first. So it is that the occasional bribe becomes the norm, the present generation shapes the next, and within a remarkably short time the ties that bind society unravel.

＋———＋

Not everyone resorted to bribery. Some resisted for moral reasons; others for lack of opportunity, of having the necessary 'chips'. Academics for example. Those in the humanities were generally able to find some private tutoring. It was far harder for the scientists – the biologists, chemists and physicists – who were often involved in high-level research. Nobody was going to slip them a couple of hundred lari for the coefficient of thermal expansion of an industrial polymer. But, if they still had a car and were prepared to swallow their pride, they had the means of a potential income.

It seemed that the driver of every other taxi I hailed in Tbilisi was a former professor. Since most of them spoke English, the ride would become an Open University course on wheels. Journalists love taxi drivers because they're such a loquacious lot; the downside is that most of them spout opinionated bollocks. In Georgia, by contrast, you could count on a high degree of intellectual enlightenment included in the fare. And a personal story with it. One former professor told me of the lengths to which he and his colleagues had gone to keep their university chemistry department functioning.

> It wasn't just for me, you understand, but for my staff and the department itself. All the knowledge we had accumulated over the years and which would now be lost. Even when they

stopped paying us, we came in. And in winter when there was no heating and we had to wear hats, coats and gloves, we still came in! But then they cut off the electricity and turned off the water . . . then, only then, we knew we were beaten.

It's little wonder that across the former Soviets there was a nostalgia for the good old days when there had been no unemployment, you got a living wage, and education and healthcare were free. A decade after The Fall, the BBC World Service did a snapshot profile of each former Soviet republic, with vox pops. One 61-year-old pensioner, Gulnara Gasanova living in Georgia's neighbour Azerbaijan, summed up the feelings of millions of her generation:

> There's a bigger choice of food now, but who can afford to buy it? I used to earn 140 roubles a month. My husband was an academic and he earned almost 500 roubles. With this money we were able to travel every year throughout the Soviet Union. The bus and the metro cost 5 kopeks. Salaries today aren't even enough for transport. If you don't have a supplementary income from somewhere, you can't survive . . . I'm now very ill but we have to pay for medicine. In Soviet times, it was free. These days people can find themselves at death's door but they still don't go to the doctor because they simply have no money.[3]

This was Azerbaijan. I had heard similar stories when working there. I had seen at firsthand the extreme gap between rich and poor. How was this possible in such a resource-rich country?

'But you have oil and gas,' I said to an Azerbaijani colleague.

He nodded. 'You're right. We have oil and gas. When communism collapsed, we also had a choice: to follow the example of Norway and share the wealth across the entire population to pay for the social needs of present and future generations . . . or we could go the way of Nigeria. We chose Nigeria.'

+ ———— +

Back in Georgia, one of my Sunday morning strolls when working in Tbilisi was down to the capital's Dry Bridge Market, so called because the water beneath the bridge dried up. Following The Fall, the market had become a hunting ground for Westerners like me to pick up items of genuine Soviet memorabilia (as opposed to the knock-off reproductions on sale in Moscow's Old Arbat where there were enough 'Authentic USSR Submarine Clocks' to furnish the entire Soviet fleet a hundred times over).

In the hope of making a few lari, the stallholders offered for sale scraps of their and their relatives' former lives. Since the stall was most often a sheet or blanket laid on the bare ground, the result looked like an artist's installation. Among the plethora of electronic components and car parts, there would be cameras, microscopes, slide-rules, opera glasses, women's wigs, WWII medals, showerheads and, on one occasion, the entire contents of a dentist's surgery, the chair included. As was once said of London's Bermondsey Market, 'If the world were tilted on its axis, anything not nailed down would end up here'.

For me, the most interesting items fell into the category of Soviet domestic, those that, with their dents and scratches, bore testimony to daily use over decades. One of my best – and cheapest – finds was a steel bottle-opener, because it explained better than any textbook how the centralised Soviet economy worked. I have it in my hand. Stamped across the top is its unique stock number,

HP-088-2, followed by its price, again stamped into the metal: 40K – forty kopeks. I can think of no commercial product in the West which would have its price so ineradicably marked in disregard of subsequent inflation or markdown. But in Soviet times, just as the hotel menu in Tbilisi was set in Moscow, so the price of even a utilitarian object like a bottle opener was fixed for eternity at the point of manufacture.

Being a regular gleaner, I had a nodding acquaintance with some of the stallholders. The fact that they could speak enough English for us to communicate reflected their former socio-professional status, now a distant and painful memory. Giorgi, with his hangdog expression, hunched shoulders and hands dug deep into his coat pockets, always had a good line in black humour. One drizzly overcast morning listening to his familiar moan, I remarked that, no matter what the economic hardships, at least he and his compatriots now had their freedom. He nearly choked.

'Yes, we have freedom – freedom not to work, freedom not to eat, freedom to travel anywhere with the money we don't have . . . If you call that freedom, we have it!'

It sounded like a line he had worked on or perhaps appropriated. But what struck me was that it was an echo of a similar line I had heard in Moscow about the supposedly good old Soviet days he was mourning. According to the joke, a hopeful shopper would ask a shopkeeper, 'Do you have meat here?' To which the shopkeeper would respond, 'No, here we do not have fish; it's at the other store they do not have meat.' Giorgi was being more ironic than he realised.

+ ———— +

And yet there are always those canny few who, endowed with native nous and a strong survival instinct, manage to exploit change, any change, to their advantage; to work the system no matter what direction it takes. In Russia, it was the 'New Russians' with their sharp suits and expensive watches who, like shiny cockroaches, had emerged from the rubble of communism. In Georgia, it was the likes of 'Katerina'.

During one of my early visits to Tbilisi, I was booked into a guesthouse in the Vera district, a leafy hillside suburb to the north-west of the city centre and a short walk down to the capital's main thoroughfare, Rustaveli Avenue. In the nineteenth century, it had been favoured by the Georgian aristocracy; then in Soviet times by the Communist Party élite, the *priviligentsia*, and now, nearly a decade after independence, by Georgia's latest upper class, those who had not merely survived the breakup of the Union but had thrived, as testified by the number of Mercedes, BMWs and four-wheel drives.

Suitcase in hand, I was greeted by the owner of the guesthouse. Katerina was in her fifties, statuesque, with jet-black hair pulled back from a white-powdered face. Speaking serviceable English, she told me she was delighted to have me stay because she felt comfortable with Westerners. We shared the same values, she said, the same cosmopolitan outlook on life. As she continued in the same vein, it became clear that Katerina was an appalling snob.

The house was grand and spacious, elegantly furnished in the heavy Georgian style and with a pleasant vine-covered terrace out the back. I was curious to know Katerina's backstory. How, while most of her fellow Georgians were living below the official poverty line, starving or slowly dying for want of medication, had she become the chatelaine of all she surveyed?

She told me she had been born in Georgia but to Russian parents, which was why Russia would always be her spiritual home. To establish her cultural credentials, she reeled off the names of two centuries of Russian writers, performing a credible swoon after each, as though the entire canon of Tolstoy's, Chekhov's and Dostoevsky's work had at that instant burst within her head like a ruptured aneurysm.

She had made a good marriage, she said, her husband being a loyal party member who rose to become the head of a state-run engineering works, providing parts for the military. I had passed the ghostly remnants of such factories on trips out of Tbilisi and I recalled being told how, when Georgia broke away from the Union in April 1991, all the old Soviet industries had folded overnight – a catastrophe for the tens of thousands who worked for them, whether manager, lathe operator, cook or cleaner. But not, it was evident, for Katerina's husband and family. So, how had they survived when so many had gone under?

At this point details became hazy. This was not a subject to be dwelt upon. I guessed, though, that the transition to capitalism and, with it, the restoration of private ownership had enabled the family to acquire legal title to the substantial property they already occupied courtesy of the former Soviet state. Doubtless with strings pulled here and palms greased there. Exploiting this windfall, Katerina had discovered an entrepreneurial flair, offering foreign visitors 'authentic Georgian accommodation' for $50 a night – what many Georgians had to live on for *a month* . . . if they were lucky. Thus, the family that had lacked for nothing during Soviet times, had found itself no less comfortable in the newly independent Georgia. This was confirmed when Katerina remarked that she and her husband, no longer restricted to Soviet countries, liked to take their holidays in Western Europe. Their most recent trip had been to Rome.

'Frankly, very disappointing,' she said, wrinkling her nose. 'Perhaps we didn't meet the right people . . . very low-class types.'

Winding back the conversation, I asked what gave her the idea to run a guesthouse. She quickly corrected me.

'Please, Michael! I don't *run* a guesthouse. I have guests.'

I wondered whether the taxman made the same distinction but, given that there was no external sign to indicate Katerina's hospitable activity and, as she had admitted, not even her friends knew about it, it's likely he had been spared the trouble.

10.

ASK THE GOVERNOR

In late 1999 I was working in Kutaisi, generally regarded as Georgia's second city and, at that time, a good three hours' drive west of Tbilisi on account of the state of the roads. Here was a chance to see close-up the post-Soviet lives of ordinary Georgians beyond the capital.

While waiting for a taxi outside my guesthouse, I noticed how all the lamp posts were tilted at rakish angles. Except they weren't lamp posts but, as the taxi driver explained, poles to support trolley-bus gantries, long gone. 'In the early 1990s they climbed the poles and stole the cable. For the copper. Now, too expensive to replace.' And so, overnight, the transport system covering an entire suburb had been taken out.

As we descended into the centre of town, there was another reminder of post-Soviet times when the driver turned off the ignition to save petrol. I learnt later that the driver of a school bus had done the same a month earlier. When he hit the brakes, there were none. Several children had died.

✦ ———— ✦

The local television journalists I was working with were keen to shoot a story about child beggars, of which there were always scores, sometimes hundreds, in former Soviet cities; often organised into gangs by latter-day Fagins. Children's charities regularly appealed to TV journalists not to film them because it gave them celebrity status among their peers. Besides, it was a rule of ethical journalism to interview children only in the presence of their parents, guardian or a responsible adult, bar exceptional circumstances. All of this I stressed to the Kutaisi team before they set off.

In the city centre they soon chanced upon a bedraggled eight-year-old standing alone in the rain, hand held out more in hope than expectation. Her name, she told them, was Christina and she earnt around five lari a day, close on three dollars. Mindful of my injunction against interviewing children without an adult present, they asked Christina where her parents were. She led them to her mother who worked nearby in the market and was happy to talk on camera. Her children had to beg, she said, because she didn't make enough from her stall to support the family. Of course, she would rather they were in school but they had to eat. And her husband? He was in prison for stealing a bag of flour. 'To feed the family,' she added matter-of-factly.

The next day I saw the market for myself. Within seconds I was assailed by a bevy of young women forcing cigarettes on me. 'Promotion! Take one, try one . . . first quality . . . German!' At well-choreographed moments they would strike and hold the exaggerated poses of Western fashion models before resuming the hustle. Shrugging them off, I moved further inside and came upon an elderly woman standing with outstretched arms; in one hand was a bunch of candles, in the other a toilet roll. It was the post-Soviet world encapsulated: luxuries like cigarettes may have been free but you still had to pay for the essentials.

Most striking, though, was the profusion of fruit and vegetables all around: apples, mandarins, pomegranates, nuts, garlic and beans in more varieties than I could count. The former fruit bowl of the Soviet Union was now selling to itself. It was clear that at this level Georgia didn't need telling how to establish a market economy. And yet Christina's mother had to send her children out to beg while their father languished in prison for filching a bag of flour.

I was still trying to understand the economic dynamics of post-Soviet Georgia when, back at base, I was invited to attend a transmission of *Ask the Governor*.

Teimuraz Shashiashvili was the governor of Georgia's Imereti region of which Kutaisi is the capital, and for three hours every Friday/Saturday night, from midnight to 3 am, he would subject himself to a public phone-in, live on camera. One of his young acolytes assured me this was democracy in action. (It was also the only time the locals could be sure of an uninterrupted electricity supply.) Offered a seat close to the governor, I realised too late that I had been brought in as a stooge and, instead, chose to make myself inconspicuous by crouching in a far corner. But there was no escape. A dozen questions in, the camera swung in my direction to reveal my undignified squat. I must have looked like the crafty crapper.

The acolyte approached, microphone in hand. 'Perhaps our foreign guest has a question for the governor from his uniquely Western viewpoint?' he wondered aloud with calculated ambiguity.

I fell back on an old stand-by. 'How does the governor see the role of the media in a democracy: to represent the government to the people . . . or the people to the government?'

The governor was already at the net. 'I expect the media to be responsible, to assist our emerging democracy to become a full one.' Smash.

A true professional would have followed up with a tactical lob, 'And what would media responsibility look like in such a situation?' But by now it was 1.20 am, far too late for a dialogue on the media's role in a democracy, emerging or otherwise.

After two weeks in Kutaisi, I was left in awe of its resilience, of the population's seeming ability to absorb and adapt to whatever life threw at them. It was reminiscent of the old British wartime spirit of 'mustn't grumble', along with a commendable dose of self-sufficiency.

One morning on a bleak 1960s housing estate, my minder-cum-fixer Jano and I encountered a man walking his pig. As we chatted, another local appeared, this time with a gun and dog. Jano asked the hunter what he'd been up to. He pointed beyond the apartment blocks. 'Shooting wild chicken in the wood,' he replied, tapping the well-stuffed bag across his chest.

Before we parted, Jano bent down to check out the pig. He and the owner agreed it would be a few months yet before *its* time came.

＋ —————— ＋

After the depressing picture I've painted of a corruption-ridden Georgia during the post-Soviet Shevardnadze era, I should add that one of the first things the new president, Mikheil Saakashvili, did on taking office in 2004 was to reform the police, and it's generally agreed, with conspicuous success. All the uniformed officers were sacked and a new force, the Patrol Police, was built from scratch with the OSCE, the Organisation for Security and Cooperation in Europe, facilitating training based on its experience with Kosovo's revamped police force. The change in public perception was little short of miraculous. From having been one of Georgia's most despised institutions in 2003, the new force was by 2009 ranked in a nationwide public survey as the third most popular after the Church and the Army.[1]

Whether that reappraisal survived the violent clashes between police and pro-European Union protestors on the streets of Tbilisi in late 2024 is harder to say.

11.

ALICE IN ABKHAZIA

One of the perks of being an international broadcast consultant is that you get sent to places you can't spell. In early 1999, a non-profit organisation committed to bringing together warring factions asked me to do some work for them in Abkhazia on the coast of the Black Sea. At the time I was working regularly in Georgia, funded by the British Government. Geographically, Abkhazia was conveniently next door; politically, it could have been a million miles away. It was a post-Soviet state like no other. For most of the world it wasn't even a state; more of an 'entity', a pariah recognised only by Russia, Venezuela, Nicaragua, Syria . . . and the tiny Pacific island of Nauru. To enter it was to 'walk through the looking glass'.

During Soviet times, Abkhazia had been an autonomous republic within the Republic of Georgia. Following the collapse of the Union, it had taken its chance and, along with South Ossetia, broken away. Thousands of ethnic Georgians fled and ended up as internally displaced persons (IDPs) – refugees in their own land – in the Georgian capital Tbilisi and elsewhere around the country. The separation had been bloody and acrimonious. I had been shocked when one of my Georgian colleagues, a gentler man it was hard to imagine, had said that the breakaway Abkhazians should be shot as traitors. He left me in no doubt that, given the means, he would personally have helped.

Predictably Russia, Abkhazia's neighbour to the north, had been a key player in the breakup, persuading the Abkhazians that they would be better off with Russia than with Georgia. It was a continuation of the old divide and destabilise policy forged (originally by Stalin) in Soviet times when Mother Russia had played the republics off against each other, sometimes favouring one, then another, to sow envy among the siblings. In 2002, The Kremlin would officially offer Abkhazians Russian passports.

After years of border conflict, the United Nations Observer Mission in Georgia (UNOMIG) was keeping the two sides apart. In fact, the only safe way in or out of the region was with the UN. A German, Martin Schumer, was to be my fixer and facilitator. An intense, monk-like figure, he was a respected UN volunteer and had played a key role in attempts to bring the sides together. We met in a cafe in Tbilisi. It was immediately clear from his pallor and the trouble he was having breathing that he was not a well man. In the event, he had less than a year to live.

Schumer had a direct, no-nonsense style. He clearly saw Abkhazia as a personal mission. We were discussing the work I would be doing with Abkhazian State Television, such as the video and editing facilities that might be available, when, apropos of nothing, he asked, 'Have you worked in war zones?' I took it as a casual, conversational enquiry, unrelated to the business in hand. If he had added 'before', I might have spared myself a shedload of stress.

I explained that I had never worked as a war correspondent but, during a varied career, I had been in plenty of conflict zones.[1] I had reported from Northern Ireland at the height of the Troubles in the 1970s (where I had learned such invaluable lessons as never to reach inside my jacket for my BBC ID when someone answered their front door) and I had found myself in the crossfire of the 1976 Thammasat

University Massacre in Bangkok when the Thai police and right wing paramilitary groups had stormed the building and killed scores of students suspected of communist leanings (my abiding memory being of lying face down while sound recordist Bill Searle held aloft his rifle mic to record the 'actuality sound' of M16 bullets whistling overhead). I didn't mention that I had also walked through a vegetable patch with Zimbabwean guerrilla leader Joshua Nkomo at his ZAPU camp on the Zambian border, only for him to reveal it was a minefield – retribution for the 'white imperialist' questions I had asked during our confrontational interview minutes earlier.

+ ———— +

We set off on a Saturday. Our UNOMIG convoy into Abkhazia was made up of five vehicles, led by a seven-tonne Mamba armoured personnel carrier, the mobile equivalent of a brick shithouse. Thanks to its shovel nose and V-shaped hull, it was able to deflect the blast of a tank-busting mine without breaking up . . . supposedly. This explained why it went first with our driver, immediately behind in a Land Cruiser, assiduously following its tracks as it weaved between the potholes. These, he explained, were where the Georgian partisans planted anti-tank mines overnight. My enquiry as to how often this happened got no response. Whether it was a case of 'You don't need to know' or 'You don't want to know' wasn't clear.

Our first stop was the UN Mission at Zugdidi, still in Georgia but less than ten kilometres from the border. I could feel the hostility when we parked in the central square. Schumer explained that this was because the locals felt the UN Secretary General Kofi Annan hadn't done enough to help the Georgians who had fled Abkhazia, many of them now living as refugees in Zugdidi.

Although it was only a hundred kilometres up the coast to Sukhumi, the capital of Abkhazia, the journey would take a couple of hours. The next stop, just inside Abkhazia, was the UNOMIG Control Point at Gali, a frequent flashpoint and now manned by the Russian Peace Keeping Force (PKF) working in uneasy alliance with the UN.

An hour later there was a 'comfort stop' . . . next to a graveyard. I could hear what sounded like cheering coming from it, but oddly tinny. To stretch my legs, I wandered across for a closer look and came upon one of those surreal sights that the former Soviet Union so often throws up. At the end of a very long cable stretched above the headstones, a television had been set up at the foot of a grave. It was showing a football match, with sound. Before a peremptory call summoned me back to the convoy, I was able to glean from a local, possibly the guardian of the graveyard, that the set was turned on and off every day, religiously. Only later did it occur to me that a more interesting question would have been whether it was tuned permanently to the deceased's favourite sports channel, or did he have to take whatever was available?

＋————＋

Schumer's office, it turned out, was in the old sanatorium of the Russian Compound – a stretch of once impressive, now neglected, buildings overlooking the Black Sea, used in Soviet times as an R & R playground for the top brass of the Russian military. The compound was guarded by Russians, but Schumer made clear he had little faith in any security they might offer. Even less in our Russian driver, a former KGB chauffeur for Soviet leaders Brezhnev and Andropov. 'They all have two jobs here – you never know who they really answer to,' he said.

I was puzzled. Schumer was a UN volunteer and UNOMIG, I knew, had their own large, well-guarded compound in Sukhumi. In the light of his concerns, why were we staying, and seemingly sleeping, here?

We arrived at the door to his second-floor office. There were actually two doors – the outer one of sheet steel with a triple lock and an inner one with its own formidable lock. Neither of them, Schumer quietly insisted, was to be left unlocked. Once inside, I noticed that the windows were fitted not with regular bars but with welded lengths of angle-iron. Schumer explained that this was to stop anyone using the balcony to get in, as had happened in his absence eighteen months earlier. As an afterthought, he added, 'And keep the curtains drawn – in case anyone decides to shoot through the windows.'

The phone on the desk had been cut off long ago. Schumer handed me a walkie-talkie, insisting that we never used names, only call signs. I was to be 'Delta Whisky'. Why such elaborate communication would be needed when we were in the same apartment was beyond me, but by now I realised that, like Alice, I had entered a world where logic no longer applied.

'You'll be sleeping upstairs in Room 333,' he announced. 'On the third floor.'

Like fuck I would. I had already decided that I would rather be inside the fortress than outside and so elected to sleep on the office couch. 'Your decision,' Schumer said. Before retiring to the bedroom, he gave some parting advice. 'In case anything happens, it's essential to keep absolutely quiet. If someone bangs on the door, don't respond.'

I comforted myself with the thought that this was all sensible security, and drifted off to sleep. At some point during the night

I was woken by a burst of Russian voices. Inexplicably, they were coming not from the other side of the double-doors but from my walkie-talkie which, on Schumer's orders, I had left 'open'. As advised, I said nothing. There was never a subsequent explanation.

✦———✦

The next morning, Sunday, turned out to be a workday for Schumer. I had assumed, without specifically asking, that his primary role was to be my fixer for the five-day consultancy I was to conduct with staff of Abkhazian State Television. In other words, I was his priority. Not so. It was now clear from the neat stacks of dollar bills lined up on his desk that his main objective was to distribute thousands of dollars to various non-governmental bodies operating in Abkhazia. We were engaged in a 'fund-running' operation – ethically more commendable than gun-running but no less risky. It also explained why we were in the Russian Compound, not the UNOMIG compound from where, with its high security, any such distribution would have been impossible.

Had Schumer mentioned any of this during our initial chat back in Tbilisi? A passing reference perhaps to supporting local NGOs – yes, something of the sort – but certainly no indication of the nature, scale or potential risk of the operation. Looking back, I suspect his war zone question had been intended as an oblique warning. So oblique, it hadn't registered.

A succession of individuals arrived throughout the day, collected their dollar wodges, signed and left.

It occurred to me as I watched the scene repeat itself that all of them must have passed through the Russian security post, in and out. How soon would it be before someone clocked what was going on? However well-intended, Schumer's operation involved a huge risk – one which I assumed he had calculated from the start and was now, without consultation, obliging me to share.

I was not happy. Following his death, I would describe Martin as 'a truly noble man – kind, moral and brave'. Which was true and, as a peacemaker, he was surely blessed. But his action on this occasion not only disregarded minimal security in a designated conflict zone but defied common sense.

There were questions. Where had the money come from? (It was significant that the recipients were required to sign.) Was the UN aware of its distribution? More to the point, did the Abkhazian government know how these NGOs were being 'supported' and by whom? If so, and if they approved, why couldn't the money be distributed officially, directly and safely? Another possibility occurred to me – an unjust thought perhaps but a pertinent one – that my visit might have been a cover for the distribution.

The whole operation was madness, as would soon become clear.

At eight o'clock that evening we learnt that one of the first recipients of the dollar handouts, the director of a centre for humanitarian programs, had been attacked in a city park by five masked, armed assailants. They had interrogated and pistol-whipped him. They knew he had collected the money but, finding none on him (he had already hidden it), they had left him, concussed and bleeding, to stumble off alone to the hospital for treatment.

I had only to look at Schumer, only to hear the rasp in his voice, his breathing now bordering on hyperventilation, to intuit what was going through his mind. The same as was going through mine. The attackers already knew large sums of money were being distributed – that much was clear. Whether or not they had known at the time of the attack where the NGO director had collected the money from was moot, but it was a fair bet they would by now. Schumer conceded that our dodgy driver would be an obvious source.

Sitting ducks at least had the possibility of flying off; we were caged. Rather, we had caged ourselves. Perhaps it comes from my working in television but, twenty-five years on, my recollection of the next twelve hours plays out in real time.

✦ —————— ✦

The office, Schumer declares, is now a target – and anyone in it. But it's close to midnight. Even if there were a possibility of alternative accommodation, what remains of the money has to be guarded. To venture beyond the triple-locked door is unthinkable. Whether we take the money with us or not, the assumption will be that we have it on us.

I am beginning to wonder whether this is some elaborate training exercise; the sort the BBC arranges for staff assigned to conflict zones, when their minibus is ambushed just off the M4 motorway and they are 'kidnapped' by Mujahideen, hooded, driven to a warehouse near Wadi Slough and subjected to interrogation, realistic enough to require a change of underwear. Unfortunately, it isn't.

So, for a second night, the office couch becomes my bed. I ask Schumer if he has a plan in the event of . . . whatever. Not exactly, he replies. The modus operandi of these criminal gangs, he explains (modus operandi? How often does this sort of thing happen, for Christ's sake?) is to fire bullets through the windows to create panic. In which case the bathroom will be the only safe place, so best to leave the bathroom door open.

'And another thing . . .' He hesitates before continuing. 'There's a possibility that, having smashed the windows, they'll lob in CS gas canisters to smoke us out.' And then? His response is less than reassuring. 'As I've said, the best policy is to keep quiet.' So, choke to death in silence.

Throughout a very long night I lie awake listening to some isolated gunfire coming from the city centre and the sound of Schumer's struggle for breath next door. The CS gas tactic is a detail Schumer had spared me the previous evening. For the first time in my life, I understand what it means to wait for 'the knock at the door' and wonder whether I should be thinking about my preferred television channel.

But any fear is mixed with anger at having been put in this absurd situation. It's one thing to go down in a blaze of bullets in some foreign hotspot doing one's job as a gatherer and dispenser of global news ('It's how he would have wanted to go'); quite another lying on a tatty couch waiting for the arrival of some thug whose idea of a wake-up call is to fire through the window and, for good measure, toss in a gas canister.

Such situations are rarely as one imagines. What you feel most is the improbability of your own extinction. It's not, 'I don't want to be here,' or 'Dear Lord, I promise to devote the rest of my life to charitable works if you get me out of here,' but rather, 'I'm *not* here . . . this isn't happening.' Nature's coping mechanism, I guess. Or, as my wife frequently observes, I'm one of those people who cannot conceive of the world going on without them. Whatever the case, I can recommend anger as an effective antidote to fear.

In the morning, neither gassed nor shot but still mightily pissed off, I tell Schumer this was never part of the brief. Two nights on death couch are enough. He doesn't argue the point and later in the morning negotiates for us to move into the UNOMIG compound. That night I sleep an uninterrupted ten hours.

My sessions with Abkhazian State Television went broadly to plan. They were in two parts. First, some political theory; how the media should be a two-way communication bridge between the government and the governed while maintaining their editorial independence (multiple diagrams on flipchart with arrows shooting off in all directions). Even as I spoke, we were all aware this fell into the 'fine in theory' category. Second, the practicalities of shooting and editing watchable news reports. There was no denying the enthusiasm of the staff and their touching gratitude that I should have come 'so far' but, having seen what passed for the State Television Centre, I was left wondering to what end they could use my advice.

At best, I realised, my presence was a diplomatic gesture, a way of assuring them they had not been forgotten. Like Schumer, I was a rare, human link with the rest of the world. Looked at from this perspective, 'at best' was good enough. Just being there was as, perhaps more, important than any knowledge or advice I might have had to impart.

During a coffee break, I watched in fascination as an old woman repaired the window in her kiosk. Tapping away with a hammer and nails, she overlapped shards of broken glass to recreate a single pane. It was a metaphor for the plight of Abkhazia itself.

On the final day, the participants presented me with a pack of souvenir photos, quote, 'to remember Sukhumi'. Shuffling through them, I was aware of the sad irony; this was as much about how *they* would have liked to remember their capital city. The Soviet-era photos showed fine Art Nouveau palaces framed by palms and cypresses looking out over a glinting Black Sea. The reality, as I had seen, was that two-thirds of the buildings had been fractured by war and neglect. Cranes – usually signs of regeneration – hung over them, but these were rusting, their heads dipped as though in mourning.

I also became a member of one of the world's most exclusive clubs, the recipient of an Abkhazian visa, number 538 – not stuck in my passport like the others because that might cause 'inconvenient questions' when moving in or out of Georgia. Instead, it was thoughtfully slipped in like a bookmark.

+ ——— +

Schumer's condition, meanwhile, had seriously deteriorated. He was having trouble not just breathing but walking. He put it down to the stress of the first two nights, exacerbated by what he suspected were fungus spores in the UNOMIG building. He needed medical treatment, urgently, but it was available only in Tbilisi. There was, we discovered, a helicopter due to fly out the next day but then we were told it had developed technical problems and spare parts were awaited.

Schumer played his ace. If UNOMIG didn't facilitate our immediate return to Tbilisi, they would be sending him back in a box. Did they really want all the bureaucratic hassle of repatriating his body to Germany? In the end, we got out the way we had come in – by road with a UN convoy.

On our return journey, we travelled up front in the Mamba APC with UN staff because we were an unscheduled booking. I noticed that the UN personnel were all wearing helmets and flak jackets, and there were four neat bullet holes in the rear window. A sign had been stuck to the bulkhead: *Sorry. On domestic escorts, we are unable to serve meals. Please ask the stewardess for refreshments.*

Laugh? I could have died.

12.

THE UNPREDICTABILITY OF THE PAST

Regimes like to make their mark – grand, multi-columned buildings bearing striking nationalist symbols – in the expectation of surviving a thousand years. Realistic for Ancient Egyptians, Greeks and Romans; less so for Nazis.

The regimes that replace them have a choice: to obliterate what has gone before or absorb it as national heritage. It can be tricky. Successive postwar German governments have been ambivalent about such sites as the Zeppelinfeld where Hitler held his Nuremberg Rallies, torn between dismantling them because they are reminders of a shameful past or preserving them as a warning for the future.

A similar choice faced Lenin and the Bolsheviks in 1917 following the October Revolution. Surprisingly, rather than raze imperial buildings like Catherine the Great's Hermitage, they spared and preserved them, although many of the Hermitage's paintings would be sold off on Stalin's orders during the 1930s. Churches fared less well, having no significance for the godless regime. Moscow's massive Cathedral of Christ the Saviour was dynamited in 1931 to make way for an even bigger Palace of the Soviets. The Second World War ensured it was never built. Instead, within a decade of communism falling apart, the old cathedral rose again; an identical copy, paid for by public subscription.

Architecturally, the transition from communism to capitalism in the 1990s was less about buildings (Moscow's ring of Stalin-era skyscrapers all survived) than about statues. Most of them were of Lenin. During Soviet times there was hardly a town or city in Russia that didn't have a centrally sited representation of the founder of the world's first communist state. In many cases they were mounted on plinths that had formerly supported tsars. More were erected in the other republics, many with curiously extended right arms and consequently nicknamed 'Long-Arm Lenins'. It's doubtful Lenin ever played charades but the effect is of him miming a railway signal. Theories about their origin differ. Some say they were an intentional echo of the twelfth century Russian ruler and founder of Moscow, Yuri Dolgorukiy – 'Yuri the Long Arm'. Others claim that the poorer republics, lacking the bronze to make the statues to the prescribed size but knowing that Lenin was traditionally portrayed in declamatory mode, arm extended, put a disproportionate amount of metal into it.[1]

As Boris Yeltsin and his capitalist colleagues were to discover, the communist-era statues – not just of Lenin but also the few of Stalin that survived Khrushchev's denunciation of him in 1956 – had iconic status for those who still clung to the old political creed. Even for those who didn't, they often had sentimental value, having long been part of the fabric of their lives. Valentina, an educated woman in her forties I met in Kazan, encapsulated the mixed feelings of her generation:

> The old Soviet leaders, yes, they may have been monsters, but their statues were like reference points when I was growing up. My friends and I would arrange to meet under one or other of them. Now, some of our squares are unrecognisable.

When you take away the statues, you take away part of my generation's childhood.

Overhearing our conversation, a young man in his twenties would have none of it:

They weren't erected by a grateful people. They had a purely political purpose – as symbols of repression; to remind us who was in charge. That's why we must get rid of them.

✦——✦

In the unlikely event of my ever being invited to present BBC *Mastermind* and faced with a contestant choosing the life of Lenin as their specialist subject, my first question would be: 'Where is the only statue of Lenin with a full head of hair?' Answer: 'In front of The University of Kazan, the capital of Russia's Tatarstan.' It shows the young Lenin clutching a book and it's there not because he was a high-flying graduate but because in 1887 he was expelled after just three months on account of his anti-tsarist activities. By 1954, however, when the statue was erected, the university authorities seem to have decided he had turned out rather well. 'We always knew he was destined for great things . . .'

What is claimed to be Russia's last large-scale statue of Lenin – and at 22 metres including the base, one of the tallest – was erected in Moscow's Kaluga Square. It was inaugurated by Mikhail Gorbachev in 1985, the first year of his leadership, when he still hoped to overhaul the system through *perestroika* and give communism a human face. Lenin, his greatcoat billowing behind, goatee thrust forward, is striding into a glorious communist future oblivious to the skateboarding kids perfecting their skills on the steps below. I remarked to Irina my interpreter that, as Lenin statues went, it was pretty impressive. She snorted, observing that Kaluga Square was sited on the Garden Ring Road, so no matter where Lenin was heading, he was destined to go round in eternal circles. If periodic local council discussions come to anything, he could be spared this Dante-esque fate and moved to the Muzeon Park of Arts (aka 'Fallen Monument Park') just south of the river where communist-era statues are accorded a dignified retirement, though, given his size, he is more likely to end up overlooking a scruffy football pitch out in the suburbs. At least there is a chance he will remain upright, unlike most of Stalin's statues.

The past, as they used to say in Soviet times, is unpredictable.

The more I travelled around Russia and the post-Soviets, the more intrigued I became, not just by the statues but by the stories they generated. Even though most of these were probably apocryphal, they invariably contained – like Soviet jokes – a barbed nugget of political truth.

According to my favourite story, back in the 1920s a statue was erected alongside the road between the Georgian capital, Tbilisi, and the capital of neighbouring Armenia, Yerevan. It portrayed Lenin and Stalin sitting chummily side by side on a bench (probably based on a well-publicised photo of them taken in Gorky). But Stalin was famously reluctant to share the limelight. As soon as he succeeded Lenin, he ordered the removal of his predecessor, leaving his own likeness in splendid self-absorbed isolation. But then, when Stalin fell from grace, he too was removed. All that was left, so the story goes, was the bench.

One winter when working in the Caucasus, I had a chance to check the story by travelling the entire length of the road. There was no sign of the bench where it was alleged to have been, nor anywhere else along the route. It too had been removed . . . if it ever existed. Yet the story of the incrementally diminishing statue remains a potent fable of the Ozymandian transience of power in Soviet times. (Coincidentally, it had a real-life parallel. In 1930s Georgia, it was fashionable among the politically aware to give their children composite first names, the most popular being 'Lenstalber' – a melding of Lenin, Stalin and Beria, the last two having been Georgian-born. When first Beria, then Stalin were discredited, the unfortunate Lenstalbers were reduced to plain 'Len'.)

Most of the stories, like that of the bench, have an element of the absurd but invariably in the service of a grim reality or warning, like that of 'two-caps Lenin'. Shortly after Lenin's death, Stalin ordered a commemorative statue of his predecessor and, on being told it was finished, went to the workshop to check it out. The covering sheet had barely revealed the head when he yelled, 'Stop!' Why, he demanded to know, was the great man not wearing that symbol of the proletarian struggle, his trademark peaked cap? Trembling, the sculptor assured him the omission would be rectified. Come the day of the official unveiling, the sheet fell to the ground to reveal a cap on Lenin's head . . . and another in his hand.

The joke is on Stalin, but it reflects the incontinence-inducing terror of those who earned his slightest displeasure, or even just feared they might. It is wholly appropriate therefore that the dread he generated in others was to be the death of the man himself. After he had a stroke at his Kuntsevo dacha during the night of 1 March 1953 and failed to appear the next morning, nobody – neither the dacha staff nor even his own guards – dared to enter his bedroom for fear of disturbing a dictatorial lie-in. By the time he was discovered, on the floor in a pool of piss (his own, this time), it was too late. He died four days later.

✦ ─────── ✦

Returning to Lenin, even more fraught than the post-Soviet debates over his bronze and stone representations have been those over his mortal, embalmed remains in the mausoleum on Moscow's Red Square.

On coming to power in 1991, Boris Yeltsin was faced with a dilemma familiar to any family stuck with an unwanted heirloom beloved by a few sentimental members of the previous generation. The temptation was to quietly lose it, and there was a recent precedent. The year before, the Bulgarian authorities had surreptitiously removed the embalmed body of Georgi Dimitrov, the country's first communist leader, from his mausoleum in central Sofia. Before anyone had time to react, let alone protest, it had been cremated. Job done.

Yeltsin, however, preferred a wither on the vine approach. The Kremlin stopped paying for Lenin's maintenance and in 1993 the goosestepping guards were removed from the front of the mausoleum. Then in 1997, Yeltsin floated the idea of a referendum. In response, the party of ultra-nationalist Vladimir Zhirinovsky announced that it would gladly buy the body and send it on a farewell tour of the provinces – a one-man show, albeit more recumbent than stand-up.

Disposing of dead Soviet statesmen has often prompted jokes of doubtful taste. When that great survivor Vyacheslav Molotov – he of the 'cocktail' fame – finally died at the age of 96, one wag suggested that, instead of burying him, they should light his hair and toss him over the Kremlin Wall.

By the time I arrived in Moscow in April 1998, the debate over Lenin's remains had reached fever-pitch. Fearing I might not get another chance, I made it a priority to pay my respects.

The marble and granite mausoleum we see today was completed in 1930, six years after Lenin's death. You can dismiss it as a piece of macabre voyeurism or enjoy it as monumental theatre. Either way, it was, and is, worth a visit. My own motivation was simply a desire to 'meet' the man who had arguably had more influence on the course of the modern world than any other. Visitors at the time, mostly foreign tourists, seldom had to queue more than a few minutes and, unlike Madame Tussaud's, it was not just the real thing but free.

As an experience, the mausoleum evokes the same mixture of anticipation and unease as a pharaoh's tomb. As your eyes adjust to the gloom, you descend two flights of porphyry steps. At each turn stands an impassive guard. No cameras, no pushchairs, and definitely no levity. Passing through a pair of massive bronze doors, you arrive in the vault of black and red marble, turn right, and progress up and around three sides of a rectangle.

There in the middle of the rectangle, in an eerily illuminated glass sarcophagus, lies Vladimir Ilyich Ulyanov, aka Lenin, with his head raised on a blue cushion, the right hand clenched, the left slightly splayed. (Some subtle carrot and stick symbolism perhaps?) I'd been told the embalming process had turned him into a waxwork dummy. Not so. Yet still I was shocked. After all those monochrome photos and newsreels of the living Lenin, I didn't expect the moustache and beard to be so startlingly orange. Red Lenin, yes – but *Ginger* Lenin?

His wardrobe had clearly been given some thought. Whereas he made his first posthumous appearance lying in state in a Bolshevik tunic with patch pockets, he had long been more stylishly attired in a dark lounge suit, white shirt and natty blue tie with white polka dots.

No longer the rabble-rousing demagogue, he had assumed the status of international statesman for all ages, all peoples and, in matters sartorial, eternally *au courant*.

Apart from the occasional touch-up, the body is given a regular eighteen-month 'service' when it is submerged in a chemical bath of glycerol and potassium acetate. In fact, along with Lenin's, there are now three or four extra bodies which, like crash-test dummies, are used for trying out new preservation techniques.

In 1953, Stalin tried to make it a double act. He had left instructions that on his demise his body was to be placed alongside his predecessor in the renamed Lenin-Stalin Mausoleum. They must have made the ultimate odd couple lying side by side on their velveteen sheets. But it wasn't to last. In 1961 Khrushchev had Stalin removed and buried beneath the Kremlin Wall. Muscovites were quick to spot a cautionary message – don't sleep in a mausoleum that doesn't belong to you.

From its first appearance, the power of Lenin's corpse to excite reverence was exploited. The fact that it showed no signs of putrefaction (most likely on account of the sub-zero winter temperatures while lying in state) was held to demonstrate that scientific socialism had achieved what the Church claimed for some of the bodies of its saints; a denial of nature's laws. As a political symbol, it had no equal. The succession of Soviet leaders who took their place on the mausoleum for the annual Red Square parades were well aware that their authority was greatly enhanced by being seen standing just feet above the founding father, if not literally on his shoulders.

Symbolism, though, can cut both ways. When Ronald Reagan met Mikhail Gorbachev in Moscow in June 1988, the two presidents did a walkabout in Red Square – studiously avoiding the mausoleum.

Gorbachev's aides had had the foresight to realise that photos of a standing capitalist beside a prostrate communist would have been too great a temptation for the Western caption writers.

When communism finally imploded, the body became a more, not less, potent relic for the true believers. The world may have changed but, so long as Lenin remained in his mausoleum, there was the possibility of political resurrection. One day the red flag would fly again. Bury him and that hope would be buried with him.

It was Vladimir Putin who finally decided the matter. Demonstrating more nous and a greater grasp of human psychology than his predecessor Yeltsin, he argued that Lenin would be more divisive below ground than above it.

'Many people have their own lives tied up with Lenin's name. For them, Lenin's burial would mean that they had worshipped false values, undertaken false endeavours, and lived their lives in vain.'[2] It was a view he would repeat in the years to come when speaking generally about the country's handling of its Soviet past.

When Yeltsin stopped paying for the body's upkeep, a charity, the Lenin Mausoleum Foundation, offered to take over. Through public donation (allegedly the equivalent of $135,000 was raised in three days) and money from Russia's seven different communist parties, the foundation paid the state embalmers for their services until 2016 when the Kremlin resumed its financial support.

In July 2001, thinking the story might be worth a documentary, I arranged a meeting with the foundation's chairman, Dr Aleksei Abramov, an elderly but still combative member of the communist old guard. We met in what he called the foundation's conference place on Schepkina Street. It was a musty, poorly lit room with photos of Second World War military heroes leaning out from the walls as though toppling forward under the weight of their medals.

Dr Abramov's argument for keeping Lenin above ground went beyond symbolism:

> It's something that is historically precious; it belongs to all mankind. After all, today's Egyptians still protect the mummies of their pharaohs; they're still proud of their forefathers. They don't say, 'Because the pharaohs weren't Muslims like us, we should throw their bodies away.'

The mausoleum, Dr Abramov contended, was meaningless without its contents. 'Imagine your grandfather being dead and buried. You go to his grave and you pay your respects. But if you take your grandfather out of the grave, it will lose its meaning.'

I forbore pointing out that there was a difference between burying my grandfather in the ground and putting him on public display in an oversized terrarium. He would have been mortified. But Dr Abramov was right. The fact that Lenin's body isn't mouldering in the grave means that for millions of older Russians his political soul goes marching on.

✦———✦

Lenin the man, the once living and breathing founder of the Soviet Union, generally gets an easy ride in popular consciousness. Lenin is seen as The Builder, the man who created the first communist state, and Stalin as The Butcher, the man who maintained it by terror. We now know Lenin was no less a butcher than Stalin, but two things have worked in his favour. First, he was waging a revolution against aristocratic power and privilege and, in his own words, you couldn't do that wearing white gloves. Ends may not justify means but they do help explain them. Second, he was in power for only seven years; there is no knowing what atrocities he might have gone on to commit, on what scale, had his term lasted the near-thirty years of Stalin's. It was Lenin after all, who believed it was better that a hundred innocent people were killed than that one person who was a danger to the Revolution remained free and a potential threat.[3]

His successor, by contrast, is more problematic. Even though Stalin is acknowledged to have been a mass-murderer responsible for the death of millions in famines, camps and purges, a cult-like fascination with the man has never died. In fact, the opposite. The indications are that, over the last decade, it has grown stronger. In 2019, the Levada Center, an independent sociological research NGO (branded as a foreign agent by Putin's government), conducted polls in 137 locations across the Russian Federation. It found that 51% 'respect, like or admire' Stalin. In a more recent survey which Levada conducted in April 2025, Stalin topped the poll with 42% as 'the most outstanding figure of all times and all nations' – well ahead of Putin, Lenin, Pushkin and Peter the Great.

On my desk, I have a ceramic plaque, the shape and size of a small saucer, which I bought in Moscow. At its centre is a pure white bas-relief set against a baby-blue ground in perfect imitation of Wedgwood Jasperware. It features not a prancing nymph or flute-playing satyr but a bust of Joseph Stalin resplendent in his marshal's uniform. No doubt it was intended as a memento but not, I think, as tourist trash. Everything about it – its quality and the fact that, unlike the matryoshka nesting dolls, I have never seen another – suggests it was made for the domestic Russian market, as an icon worthy of reverence. The most surprising thing about it is the imprint on the back which indicates it was made in the year 2000.

My own first encounters with the man and his myth were in the country of his birth, Georgia, on a visit to the Romanov Summer Palace at Likani in the Samtskhe-Javakheti region of the country. The palace was built at the end of the nineteenth century in a striking Moorish style with broad shade-casting eaves. Stalin stayed in it on two occasions – in 1921 with his second wife Nadezhda (the one who shot herself) and again in 1951, two years before his own death.

I joined a guided tour of foreigners. The highpoint was the room Stalin had used as his office and what our English-speaking guide described as 'the two historical nails' – one by the door, the other in the side of the desk. These, the guide informed us, had been hammered in by the great man himself.

That fact alone seemed hardly enough to make them historical. Was the guide perhaps making some abstruse point about Ioseb Jughashvili's adopted nom-de-guerre: Stalin – literally, *Man of Steel*?

Well, no, he answered. The nails were to hang his cap and coat on – his coat by the door, his cap by the desk. Pointing to the latter, he invited us to examine it. From a respectful distance, we all duly stared at this inch-long piece of metal with a reverence that might be accorded the nails of Jesus' crucifixion. We were told we could photograph it – which, I'm embarrassed to say, I duly did.

It was only afterwards that I realised how easily we had been sucked – rather, suckered – into the Stalin cult. Had I really taken a photo of a nail because Stalin had hung his cap on it? Or was it the fact that, rather than call the palace's odd-job man, as would any normal dictator, he had hammered it in himself? *With his own hand.* Would I have taken a photo of a paintbrush because Churchill had used it to create one of his oils? Unlikely.

(It was worse than I remembered. Checking back through my archives, I came across not only the photo I took of the nail but, to my appalled disbelief, another with my own cap hanging from it.)

✦ —— ✦

Some months later, Jano Zhvania, my Georgian friend, Internews colleague and personal bodyguard (over six feet tall with a black belt in karate), suggested a visit to Gori, Stalin's birthplace. For those who worship the man, Gori is the ultimate place of pilgrimage. Even though it was December and not many, if any, degrees above freezing, I accepted without hesitation. Recalling my conduct at the Likani Palace, however, I determined to rein in my worrying tendency to idolatry.

These days you can drive from Tbilisi to Gori in about an hour and a quarter. Back in the early 2000s, it took a good two hours because of the state of the road. It could be a terrifying experience as oncoming trucks and buses crazily zigzagged in their attempt to follow what remained of the asphalt, pulling over to their side only at the last moment.

Fortunately, Jano was a great distraction from the possibility of becoming roadkill; an engaging travel-companion with a seemingly inexhaustible memory of Soviet times. He had been brought up in Zugdidi in the west of the country, just thirty kilometres from the Black Sea. To the south, about 100 kilometres away, was Turkey – close enough for Zugdidi residents to pick up Turkish television. One of Jano's earliest childhood memories was being puzzled by how short the Turkish films were. Only when older did he realise he had been watching the commercials – unknown to viewers of Soviet television.

We were near the halfway stage of the journey, passing a succession of dilapidated factories with every window broken. Jano was telling me how, like all young Georgian males, he had been conscripted into the Soviet military. Being bigger and brighter than most, he had been trained as a tank-driver and, he added, had taken part in the Third World War. Assuming this to be a linguistic lapse, I attempted to correct him. 'No, no,' he protested, 'it's what I am meaning – the *Third* World War!'

He explained that between 1986 and 1988 he had been stationed in East Germany, near Dresden. His tank was a T-80. Jano was so proud of it that, against orders, he hid a carefully folded black and white photo of it in his epaulette. And he still had it, now tucked into his wallet alongside photos of, he was keen to stress, his *equally* beloved wife and two sons. As proof, he pulled it out to show me before continuing.

One night Jano and his crew received an order to proceed without delay to the border with West Germany, their T-80 loaded with live shells. There had been similar orders before but always as part of a Warsaw Pact exercise and never with live ammunition. Since there had been no mention of any exercise, the natural assumption was that this time it was for real. They were going into battle.

Arriving at the border, nerves taut and adrenalin flowing, they were surprised to be confronted in the middle of the road by a jeep bearing British and American flags. There followed several seconds of discussion among the crew whether they should shoot or salute. Had they opted for the former, they might well have started a Third World War.

It turned out to be part of a confidence-building 'verification exercise' where the opposing sides lined up, facing each other across the border, to show the other side their military hardware; a superpower game of *I'll show you mine if you'll show me yours.* Amazingly, Jano's Soviet commanders had felt no need to tell those lower down the chain. More than a decade later, he was still haunted by the memory of this, the day the world ended . . . nearly. The possibility of a misunderstanding or miscalculation starting a global confrontation is frequently mooted but stories like this make one realise the potential is far, frighteningly, greater than imagined.

For Jano and his crew, it was probably an even narrower escape than they realised. Launched in 1976, the T-80 was hailed at the time as the best in the world. It was the first Soviet tank to be powered by a gas turbine engine, giving it an impressive top speed of 70 kph. Although never put to the test in a Third World War, it went into service in the mid-1990s against Chechen separatists. This revealed that, on account of a design flaw, a well-placed rocket-propelled grenade could blow the turret clean off. Its reputation was dealt a further, perhaps terminal blow, when in 2019 a Russian video appeared on YouTube showing how the barrel, when equipped with a machete strapped to its business end and gently lowered, could cut through a watermelon placed on a picnic table. No longer hailed as the best tank in the world, the T-80 is now reputed to be the world's most over-engineered fruit knife.

+———+

Having read up on the place, I had a good idea what to expect in Gori. There is the armour-plated railway carriage which took Stalin to the Yalta and Potsdam conferences (he had a fear of flying).

It's fitted with an air-conditioning unit, a full-sized metal bath and the ultimate selfie-opportunity for today's visitors – his personal flush toilet. A few metres from the carriage is the Joseph Stalin Museum and, in front of it, the secular equivalent of the Bethlehem stable: the peasant's hut in which Ioseb Jughashvili was born, long ago encased in a ridiculously over-the-top neoclassical pavilion.

What we hadn't expected was to find the museum closed because the town's electricity supply was off, a common occurrence in Georgia during the early years of its independence. Resourceful as ever, Jano asked around and, finding a local teacher who conducted the occasional school visit, he engaged her to give 'a very important English visitor' a personal tour.

By now, it was late afternoon and not just freezing but getting darker by the minute.

Wrapped in a heavy overcoat and bearing a flashlight, Keti, our thirty-something guide, got one of the resident guards to unlock the main doors as she explained to us that she had been born and brought up in Gori and went to the nearby school that overlooked the museum.

The museum was completed four years after Stalin's death. Despite Khruschev's denunciation in the interim, it is an unashamed celebration of Stalin's life with an all-pervasive whiff of something more: veneration. To capture that whiff, join me on the tour . . .

In the entrance hall, we are welcomed by the great man himself – a marble effigy, well over two-metres-high, picked out by Keti's flashlight at the top of a flight of red-carpeted stairs. It's a stunning *coup de théâtre* even if in life Stalin is generally reckoned to have been 165 centimetres tall (whether including stacked heels is unspecified).

As we move from room to room, her flashlight shafting through the gloom, Keti matches her words to significant objects and pictures that emerge like ectoplasm. She takes us through the successive stages of Stalin's extraordinary life: son of a cobbler, trainee priest, poet, revolutionary and (all in the cause) bank robber; repeatedly exiled or imprisoned by the tsarist regime; Lenin's fellow Bolshevik before succeeding him as leader of the Soviet Union and hailed as its saviour during what Russians call The Great Patriotic War.

I am struck by a photo of Soviet soldiers kneeling, like figures in a nativity scene, in front of the hut of his birth, before going into battle. Noting my interest, Keti remarks that Churchill was a great admirer of his wartime partner and directs the flashlight at an alleged Churchillian quote, in its original English, high up on the wall: 'When he came, Russians had only hoes; when he left, they had nuclear reactors.'

We pass through a succession of rooms crammed with personal items (including Stalin's shaving kit) and gifts presented to him during his leadership, ranging from the kitsch to the grotesque, before ending up in a spacious hall, now in total darkness. We are in the Holy of Holies. Keti's beam drops to floor-level, illuminating an object surrounded by a semi-circle of pillars. Stalin stares back at us as though emerging from a coalhole. It is his death mask.

Returning to the entrance where we started, Keti asks if I have any questions. There is only one and it's personal. In fact, by now I am as much interested in her as I am in Stalin.

Here is a young woman, educated and informed; born, I'm guessing, less than two decades after Stalin's death. For the best part of an hour she has been talking about him as if he were as remote in time as Ivan the Terrible. I can understand that she might feel a certain civic pride on account of her hometown being the birthplace of an undeniably historical figure, but she must be aware that there are people still living (this was December 2000) whose lives had been forever changed by his actions, quite apart from those millions of dead who might still be alive but for him. So how does she, a Georgian and, no less, a teacher, view Stalin from a *moral* standpoint?

She takes her time before replying. 'Stalin was a phenomenon. Strength is necessary sometimes. Only the historical perspective will allow a complete judgement.'

On the one hand it's a cop out. Given what we now know, it's hard to imagine any historical perspective that will recast Stalin as anything other than a mass-murdering monster. As for 'strength', are we talking about courage or brutality? But, on the other hand, her description of him as 'a phenomenon' – like a force of nature, neither good nor bad because utterly amoral – resonates. It reminds me of the cynic's definition of religion – man's attempt to communicate with the weather. Judgement of men like Hitler, Pol Pot and Stalin is ultimately futile. They are beyond evil. The best we can do is record their crimes to ensure they are never forgotten, in the hope of never being repeated.

For many Georgians, Stalin may be the local boy made bad, but he is still *their* boy. There is an unspoken pride in having produced the second and longest-serving leader of the Soviet Union, the man who, they will argue, despite his faults, defeated Hitler and the Nazis. But it's a reputation that ebbs and flows with events.

In the twenty-five years since my visit to Gori, there was first the Rose Revolution in 2003 that ousted Eduard Shevardnadze and put Mikheil Saakashvili in power, followed five years later by the Russo-Georgian War when Russian forces bombed the town and occupied it for ten days, rekindling memories of Soviet repression during Stalin's time. It prompted a long-delayed reappraisal of the local boy.

The Joseph Stalin Museum now has a section which, attempting to present a more balanced view, acknowledges his darker side, and in the middle of the night of 25 June 2010, a municipal crane finally removed Stalin's six-metre-high bronze statue from Gori's main square. It is believed to have been the last large-scale statue of Stalin in the former Soviet Union still standing in its original location.

And yet the man remains a subject of seemingly inexhaustible fascination; his reputation in some quarters still deemed worthy of protection. In 2018, Armando Iannucci's coruscating comedy *The Death of Stalin*, a co-produced British-French-Belgian movie that tells of the jockeying for position following the leader's death, was banned by the Russian authorities. Two days before its scheduled release, the Ministry of Culture revoked its screening licence in response to the unanimous disapproval of certain 'Russian cultural figures'.

It wasn't as though this was the first time Stalin had been negatively depicted on screen. In 1987 during the period of *glasnost*, Mikhail Gorbachev famously gave the go-ahead for the belated release of *Repentance*, Georgian director Tengiz Abuladze's film about a cakemaker who repeatedly digs up the body of the local mayor, a barely disguised Stalin surrogate, so that the memory of his brutal past will not be buried with him.

But *The Death of Stalin* broke a taboo. The problem was not that it showed the tyrant in a negative light but that it was funny . . . seriously funny. The Russian journalist Andrei Arkhangelsky put his finger on it. 'We can criticize Stalin but we must not laugh at him.'

13.

KEEP ROLLING!

The late Russian cultural historian Dmitry Likhachev put it best: 'Television permits us to see things not only at a great distance but at very small distances too . . . It allows us to see the face – the living face of a man point-blank when that face can neither lie nor pretend. Television is the great exposer of lies, pomposity, stupidity.'[1]

Compared with the written word, television can be superficial. But, as Likhachev says, it also has a unique ability to be both mind-reader and lie-detector. Never more so than when applied to our leaders. It is this that makes it such an invaluable tool in protecting and preserving democracy.

Think of 9/11 and the shot of George W. Bush reading a book about a pet goat to a class of Florida children as, for what feels like an interminable near-seven minutes, he seemingly struggles to take in the news that the United States is under attack. You can read the thought bubble: *Remind me, who's the Commander-in-Chief? Oh, shit!*

Or the end of an interview with Tony Blair, looking back over his decade-long, three-term premiership. 'How many people in their lives will get a chance to do something like that?' he asks rhetorically. He then specifies a leader's ability to affect people's lives for good, and without mentioning Iraq, 'sometimes even affect them for ill'. The interview ends but the camera keeps running. For a further eleven seconds, Blair, his mouth hanging half open, goes into a defocused, quasi-catatonic state in which he seems to be reassessing his entire political career. Finally, with an awkward smile, he snaps back into the present: 'That's that, then . . .'

In television, nothing happening can be as significant as something happening. It's the dog that doesn't bark. An experienced camera-operator instinctively knows when to 'keep rolling'. In the days of film, when the standard 400-feet 16mm roll lasted a little over eleven minutes and cost £200, it could be a fine judgement call. Less so these days when the typical video cassette or memory card lasts an hour or more – and can be re-used.

Tellingly, the Russian word for a camera lens is *obyektiv* – objective. There are times when all the cameraman has to do is point, record . . . and keep rolling.

Keep this thought in mind for what follows.

†———————†

In the late 1990s an exhausted and ailing Boris Yeltsin was casting around for his successor as president of the Russian Federation. He claimed to have considered twenty candidates over four months. After giving six of them try-outs in the role of prime minister, he and 'The Family', as they were known, settled on Vladimir Putin. On New Year's Eve 1999, the last day of the old millennium, Yeltsin took the world by surprise with the announcement. More than that, to mark the moment, he made Putin acting president with immediate effect and, to wrong-foot any contenders, he brought forward the upcoming presidential election to 26 March 2000 – less than three months ahead.

No one could have done more to ensure the succession of his preferred candidate.

Enter Vitaly Mansky, the Head of Documentaries for Russian state TV, together with his hand-held camcorder, one of the new generation of compact models, little bigger than a beer-can, with a flip-out screen and top-mounted directional microphone the size of a cigar. By comparison with the standard TV camera, it is tiny and seemingly innocuous. Wherein lies its power, for in terms of the damage it can wreak, it will turn out to be Mansky's secret weapon.

Mansky is given the job of shadowing acting president, now candidate, Vladimir Putin during the election campaign. Officially, his footage is for the State Archives but, since he has been seconded to Putin's election team, it will also handily provide material for a Putin promotional video to be screened in the run-up to the election.

Nearly two decades later in 2018 – by which time Mansky has moved to Latvia – the footage will resurface in an extraordinary documentary titled *Putin's Witnesses*. Mansky had decided Putin was a dictator. Reckoning that his greater duty was to history than to the president, he had jumped ship, taking some of the most precious cargo with him. If you want to understand why television is such a powerful medium, how it can be discreet and intrusive in equal measure, look – or, rather, *watch* – no further.

I predict future writers of Russian history will be indebted to Mansky as the digital Boswell to successive presidents Yeltsin and Putin, for he turned out to be a master of the 'keep rolling' school of documentary makers. George W. Bush famously glimpsed Putin's soul and declared him to be trustworthy. Personally, I would rather take Mansky's cinematic assessment.

It is election night, 26 March 2000 . . .

The Yeltsin family are to be filmed at home by Mansky and his documentary crew as the results come in. It's fair to assume that Yeltsin's media-savvy daughter and adviser, Tatyana (think Ivanka Trump), will have given the go-ahead. Where's the harm? As Putin's political patron, her father is undeniably a key character in the story: both puppet-master and kingmaker. No question, he is still a significant public figure, even if increasingly afflicted by age, heart problems and the accumulated effects of alcohol. The only risk is embarrassment.

In the event, Yeltsin holds up well, showing interest in the evening's proceedings and, though his speech is laboured, still articulate. The embarrassment comes from a wholly unanticipated quarter.

At this point, a quick bit of background . . .

Over the previous months following Putin on his campaign trail, Mansky has not only mastered his diminutive camcorder but has developed a shooting technique for unpredictable and potentially sensitive occasions. As a documentary director, he still works with a professional cameraman wielding what is ostensibly the primary camera – a bulky piece of shoulder-mounted kit the size of a ghetto-blaster and, with its winking red light, impossible to miss. But Mansky has learnt that there are situations when the cameraman is more useful as a distraction, a decoy, to enable him to sneak in and get up close and personal with his own camcorder. The visuals aside, the camcorder's directional microphone proves particularly useful in picking up low-level snippets of speech.

Back to the unfolding scene in the Yeltsin living room . . .

✦ —— ✦

As the results come in, it is clear Putin is ahead. When he passes the 50% mark, it's suggested that Yeltsin should phone Vladimir Vladimirovich (Putin) to congratulate him on what now looks like certain victory. Yeltsin picks up the phone and is put through to Putin's campaign office. He asks to speak to the man who is about to become president in his own right and is told Putin will phone him back. Yeltsin replaces the handset and everyone in the room waits.

The seconds pass . . . then the minutes. Mansky's camcorder keeps rolling.

In an increasingly uncomfortable situation, there is a call from Putin's campaign office to reassure Yeltsin that the message will be passed to Putin and that, as promised, he will return the call. The implication is that he is out of the office but expected back soon . . . any time now.

When there is still no return call, the family – Yeltsin, his wife and daughter – fill the silence by speculating whether Putin is changing his clothes, taking a bath . . . or maybe a shower? And of course he would then have to get dressed which would take time. Or maybe – Yeltsin himself surmises – he is just 'hanging out', even 'bossing about', whatever that means. It is toe-curling, and all being recorded with devastating objectivity.

After *an hour and a half* and still no return call, the embarrassment is turning into humiliation. The family can't sit there all night waiting for the phone to ring. Still less can they be videoed waiting. Glancing at his watch, Yeltsin declares, 'Let's not wait. Let's say goodbye.' There's some awkward scraping of chairs. Nobody in the room says what everybody is thinking: that it is unconscionable that Putin would not respond to the call of the man who has done so much, and risked so much of his political reputation, of his legacy, to put him in power. It's a matter not just of respect but common courtesy.

Putting the best gloss on the evening, Yeltsin declares that Putin's victory will be 'good for free elections, the freedom of Russia and for the freedom of the media'. With this last thought in mind, he moves across the room to a stills photographer, grasps his hand and declares, 'If Putin wins, the freedom of the media will be ensured by all means!' The photographer looks unconvinced. 'Let us hope,' he responds. His expression says, 'Yea, yea.'

Immediately behind the photographer is the man who will have the job of implementing the new freedom of the media. He has been in the room all along, keeping an eye on the filming but careful to stay in the background, perhaps because he, more than most, understands the power of television.

He is Mikhail Lesin, the oyster-eyed minister for the press, broadcasting and mass communication under both Yeltsin and, for the last three months, Putin in his acting capacity. He has already brought Russian state television under one roof to give the Putin administration more control over it, and in the months that follow the election he will start bringing all the independent networks broadcasting nationally under the Kremlin's authority. In short, what Yeltsin has just said about freedom of the media being ensured is totally at odds with what Lesin has already done and is committed to keep doing. Even so, as they say their farewells, Lesin takes Yeltsin by the arm and, with Mansky's camera recording, says, 'We will provide the freedom of the media.' Orwell would have relished the moment.

Recalling the evening some years later, Mansky said he was amazed that at no point during the hour-and-a-half wait for Putin's return call did anyone in the room say, *Stop filming!* or *Delete that material!*[2] The one man who could have done, who had the power to intervene and save Yeltsin's face, was Mansky's ultimate boss, media minister Mikhail Lesin. He said, and did, nothing.

It's hard not to speculate whether this masterful inaction was part of the longer-term strategy. Yeltsin was yesterday's man, clearly already low on the new president's priority list – if on it at all – and, as Russia and the world would soon discover, whatever he may have thought or not thought was now irrelevant. Perhaps putting that irrelevance – worse, humiliation – on public display was something Lesin was all too happy to allow.

+———+

Forward nine months . . .

Mansky and his camcorder (and, as previously, with his professional cameraman in tow) are back with the Yeltsins, this time to record the family celebrating New Year 2001. And without the Rasputin-like figure of Mikhail Lesin hovering behind the sofa. It's exactly a year since Yeltsin named Vladimir Putin as his successor with immediate effect and nine months since Putin was elected president in his own right. As for the earlier episode with the un-returned phone call, those involved seem to have persuaded themselves that it wasn't as bad as it may have felt at the time.

Former president Boris Yeltsin stands at the head of the table to toast the incoming year. The clock strikes, glasses chink, kisses are exchanged. It's the time-honoured ritual of celebration, renewal and hope. As Yeltsin sits down, the strains of the Russian national anthem can be heard coming over the television.

But something is wrong. This is not Glinka's *Patrioticheskaya Pesnya*, the nineteenth century composition that Yeltsin had brought in during his presidency, part of his effort to root out all remnants of the communist era. Instead, it is Vladimir Putin's sanctioned reworking of the old Soviet anthem, *Soyuz Nerushimi* – same tune, modified lyrics. It's clear from his expression that Yeltsin has registered the change. Mansky moves in. Bringing his camcorder close, he asks in a conspiratorial whisper, 'Did they restore the anthem without your knowledge?' Yeltsin gives the slightest of nods which, if his face weren't filling the screen, might have passed unnoticed – like that of a prisoner being asked in the presence of his guards whether he's been beaten. 'Do the new words save it?' Mansky presses. Yeltsin closes his eyes and cryptically responds, 'It's red-*ish*'.

Yeltsin is referring to the tune rather than the words, which, if anything, now have a religious flavour. The opening lines of the Soviet original, 'Unbreakable Union of freeborn Republics, Great Russia has welded forever to stand' have been replaced by, 'Russia our holy nation, Russia our beloved country. A mighty will, great glory – these are yours for all time!' It works better in Russian.

There are few more sensitive, more divisive, subjects in Russia's transition from totalitarianism to democracy than the old Soviet anthem. It's the hammer and sickle in musical form. Yeltsin understood its power, the swooping and soaring melody up and down the scale, the potentially dangerous nostalgia that it evoked. Which is why, in his determination to make a clean break with the past, he replaced it with the Glinka, just as he had tried, though failed, to bury Lenin and close the Mausoleum.

Putin's response to the Lenin issue had been to avoid a head-on confrontation by putting any decision in the PENDING tray – sometime, maybe never. The old anthem was another matter, and trickier because Yeltsin had already replaced it. Its restoration, the music if not the words, was the clearest indication of the ideological rift between the two men. And, as Mansky got Yeltsin to reveal, his successor hadn't even bothered to tell him. In fact, Putin had personally launched the first performance of the new version, with full choir, at a Kremlin reception the previous evening, 30 December 2000. One can only assume that neither the former president nor any member of his family had been invited.

✦ ———— ✦

As a result of Mansky's cinematic work during and after the Yeltsin-Putin transition, it is proposed that a documentary should be made and broadcast on the first anniversary of Putin's presidency, with a view to affording Russian viewers a fly-on-the-wall glimpse into the workings of government.

By now, the hand-held camcorder has become Mansky's weapon of choice and no longer his 'stealthy stiletto'. Given unfettered access throughout much of the Kremlin, he now wields it openly to the discomfort of Kremlin staff, as is clear from their expressions when the camcorder's twitching snout appears around the door.

Yet, judging by the footage, the president himself is totally at ease with the arrangement. While other leaders might have found it intrusive, Putin – in the supreme loneliness of supreme power – gives the impression of appreciating the company. Most revealing are the out-takes. They show Putin indulging Mansky as 'a licensed fool' in the Shakespearean sense, throwing out provocative statements and then encouraging the cameraman/director to challenge him, to speak truth to power.

At other times the camera itself becomes the president's personal chronicler and confessional. Aware of it at the periphery of his vision, he checks with Mansky that it's recording and then, with no prompting or cueing, delivers a soliloquy about the challenges and frustrations of the top job:

> You do understand, whenever I have to take certain decisions, some people will always think that these actions are wrong, including the ones who voted for me. I believe I have to explain to all, absolutely all the motives of my acts. But I must act as I deem necessary.

Again, pure Shakespeare. *Macbeth*? *Richard III*?

The restoration of the Soviet anthem turned out to be more controversial than Putin had expected, and it is clear from his to-camera musings that he feels his decision is one of those that has not been adequately understood by the Russian people. In fact, he is so keen to explain his reasoning that, having done one explanation, he summons Mansky back the next day for a second take. What comes across is an unexpectedly sensitive side to the man later credited with eliminating his political adversaries by whatever means at whatever distance:

> Most of the population harbours a certain nostalgia. You must not deprive people of everything. There is a moral issue here. This is what I think about when I remember my parents. This (the Soviet anthem) is a part of their life. Should we just dump it all on the scrapheap of history, as if they had never lived? It would be very cruel toward our parents.

How then to square Putin's tender concern for the feelings of his parents and their generation with his cavalier treatment of the man who could well be described as his political father?

For three years as, successively, deputy chief of staff, head of the FSB (formerly the KGB), prime minister and finally acting president, Putin had been Yeltsin's man. At the hand-over of presidential power, he had even pledged himself on television to a continuity of policy and action, making specific mention of press freedom:

> There has been no vacuum, nor will there be one. I want to warn that any attempt to exceed the limits of the law, and Russia's Constitution, will be decisively crushed. Freedom of speech, freedom of conscience, freedom of the press, the right to private property – all these basic principles of a civilized society will be reliably protected by the state.[3]

But once Putin could claim the presidency in his own right through the ballot box, everything changed. As Mansky says, 'The successor got his sea legs quickly enough, distancing himself more and more from his creator.'

The close-up of Boris Yeltsin's expression listening to the restored anthem reveals what is now clear to all. Putin has played the old man to perfection (daughter Tatyana too, for she would have been involved in the choice of her father's successor). Words intended to reassure were calculated to deceive. Leaving nothing to chance, Putin guaranteed Yeltsin – and, by extension, The Family too – protection from any charges relating to his time in office. Generous? Perhaps, but also a way of gagging them post-transition. They would have known that any overt criticism of the new regime, any rallying calls to the old, risked the withdrawal of that protection.[4] You can take the man out of the KGB but . . .

14.

THE GRIP TIGHTENS

In the years since being recorded by Mansky, Putin has shown himself to be like the Victorian circus performer who could ride three horses simultaneously. He has kept the embittered communists sweet by saving symbolic remnants of the Soviet era – not just the anthem and Lenin, but official remembrance of the Great Patriotic War and respect for those who fought in it (the red flag no longer flutters above the Kremlin but the illuminated red stars still twinkle). He has repaired relations with the Russian Orthodox Church, supporting religious freedom and personally – very publicly – participating in their rites on significant holy days. And, the greatest challenge, he has kept the general population on side by restoring Russia's self-esteem and international standing. No longer a humiliated husk of a nation dependent on Western know-how to rebuild, Russia is again a force to be reckoned with, whether annexing the Crimea, intervening in Syria, engineering European dependence on Russian natural gas or, most recently, invading Ukraine. And if that has pissed off those in the West who boasted of winning the Cold War, so much the sweeter.

Russia may have lost its political siblings, the Soviet republics, along with the Eastern Bloc satellites that, in the form of the Warsaw Pact, constituted a defensive wall against the West and any future German aggression, but losing an empire has its upside. Freed of burdensome costs, responsibilities and the constant familial bickering, a leader can concentrate on the core. And, in terms of size and resources, the Russian Federation is a considerable core, a landmass representing roughly three-quarters of the old USSR.

No surprise then that he has raised no objection to being cast as a new tsar. St Petersburg, built by one of the greatest tsars, was his birthplace (then called Leningrad) and his first political base. He may have been brought up in a communal apartment with water running down the walls but, stepping outside, he would have been surrounded by Peter the Great's imperial pomp. He still wears a conventional lounge suit (when not in judo gear or stripped to the waist on horseback) but is regularly shown walking through gilded halls and marble palaces, with his familiar rolling gait, left arm swinging, right arm rigid by his side (a remnant, allegedly, of KGB training; the need to keep the right hand close to the sidearm). He is the epitome of the strong-man – in Russian, *tverdaya ruka*, 'the firm hand' – and that seems to suit most Russians just fine. No surprise perhaps that those who lived through the eighteen-year stagnation of Brezhnev's rule, followed by the uncertainty of Gorbachev's sweeping reforms and the loss of empire, leading to the free-wheeling chaos of the Yeltsin era should, when offered the choice between law and order, choose order, while giving their president an approval rating that Western leaders can only dream of. The law is still there but, with United Russia's iron grip on parliament, it can be written and rewritten according to the president's wishes. Thanks to just such a constitutional amendment, backed by a popular referendum, Putin could be in the Kremlin till 2036, by which time he will be 84.

Back in the early days of the new millennium when Putin was still testing the limits of his power, it was inevitable – if only in hindsight – that he and his media lieutenant Mikhail Lesin would set their sights on the foreign NGOs and Western consultants brought in by Boris Yeltsin. Top of the list: those involved in promoting democracy, human rights and independent media.

My first inkling of the change came in April 2002. My Russian visa had expired but relations between the UK and Russia were going through one of their periodic lows. The Russian Embassy in London's Kensington had capped the issuing and renewal of visas at a hundred a day. Applicants were camping outside overnight. But, as luck would have it, I was booked to work in Armenia for six weeks before my scheduled return to Russia. Armenia, unlike its neighbour Georgia, had maintained good relations with Moscow and so it was decided by my joint employers, the Thomson Foundation and Internews Network, that I would renew my visa at the Russian Embassy in Yerevan with fingers crossed, and fly on directly to Moscow. It was worth a try.

Once in Yerevan, it was with a sense of foreboding that I presented myself at the visa division of the impressive brownstone Russian Embassy in Lusavoricha Street. The potential flaw in the Thomson/Internews stratagem was that I was still a UK citizen in need of a Russian sticker and stamp in my passport. If Russia was unhappy with the UK, they could be just as unhappy – and uncooperative – in Yerevan as in London.

Like few other items of officialdom, passports can induce an instant quickening of the pulse – in the worst case in a lawless land when offering one at an isolated checkpoint manned by drunken, trigger-happy soldiery. But even when stopped in a crowded street and subjected to an identity check with a gruff demand for

Documents! On one such occasion in Tbilisi, a plain-clothes member of Georgia's Special State Protection Service pulled a pistol on me after believing, mistakenly, that I had taken a photo of a cluster of antennae on top of what was evidently a sensitive building. In the end, the matter was resolved by my demanding to see *his* documents (for the record, Operative Agent, No. 000167), a reaction seemingly so unexpected that he backed off. It could have been worse. Had it not been a Sunday, a rest day for our Thomson-provided armed bodyguard, there might have been an exchange of something more serious than words.

One of the most bizarre but true stories to come out of the Cold War concerns the ease with which the Russians were able to unmask American spies, despite their being provided with impeccably forged Soviet passports. The CIA spymasters in Langley were baffled, confident they had got everything else right: clothing, cover story, language, even regional accents. There was *something* about the passports. The give-away, it would turn out, though only after the Cold War, was the pair of staples that held them together. Whereas the American forgers had used non-corrosive staples stamped from Pittsburgh's finest steel, the genuine Soviet staples were so low-grade that they rusted the moment they were issued, staining the adjacent paper a telltale brown.

Obtaining visas, even with a genuine passport, from the embassies of former Soviet republics could be a tense business. (But salutary too in that it gave you, the Westerner, some small idea of what it was like for the citizens of the country in question when dealing with their bureaucrats.) There was always an awareness that you were dealing with an individual who could use their modicum of power to make your life difficult, should they so choose – whether deliberately or on a whim. Additionally, there was no knowing what was on the departmental computer at their elbow, what flag might have been put against your name. As the supplicant, your only aids were chatty charm and a dog-like 'roll over and tickle my tummy' submissiveness.

Back at the Russian Embassy in Yerevan . . .

Before approaching the visa desk for my renewal, I had filled out the obligatory form, explaining my reasons for revisiting Russia, along with details of my employer. An overweight official with sweat-beaded neck like a cider press now examined it. He huffed, puffed, consulted his screen, scowled and, as I feared, raised an issue.

'Your employer's name. It is not correct.'

'I don't understand.'

He stabbed a fat finger at the relevant box on my form. 'It should be Volga River Cruises.'

'There must be a mistake,' I said. 'I work for Internews Network.'

'Not no more you don't. Now you work for Volga River Cruises.'

Was it conceivable there were two Michael Delahayes applying for visas, the other working for a cruise company? I tried to argue the point but the official was already looking over my shoulder.

'You talk to your people. If you want visa, you return tomorrow.'

Back in the Internews Armenia office, I recounted what had happened. Half an hour later there was a call from Internews' Moscow office with apologies. All foreign or foreign-funded NGOs in Russia were now required to go through more bureaucratic hoops. Internews was currently 'between licences' and was using Volga River Cruises for the purpose of visa applications. Somebody should have told me. Repeat apologies.

'You mean I have to lie?' I asked. *Konechno,* was the response. Of course.

Next morning I returned to the embassy, wondering whether I should be wearing a jaunty sailor's cap. More soberingly, it also occurred to me that both I and Internews might have been set up.

Such a thought was not entirely fanciful. We may have been in *post*-Soviet times but within four years of the collapse of the USSR, the feared KGB had morphed into the FSB, a change of initials but an agency of the state still responsible for counterintelligence and surveillance. Equally to the point, one of its recent directors, himself a long-serving former KGB officer, was now president of the Russian Federation.

So here I was, for the second time in as many days, about to cross the threshold of Russia's Armenian embassy in the knowledge that Russia was back in the business of blackmail and entrapment. I was also mindful of being not in a Russian embassy in Paris or Rome, but in a former Soviet republic that maintained close ties with Moscow. Get the paperwork wrong in such a situation and there could be serious consequences – as the director of Internews Russia would discover in 2007. Believing the euros she was carrying didn't require declaration on a routine airport immigration form, she was charged with a criminal offence and had to flee the country. The incident resulted in the wind-up of Internews' entire Russian operation. More later.

Aware that my reappearance at the embassy might end with my arrest for attempting to enter Russia under false pretences, I filled out another visa renewal form and, pen less than steady, followed the latest instructions. Employer: Volga River Cruises. The same official was on duty. Whether a cause for comfort or alarm, there was no knowing.

Welcoming me like an old acquaintance, he read through my application, beamed and with a decisive thump of his official stamp renewed my visa on the spot. He handed me back my passport.

'A magnificent river, the Volga – the longest in all Europe, as I'm sure you will know.'

As matters turned out, it was to be my last visit to Russia. It was also the visit when I would meet media minister Mikhail Lesin face-to-face.

✦————✦

It was May in Moscow. Spring seemed to have lasted barely a fortnight. Now, judging by the blooms in the Alexander Gardens beneath the Kremlin walls, it looked like we were on the cusp of summer. Normally in matters meteorological one could rely on the chamber ensemble of the Moscow Conservatory who, exploiting the acoustics, regularly busked in the underpass leading from the Lenin Library to the gardens. But even they seemed undecided, hedging their bets by alternating between Vivaldi's 'Spring' and 'Summer'.

With a feeling of renewal in the air, Internews' staff had been invited to a barbecue which media minister Lesin was hosting for the foreign press at a state-owned country club outside the capital. It was a generous gesture but regarded with some suspicion. Internews' mission in Russia was to promote, through moral, financial and practical support, independent media at regional level to counter the minister's efforts to bring all the media at national level under government control. That may not have been how it had started out under Boris Yeltsin but it was certainly the reality now. In fact, it was Lesin, acting as Putin's media henchman, who a year earlier had overseen the final transfer of Russia's biggest independent network, NTV, to the state-owned Gazprom-Media. So, in issuing the invitation, was he hoping to size up or to soften up the opposition? Or, not beyond possibility, to psych it out?

A dozen of us crammed into a minibus and, as we headed west out of the city, past the high-rise apartments of Moscow's middle-class and through the birch forests of 'dachaland', formerly the holiday haunts of the old Soviet Politburo, I noticed that all my male colleagues were wearing suits and ties. I had never seen them looking so smart; in fact I was surprised some of them even owned suits. Having been told this was to be a barbecue, I had chosen the sort of attire that might be appropriate if invited to George W. Bush's ranch at Crawford, Texas: jeans, a leather bomber-jacket and open-necked shirt; borderline 'smart casual'. When I asked why I hadn't been alerted to the dress code, a senior female colleague snapped that I shouldn't need to be told what to wear for a ministerial meeting. How long had I been working in Russia? She left me in no doubt that I was guilty of a sartorial transgression just short of a diplomatic incident. I felt like the victim of a practical joke who is invited to a fancy-dress party only to discover on arrival in a chicken costume that everyone else is dressed normally. The driver offered me his tie. If it didn't work, he added, I could use it to hang myself. Russian humour – love it.

As we prepared to decant from the minibus, it was clear I would have no chance of hiding in a hedge. The door slid back to reveal Minister Lesin, waiting to welcome us in person – impeccably attired of course in suit and tie. Introducing myself, I apologised for looking like a plumber. He laughed it off: Russia always had need of plumbers! And journalists? Not so much, I suspected.

There were fifty or sixty of us, as I recall. The minister made a commendably short speech of welcome, then, in a calculated gesture to show us foreign hacks that he was a regular guy at heart, he threw off his jacket, unknotted his tie and, collar unbuttoned, took his place alongside the catering staff to turn the kebabs. I'd like to think it was to make me feel better but I doubt it.

I remembered the barbecue strip-down thirteen years later when I read the reports of his death, partly because it too featured a degree of undress.

+ —————— +

After five years as media minister, Lesin was appointed Putin's personal adviser for mass media relations and launched his greatest legacy: Russia Today, or RT as it became, the 24/7 satellite news channel that 'acquaints an international audience with the Russian viewpoint' and with its Moscow spin challenges the worldview of the BBC and CNN.

Alongside his political rise, Lesin had always been an astute business operator and by 2011 he was rated a multi-millionaire. He started to split his time between Russia and California where he had moved his family and acquired substantial property assets. Before long there were accusations in America of money-laundering and in Russia of unpatriotic behaviour. (It didn't help that, like so many of the oligarchs whom Putin had forced into exile, Lesin was Jewish.) He was out of favour with both Washington and Moscow, and his enemies were circling.

In early November 2015, he booked in to a Washington hotel. There followed a three-day bender of Stakhanovite proportions during which, in a somnambulant state, he would wander the corridor in his shirt and underpants. On the morning of 5 November, he was found dead in his room. He was 57. Initial reports suggested a heart attack but further examination by the US authorities concluded he had died of, quote, 'blunt-force injuries to his head, with contributing causes being blunt force injuries of the neck, torso, upper extremities and lower extremities, which were induced by falls, with acute ethanol intoxication'.[1]

Though few doubted the intoxication, many questioned the circumstances, how so many injuries could have been self-inflicted.

15.

DINNER WITH ZAZA

The life of an international broadcast consultant is like that of any other freelancer. Planning is impossible; the future, beyond the next six months, is a blank. You never know what will turn up but, when it does, the impulse is always to accept for fear that, if you don't, you won't be asked again, or the consultant who does get the gig may turn out to be more to the client's liking, or just better.

As a result of this mild paranoia, I was spending months at a time away from home and family. As my wife Anni put it when asked, I was 'big in the Caucasus'. Fortunately, daughter Rachel was by now grown-up, living an independent life, and Anni had always been happy with her own company and piano. Unlike some marriages, ours could manage the separation. One morning Anni bumped into a friend in the local Marks & Spencer. The inevitable question came up.

'And where's Michael?'

'Siberia,' Anni replied.

The friend shook her head. After a two-beat pause, she asked, 'How do you *do* that?'

When I was working abroad as a BBC reporter, invariably with a producer, the practice was to keep our distance from British embassies and consulates, to make clear the corporation's independence and avoid any assumption of the BBC's alignment with the foreign policy of the current British Government or, worse, suspicion of collaboration with it. It has been not unknown for British journalists – *print* journalists – to act as spies.[1] Perhaps with good reason, Russian governments, both Soviet and post-Soviet, have long put Western journalists close to the top of their suspect lists. Even if they turn out to be innocent, they can still make handy bargaining chips for swaps, as has been evident in recent years.

When you are working as a media consultant, however, you find yourself in an ill-defined crossover world. You are neither a journalist (although there is nothing to stop you knocking off the odd newspaper or magazine article) nor a diplomat, but your work is mostly funded by government departments or agencies – British, American, EU – that have a clear diplomatic objective in mind; whether to improve relations with the country concerned or, more specifically, to improve its record on human rights and media freedom. As a result, wherever I worked, I was in regular contact with the British Embassy, High Commission or British Council and, in respect of my role and its funding, it would be fair to say I often found myself representing my country abroad and promoting its values.

But such proximity to one's own government held dangers in the post-Soviet world of the early 2000s, offering a tempting opportunity for an unstable regime, should it decide a Western spy story might serve its purposes. And a plausible one. Roaming the former Soviet republics as a consultant, free of the monitoring to which tourists and particularly journalists were subjected, would have made the perfect cover for clandestine activity. I had a particular problem with an Australian acquaintance, an academic specialising in Russian history, who would assure mutual friends in Adelaide that I was an undercover agent for the British Government. It wouldn't have mattered except that he was in regular contact with fellow academics in Russia who might have felt the 'information' was worthy of wider circulation.

For the record, I was never asked to do anything remotely risky. The only uncomfortable incident was entirely of my own making and far from the former Soviet Union. While conducting a human rights course in Namibia, southern Africa, funded and hosted by the British High Commission, I thought of a novel way to illustrate what freedom of speech meant in practice.

'There is,' I declared, 'a part of Hyde Park in London called Speakers' Corner where everyone has the freedom, established by a law of 1872, to stand on a box and say whatever they want in public, for all to hear.' The impact was less than I had hoped; perhaps the law of 1872 had been a detail too far. So, adopting a shock tactic to ram home the point, I went on, 'For example, I could get up and shout, "Fuck the Queen!"'

The instant the words left my mouth, the next morning's headlines flashed before me: VISITING BRIT TELLS JOURNALISTS, F- THE QUEEN! I spent an excruciating twenty-four hours anticipating my recall to London for a Dreyfus-style dressing down by a Foreign Office functionary. Fortunately, the participants were not as sharp journalistically as I had feared. (So much for my training.) It should also be added that I was probably over-egging the point. I note on the current Royal Parks website, the line, 'Anyone can turn up unannounced to speak on any subject, *as long as the police consider their speeches lawful*' (my emphasis). Hmm. 'I don't care much for Her Majesty' doesn't have quite the same punch.

(Oleg Dmitriev, my colleague at Internews Russia, was fond of a story about a Russian and an American sparring over their respective freedoms. 'I can stand in Times Square, New York,' says the American, 'and shout, "Fuck Ronald Reagan!"' 'So?' responds the Russian, 'I can stand in Red Square and shout, "Fuck Ronald Reagan!"')

✦ ——— ✦

For all that I never felt any pressure, a British Embassy or High Commission would sometimes pass on a request. In June 2001 while I was working in Georgia, our ambassador, Deborah Barnes-Jones, asked if I would meet the Director General of the country's state broadcasting channel, Zaza Shengelia. He was keen to know about the BBC model and how it was funded.

The first time I had seen the Georgian State TV Centre had been nearly three years earlier in December 1998 on my first visit to Georgia. What I most clearly remembered was the ubiquitous eau-de-nil paint on the walls, reminiscent of a hospital, except that the smell was of dust rather than disinfectant. A number of other images had stayed with me: the antiquated Soviet-era studio cameras, circa 1950 and worthy of a museum (parts from one being cannibalised to supply spares for the others), the clocks stopped in both Studio 1 and Studio 2 (at different times), the dead strip-lights down the corridors that had never been replaced, and the technician slumped over a control deck, out to the world and not caring who saw. The atmosphere had been one of lethargy and neglect. It was the morning after the post-Soviet party.

Preparing for my meeting with Shengelia, I knew that giving the institution a makeover would be about more than upgrading the building and its equipment. It would require a total re-think of its aims and values.

One of the requirements for any country wishing to claim the status of a Western-style democracy is to transform its 'state broadcaster' into a 'public service broadcaster'. This is about more than semantics. At its heart is a fundamental but seldom recognised truth: that a functioning democracy requires an informed electorate. Posting a folded piece of paper into a box is just the most visually symbolic part of the process, a handy, rather lazy, media cliché (of which television news is particularly guilty). Even if elections are openly and fairly conducted with a genuine choice of candidates, the exercise remains little more than window-dressing if the voters haven't had access to the facts necessary to inform that choice.

Hence the essential role of the journalist in a democracy. In fact, *two* roles: to inform the electorate, and to monitor the elected. The first before an election; the second throughout the period that follows.

✦ ———— ✦

'Democratic' is a word capable of contradictory interpretations; perhaps the most blatant example of Orwell's 'doublethink' by which a word can simultaneously mean itself and its opposite. Totalitarian regimes love it. Hence, the former *Democratic* Republic of East Germany and the present *Democratic* People's Republic of North Korea. To which you could add the *Democratic* Republic of the Congo, though better termed 'dysfunctional'.

Back in 1978 when working for the BBC, I had an illuminating interview with Zambian president Kenneth Kaunda. The occasion was the upcoming presidential election. In 1973 he had turned

Zambia into a one-party state but – a political fig leaf – the Constitution still required that the President of the Republic be elected every five years, allowing the possibility of a new leader of the one-party 'democratic' state . . . in theory.

But under Kaunda's rule, not in practice. In the 1978 election (as well as the two subsequent ones), all other candidates were eliminated by one technicality or another, leaving KK, as he was known, unopposed. In effect the election was to be a vote of confidence with a 'YES' and 'NO' choice on the ballot paper. For those who couldn't read, YES to Kaunda's continuing as president was represented by a soaring eagle; NO by a rabbit. (The Zambian Electoral Commission had at least had the guts to ban the original image, a snake.)

Sitting opposite this most genial of men on the lawn of State House, Lusaka, surrounded by strutting peacocks, I opened the interview with what I thought was a zinger.

'Mr President, democracy enshrines the concept of one man, one vote. How do you justify interpreting that to mean that there should be only one man to vote *for*?'

Kaunda laughed and, with a dismissive flick of his trademark white handkerchief, replied, 'Ah, Michael, you don't understand African democracy . . .'

The same had been true of what some liked to call Soviet democracy. Sure, there were elections, or 'choices' (*vybory*), as they were called, but the only choice was whether you endorsed a party-approved candidate, or not.

Which brings us back to the importance of a public service broadcaster. A state broadcaster is by definition an arm of government. As such, it typically selects the facts favourable to that government's agenda. If a fact is inconvenient, it is either not reported or, if unavoidable, reported only to be denied or rubbished.

To get a more accurate and balanced view, therefore, the voter must rely on alternative *non*-governmental sources, whether television, radio, print or online (including these days social media). The result is not objectivity but its second-best – pluralism. That is, a range of views across the political spectrum on which the voter must make a value judgement with a fair chance it will be wrong.

Always assuming there *is* a genuine range. Not just in the former Soviets but in many mature Western democracies the diversity of views is worryingly limited. The UK's *Guardian* newspaper, for example, with its 'progressive' left-inclined editorial line, is greatly outnumbered by well-financed rivals with right-inclined agendas, whether political, commercial or both. Think the Murdochs' News Corp.

One of the fascinating footnotes in Australia's media history is that it was the former Liberal (Australian for 'centre-right') prime minister, Malcolm Turnbull, who helped create, thanks to a wealthy contact, a digital offshoot of the *Guardian*, *Guardian Australia*. It launched in 2013, two years before Turnbull became prime minister. As he wrote in his biography, *A Bigger Picture*, 'I was beginning to despair about the state of Australian journalism . . . I wasn't especially concerned about the political slant of one outlet or another, but more about the fact that newsrooms were shrinking and editorial standards were dropping to the loopy standards of the twittersphere'.

Although Turnbull's primary concern may not have been the political imbalance of Australia's media waterfront, *Guardian Australia* has made a considerable contribution to editorial diversity while maintaining its own independence.

The struggle for genuine plurality – that is, diversity – is why the public service broadcaster is such a vital element of democracy with a charter, like the BBC's, that requires 'the British values of accuracy, impartiality, and fairness', along with the implied requirement that it will hold the government of the day to account and call out blatant propaganda. In the words of the BBC's former Director of News, Fran Unsworth, 'Under our charter, the job is to provide impartial news without fear or favour, and not to be beholden to commercial or political interests'.

But here's the thorny question: how is such a source of accurate, impartial information to be financed, and by whom? If directly out of the public purse, that is by the government itself, there is always the 'he who pays the piper' problem; that the strings of the purse will be tightened or loosened according to how well those in power feel their actions are being represented and reported. On the eve of Australia's general election in September 2013, Tony Abbott, the leader of the opposition Liberal and National parties, generally referred to as the Coalition, promised live on air that there would be no cuts to the government-funded public service broadcaster, the ABC. The Coalition won by a landslide and in their first budget announced rolling cuts to the ABC over the following four years. Abbott's explanation: 'Things have moved on, circumstances are different.'

The only way to protect funding is to have some sort of breaker between the national broadcaster and the government. The UK does this (at the time of writing) by means of the TV licence scheme. Any household that watches or records a television program, *whether or not it's a BBC program*, is required by law to have a licence. The fee is collected not by the government but by the BBC through its Finance and Business Division. By such means, the public directly funds the corporation. As the BBC is fond of reminding its listeners and viewers, 'It's your BBC'.

The licence-fee model is not perfect. Like democracy, it is arguably the worst system ever devised, except for all the others that have been tried. Taking the UK as an example, it has two major weaknesses.

First, it is the government of the day that, following negotiations between it and the BBC, periodically decides the amount of the licence fee – crucially whether it should rise with inflation. This means the government with its greater clout still has its hands, if not actually on, then hovering over the purse strings.

Second, the UK's media landscape has changed over the years with now many more players. It is therefore harder to make an argument in defence of a guaranteed income for one broadcaster raised by what is in effect a tax that, if you fail to pay a fine for evasion, can land you in prison, when all the others have to find ways to fund themselves by advertising, subscription or foreign sales.

Armed with a bundle of facts, figures and possible scenarios, I phoned the Director General of Georgian State Television and Radio. I had never met the man but knew him by repute. If anyone in Georgia was 'Mr Entertainment', it was Zaza Shengelia. He had done the lot, during both the Soviet and post-Soviet eras: organised music festivals, co-founded an independent television channel, created a record company, even for his sins judged the Eurovision Song Contest and – the ultimate poisoned chalice – had been called upon to sort out the national broadcaster.

'Where'd you like to meet?' he asked, going on to list some of Tbilisi's best-known eateries. I chose a Mexican restaurant on Perovskaya (now Akhvlediani) Street, partly because I had never eaten there but also because it was hard to miss. To distinguish it from all the Irish pubs in the street, a welcoming stooge was posted outside in a poncho and oversized sombrero. We settled on 9 pm.

———

Zaza had reserved a corner table at a distance, I was relieved to see, from a large TV hanging ominously on the other side of the room. If there's one thing I hate more than muzak in a bar, cafe or restaurant, it's the audio-visual intrusion of a television. What is odd is that Italians, the ones you'd think least in need of conversational gap fillers, are probably the worst offenders, with not far behind it seemed, the Mexicans, or at least the Mexican Georgians . . . or Georgian Mexicans.

Over dinner Zaza and I discussed the various models for financing a public service broadcaster. We agreed that a possible for Georgia was the one that added a TV licence element to the household electricity bill since anyone who had a television would need electricity and would be paying for it. Like the BBC system, it would keep the government at arm's length. However, such a system assumed reliable metering and billing, which in the post-Soviet republics a decade after the collapse of the Union was still problematic. Even so, of all the models, we agreed it was the one most worth pursuing.

We had pretty well covered the ground when Zaza caught the eye of a waiter. It was coming up to ten o'clock, time for the late evening news on the state broadcaster. Without anyone else being consulted, the television was switched from Rustavi-2, the popular commercial station, to the state channel. Zaza said there was something he wanted to show me.

As I focused on the screen from some ten metres away, he explained that the two dilapidated studios I had seen in 1998 had been knocked into one to act as a single, refurbished news studio. What did I think?

I was impressed. Half close your eyes and it could have been the BBC's *Newsnight* program. The new French-designed set, Zaza explained, had cost $60,000. He drew my attention to the centrepiece – a large, apparently floating, transparent Perspex triangle with lights running around the edges. The anchor sat on one side, with the guests arranged along the other two. It looked as though a UFO had dropped through the roof and was attempting to land. All it lacked were a few puffs of CO_2.

As Zaza continued to enthuse, it was clear that this was his baby, a powerful twenty-first century symbol of the regeneration of Georgian State (soon to be Public) Television under his directorship. He was keen to know my professional opinion, particularly of the centrepiece. Was it beautiful, or was it *stunningly* beautiful?

I hesitated. First, because studio design is not my speciality; my consultancy work focuses on the editorial side rather than the presentation. Second, because how well a set works – for example, how much room there is for the cameras to move around and reposition themselves, whether manned or automated – cannot be judged by looking at the two-dimensional screen of a domestic TV, no matter how big. To use a theatrical analogy, you need to see into the wings.

But what capped both these reservations were the differences in national cultures.

A couple of years earlier, I had learnt a salutary lesson when doing some documentary training in Damascus. Waiting in my hotel room for the interpreter, I turned on the television. Up came a quiz show – three figures in traditional Syrian dress, each in his own arched niche and, facing them, seated at a desk, a quizmaster who asked each in turn a question while every so often talking to someone on a telephone. The entire studio was ablaze with gaudy, multi-coloured strip lighting. The phone, I assumed, was an element borrowed from *Who Wants to be a Millionaire?* – to 'phone a friend'. When my interpreter arrived, I asked him to explain the rules. He laughed.

'Well, it's a quiz show, right?' I sought to confirm.

'Of sorts,' he responded. 'It's called *Ask an Imam*. Viewers ring in with their questions about the Quran. The guys in the niches are the imams.'

The moral? When in another country, never judge a TV program by its set. The viewers' tastes may not be yours.

For all the above reasons, I sought to evade Zaza's question. I said I would need to see the set, particularly the central desk, from all angles to make any observation that might be of any conceivable value.

But Zaza wasn't going to take 'can't' for an answer. Picking up his mobile, he phoned the studio gallery – I assumed the director or the program editor beside him. Since the exchange was in Georgian, I had no idea what was being said. All I knew was that the program was going out live on air before our eyes.

To the evident mystification of the anchor, the red tally light that indicates which camera is transmitting started to jump between the three cameras as the vision-mixing director cut between them to show different aspects and angles of the studio and its extraterrestrial centrepiece. At one point Camera-2 might even have sashayed across the floor to get a better shot into the wings. All this for the benefit of a UK consultant sitting a kilometre and a half away in a downtown Mexican restaurant with a Corona beer in hand. I was going to say, exclusive benefit, but this was being broadcast nationwide as the anchor, valiantly continuing the studio discussion, struggled to understand why the shots on her monitor bore no relation to the exchanges between her and her guests.

There appeared instead, twenty years before its time, the equivalent of one of those videos produced by today's high-end estate agents – the sort that invites potential buyers to admire their latest desirable offering with its elegant hallway, state-of-the-art kitchen and spacious living area.

And if the anchor and her guests were confused, heaven knows the effect on the viewers at home. In my memory this went on for several minutes. In reality it was probably no more than thirty seconds before I declared the new set to be more than fit for purpose. Indeed, *stunning!*

There was something quintessentially Georgian about the whole episode. Yes, it was a crude demonstration of power. But in Georgia, if you've got it, you don't just use it, you have the fun of showing others how you use it.

The next year, 2002, when helping to set up a new TV station in Tbilisi, our four-strong band of UK consultants were invited to a picnic by the station's management with security to be arranged by another invitee, the local chief of police. Imagining an approximation of Manet's *Déjeuner sur l'herbe*, we were puzzled by the security element until informed that the venue was the Pankisi Gorge, an active conflict zone on the border with Russia where Georgian troops were fighting Chechen militants. It was hard to think of a less suitable place for a spread of skewered meat, pickles and regional cheeses. A barbecue on a Belfast barricade in the 1970s?

As we entered the gorge, I noticed that armed security officers had been stationed every few hundred metres along the road, each saluting as our Audi-Merc-BMW motorcade sped past. When the picnic concluded, after three hours and a succession of obligatory toasts, the police chief turned to me. 'You see, perfectly safe!' How many had been needed to ensure our safety, he didn't specify.

As for Zaza, I very much doubt that he had planned his intrusion into the evening news but, having decided this was the simplest way to show me what I said I needed, he just did it. Since he could, why not? I tried to imagine a BBC director general doing something similar – and failed. In fact, if precedent is any guide, the situation would likely have been reversed.

On the night of a UK General Election in the 1970s, the BBC's director general at the time invited a dozen influential guests to dinner in his suite on the sixth floor of Television Centre. As the Election Special program went on air with the first results, he decided to take his by now rather-too-merry band down to the studio to watch the action from the gallery. The moment he and his party entered, the studio director swung round and told his boss that he had enough to worry about without he and his boozy mates breathing down his neck (or words to that effect). The DG murmured an apology and, along with guests, backed out. The studio director, Keith Clements, went on to have a distinguished career in BBC management, his reputation enhanced by repeated tellings of the episode.

+ ——— +

During his six years as Director General of Georgia's national television and radio service, Zaza Shengelia oversaw its transition from state broadcaster to the renamed 'Georgian *Public* Broadcaster', better known by its initials, GPB. Under his leadership, it also became a member of the European Broadcasting Union.

Twenty years on, the GPB is wholly funded by the state while required by law to provide 'information that is free from political and commercial bias', with all the built-in tension such a linkage implies when 'state' and 'government' so often overlap. Different formulas have been tried: making funding a percentage of the country's gross domestic product and, the latest starting in 2026, tying it instead to the number of employed citizens.

Many other, probably most, countries have state-funded national broadcasters. But Georgia is not any other country. Given its post-Soviet history of rolling, episodic political turmoil, it has always been hard to see how the GPB could avoid, still less counter, government pressure and interference. The insidious alternative is self-censorship, such as steering clear of investigative programs that might embarrass the government or depriving opposition voices of airtime on talk shows about hot-button issues – both of which charges have been levelled at the GPB. Most recently, the broadcaster has been criticised for sacking journalists who speak out about what they see as its lack of editorial independence, notably in its reporting of the 2024/25 mass protests against the government's anti-EU stance.[2]

Those more generously disposed point out that, though the GPB might give the government a far too easy ride, it is less politically biased than its commercial rivals. Which takes us back to a point touched upon earlier in this chapter: how pluralism works in practice. And a pertinent question: How is a media environment that manages to be both pluralist *and* politicised contributing to media freedom; let alone public enlightenment?

Zaza likes to claim the GPB is based on the BBC model, one of the many we discussed in downtown Tbilisi back in 2001. Perhaps, but only in the way an aircraft carrier is based on a Roman trireme.

16.

THE TROUBLESHOOTER

Question: What's the difference between a trainer and a consultant? The glib distinction is that a trainer is fixed to the spot and gives answers while a consultant moves around and asks questions.

Standing before a whiteboard, facing rows of eager, upturned faces as you dispense expert knowledge acquired over the decades may be good for the ego, but any impact you have is going to be dependent on the bosses of those you've trained giving them the chance to put their newly acquired skills into practice.

Sadly, and all too often, the attitude of bosses in the post-Soviets when their staff returned to work was *that was training, this is reality.* In the case of reporters, that usually meant going back to doing two, maybe three stories a day. (The standard practice of paying reporters by the story only encouraged the sacrifice of quality to quantity.) When I was subsequently made aware of this by emails from those reporters, I wondered whether I had trained them just to be frustrated. I had shown them the promised land only for them to be denied entry. The one upside was that, very occasionally after a course, I would hear that a boss was furious because the reporter or cameraman he had sent us had promptly resigned on their return and moved to another station. Progress sometimes comes in unlikely forms.

Far better in terms of effecting real change is to work alongside journalists doing their jobs in real time. As a consultant. But most rewarding is to be called in as a 'troubleshooter': to fix an issue which those on the ground acknowledge exists but cannot identify.

+———+

Afontovo TV was the station. I liked the name the first time I heard it. It had a soft, Italian timbre: *A-fon-tov-o*, with the accent on the second syllable. A small hilltop town in Tuscany perhaps, famous for its *porcini* and *vino nobile*?

It turned out to be in the aluminium-smelting heart of Siberia – the city of Krasnoyarsk, the capital of a region eleven times the size of Britain and over 4000 kilometres due east of Moscow. To get there, you had to fly out of Domodedovo Airport (aka Domo-*dread*-ovo) and submit yourself to the tender mercies of KrasAir. As I would discover on both the outbound and return flights, Krasnoyarsk's regional airline offered passengers a unique take on the drinks trolley.

Most of those who flew KrasAir were heavy-set business types shuttling between Moscow and Krasnoyarsk's aluminium plant. From the prodigious amount of alcohol they consumed before boarding, you would have thought they manned the furnaces. By take-off, it wasn't only the aircraft that was tanked up. At this time, late 1999, KrasAir was still operating Soviet-era Ilyushin and Tupolev planes with, by today's standards, relatively little insulation between the cabin and the exterior skin. When the warm exhalations and perspirations of the onboard business contingent met the cool of the overhead panels at 30,000 feet, the aircraft became a flying alembic as drops of condensed vodka formed and dripped on those below.

Russia's regional airports never failed to amaze. On another flight in the depth of winter, our aircraft had been held for over an hour on the tarmac. The danger in this situation is that ice will form on the wings and fatally compromise take-off, which is why it's standard practice to spray glycol on them. I drifted off to sleep and woke to see a babushka standing on the wing, casually sweeping the snow off with a domestic broom. Never had the combination of a wing and a prayer seemed so apt.

✦ ———— ✦

In anticipation of my arrival in Krasnoyarsk, Afontovo's operations manager, Larisa Malinova, had helpfully emailed me some background information.

By most measures, Afontovo TV was doing OK. Up against two government-owned and three independent stations, it had the biggest audience share of the independents. (To be clear, Afontovo was independent in the sense that it was neither government-owned nor government-controlled. Its majority shareholder at the time of my visit was Vladimir Gusinsky's Media-Most company, which enabled Afontovo to broadcast network material, along with its own regional windows such as news bulletins and a breakfast program. There was no evidence of Gusinsky interfering in its news output.) The station had its own advertising agency which not only offered potential clients on-air slots but also its own facilities to produce the ads for them. That said, the economic collapse of August 1998 had resulted in an 80–90% cut in local advertising revenue while the station's income had dropped from $250,000 a month to $50,000.

But Afontovo had survived and, with the prospect of better times ahead (Boris Yeltsin was still president), it had an invaluable asset:

its own transmission tower. This meant that, unlike most other independent stations, it didn't need to lease a state-owned transmitter, making it immune to the sort of pressure that could be applied when the lease came up for renewal.

The immediate problem – the reason for my presence – lay with its evening news bulletin, *Novosti Afontovo,* lasting forty minutes and aired six days a week. In the past it had been pulling in a respectable 60,000 to 80,000 viewers but, according to the latest Gallup sample, the figures had slumped to below 30,000. In short, it was being hammered. The scheduling didn't help. It was up against three other evening bulletins and going on air at 8.30 pm, the last in line. To just rehash what had gone before wasn't an option. To borrow one of the BBC's favourite buzz words, the bulletin had to make itself 'distinctive'. But how?

Unusually for a station boss, Afontovo's co-founder and general manager, Alexander Karpov, took a particular interest in his news division. Alexander, then in his late thirties, was a shining exception to most station bosses I had met in that he believed the public deserved a serious, informative and objective news service; that indeed democracy depended on it if it was to survive in Russia. And no hidden adverts, no flattering stories about local companies surreptitiously slipped into the bulletins in return for a backhander.

In their determination to keep the news not just 'clean' but watchable, Alexander and Larisa welcomed advisers and consultants. What was needed, they agreed, was a fresh pair of eyes. Shortly before my arrival, two top news editors – one from Tomsk, the other from Ekaterinburg; both of whom I knew and respected – had been brought in to lead a two-day seminar, attended by the entire Afontovo news team. The effect, Larisa said in her briefing notes, had been positive but the improvement had lasted barely a month.

Now it was my turn, with eyes both fresh *and* Western, along with the luxury of five days on site to get to the root of the problem, whatever it was. I was under no illusions; I was going to have to earn my fee. Adding to the pressure, I learnt that Internews Russia had described me as the man for the job.

I checked the list of the news division's staff and equipment that Larisa had sent me. Both, compared with equivalent regional news operations in the UK, looked more than adequate. And, always relevant, the evening bulletin was fronted by an experienced and, by all accounts, popular news anchor. (It's amazing how many viewers, irrespective of nationality, will watch the news for the anchor rather than the contents.)

Going out last in line at 8.30 pm was obviously less-than-ideal but I could understand the reasoning. To move to an earlier slot might put the bulletin head-to-head with one of the national network bulletins. By concentrating on local and regional news, it should have been possible, serving a city of close on a million people, for the Afontovo bulletin to carve out a significant slice of that potential audience.

Reading through what Larisa had sent me, I had expected a red flag or two to pop up. There were none. It was a mystery. Given the staff, the equipment, the facilities, the anchor and, not least, the support of the station's boss, there was no obvious reason for the Afontovo bulletin to under-perform. The root of the problem, I concluded, had to be organisational, and that would be hard to pinpoint, let alone fix. To take an automobile analogy, it's the difference between a mechanical failure where the parts are readily identifiable and accessible – engine, gearbox, transmission, steering, brakes, and the like – and an electrical fault, at any point along more than one-and-a-half kilometres of cabling.

The first day got off to the worst possible start. I had flown from London, overnighted in Moscow, arrived late evening in Krasnoyarsk (vodka infused, courtesy of KrasAir) and stumbled straight into bed, by when I must have been half-a-dozen time zones out of kilter. Little surprise then that I slept through my alarm the next morning and only surfaced when Larisa rang up from reception with engine running. As we clipped kerbs in our dash to the Afontovo studios, I mentally crossed staff punctuality off my advice list. Arriving late and unshaven, I must have made a deeply unimpressive sight. (This was a decade before George Clooney made designer stubble fashionable.) The man for the job. You think?

But I was in luck. Any half-way competent consultant would have identified the problem within ten minutes of sitting in on *Novosti Afontovo's* morning meeting. As indeed, would have the advisers brought in from Tomsk and Ekaterinburg if, rather than conducting a seminar with whiteboard, coffee, tea and biscuits, they had had the chance to venture on to the shopfloor and monitor the news operation in action.

The morning meeting, such as it was, lacked any sense of purpose, let alone buzz. (In fact, I wondered whether it had been staged for my benefit. As the week progressed, it disintegrated to the point of non-existence.) It was led by the news editor, with the program producer playing second fiddle. Present in the newsroom but participating only in so far as they were pointing in the right direction were the news organiser, assignments manager and a couple of others, their roles unclear. After going through the day's list of 'possibles' and selecting the items for that evening's bulletin, the news editor and program producer hit their phones to set up the stories. That done, they rang the half-dozen on-duty reporters to brief them on the ones they had been assigned: what it was about, where to go and who to talk to. 'Oven-ready' would be one description; 'half-baked' might be more accurate.

In a UK or US newsroom, by contrast, the purpose of the morning meeting is, figuratively, to fire up the boiler. It's the most important meeting of the day. The news editor will have that day's 'prospects list' prepared by the Forward Planning Unit, and – along with the news organiser and/or assignments manager (INTAKE) and the program producer (OUTPUT) – will go through it, discussing and selecting items for the evening's running order and allocating reporters.

And here's the difference. Researching and setting up the stories is left to the reporters. That's their job and always has been, long before Woodward and Bernstein. The reporters are the hunter-gatherers of the news operation, expected to use their initiative and their contacts to deliver the best story to the best of their ability. In fact, some news editors in some newsrooms will insist that the reporters (particularly the specialist correspondents) attend the morning meeting either in person or over a conference call, in the expectation that they will pitch their own stories or add value and angle to those already listed. The news editor, particularly one who has watched *All the President's Men* too often, might even go round the room, actual or virtual, and ask each reporter and correspondent in turn what they bring to the day's table.

I can vouch from my own experience as a reporter that the editorial finger swinging in your direction concentrates the mind mightily. As a way of deflecting interrogation, one of my female colleagues would invariably respond, 'Right now, we should be taking a look at China.'

Heads would nod sagely, pencils would scribble purposefully and, because nobody had a clue what might be happening in China, the moving finger would move on. Worked every time.

By contrast, Afontovo's reporters were being treated like thoroughbred racehorses; kept locked and blinkered in their stables and let out only when it was time to hit the track. As became evident in the days that followed, the fact that they had not personally researched and set up the stories often resulted in their getting the wrong angle, interviewing the wrong people, or failing to realise till too late that there was no story. Their roles had to be redefined, giving them the necessary 'ownership'.

When I asked the news editor why he and the program producer were setting up the stories themselves, his response was, 'High-ranking public officials and company bosses won't talk to reporters'. I didn't have the facts to challenge the assertion but I found it hard to believe that the head of a school or hospital or even the managing director of the local aluminium works would refuse to talk to a reporter from the city's premier independent television channel. More likely, I suspected, the news editor was a micro-manager who found it hard to delegate. Later I learnt he had worked as a reporter himself, which might have explained why he was trying to do the job of every other reporter.

But by midweek something else had become apparent. The news editor told me that about a third of the bulletin's stories were planned before the day of transmission. I didn't know what he meant by 'planned' but from what I could see far too many stories were being researched, set-up, shot, edited and transmitted on the day. The result was a state of perpetual crisis management. It's part of a mindset I have encountered elsewhere; that 'news happens and therefore there's little or nothing to be done in advance'.

It's a myth. Very little news just happens. Mercifully, 9/11 and the 2004 tsunami are the exceptions. Most news is known about *before* it happens. Just think of all the court cases, official announcements and inquiries, campaign launches, national celebrations and anniversaries, concerts, exhibitions, sporting events – in fact everything from elections to eclipses – when the dates are known a day, week, month or, in the case of anniversaries, a whole year, decade or century in advance. Even 'spontaneous' demonstrations, protests and marches are usually flagged a day or two before to alert those it is hoped will join. As for court cases and official inquiries, these are stories which can be predictably revisited day after day, week after week, as they progress.

When broadcasting a forty-minute nightly news bulletin like Afontovo's, planning must be part of the process. Either in the form of a Forward Planning Unit, as favoured by Western newsrooms, or at least the appointment of a dedicated forward planning producer. (No, I've never heard of 'backward planning' either, but 'forward planning' is the accepted terminology.) The planning producer's job is to log all the events coming up in the next week and beyond, present them to the news editor at a regular weekly meeting and, together, triage them into unlikely, possible, definitely. The result is a seven-day prospects list. Using this, the news editor can assign in advance reporters to the selected stories and additionally allocate a cameraman for any of the stories that might benefit from some pre-shooting. 'Planning' is one word for it. Perhaps a better one is 'anticipation'.

This way, even on the slowest news day, the cupboard will never be bare; there will always be standbys on the shelf, transmission-ready, thus avoiding the daily miracle of trying to get every story to air within a twelve-hour timeframe. The other benefit is that you can keep your picture editors busy in the mornings working on the pre-shot material, instead of having them twiddling their consoles as they wait for the on-the-day footage to swamp them after lunch.

Back in the Afontovo newsroom the rest of the week progressed well. We let the reporters off the leash and, with boss Alexander's personal participation, we held half-hour post-mortems after every evening bulletin to submit each story to some constructive analysis. In any other industry, such retrospective appraisals would be regarded as normal quality control, and yet in the daily treadmill of television news they are often regarded, if they happen at all, as just an occasion for put-downs and point-scoring.

By the end of the week, there was a feeling that progress had been made. Individuals now had a clearer idea of their roles within the team. We had identified at least two natural hunter-gatherers among the reporters and the last-minute scramble to get on air had been transformed into an almost orderly operation thanks to the appointment of a planning producer. I felt I had earned my fee.

The question, as always, was whether the improvement could be sustained. I got the answer from Operations Manager Larisa in an email eighteen months later. It can be summarised in four words: up to a point.

The evening bulletin had been moved half an hour earlier to 8 pm but was now going head-to-head with, and often losing to, a rival bulletin. The appointed forward planning producer was sometimes required to work as a regular, rostered producer, diminishing her effectiveness. As a result, the on-the-day, last-minute mentality had reasserted itself. In fact, the news editor seemed to have become a planning sceptic, arguing that there was no knowing what may happen during the day. True, but that is no reason not to prepare beforehand what you *do* know.

To boost its public profile, the News Division had been given its own section on the Afontovo website but the news editor delayed the upload of 'hot' stories – what most people would call news – till late in the day for fear the competition might see them and cover them better. It was an indicator of the station's future trajectory.

All of this was against the backdrop of some ominous movements at the national level. Three months after my consultancy, on New Year's Eve 1999/2000, Yeltsin had appointed Vladmir Putin as acting president and, as explained in an earlier chapter, Putin's media minister Mikhail Lesin had set about bringing Russia's media under Kremlin control. Number one target was Vladimir Gusinsky's Media-Most, the company with a majority shareholding in Afontovo TV. Gusinsky was forced to sell his empire to Gazprom-Media, a subsidiary of government-controlled Gazprom. Afontovo escaped. With the help of a local bank owner, Alexander Karpov persuaded Gusinsky to sell the Afontovo shares back to him before the take-over.

But to re-equip the station, Karpov still needed a deep-pocketed investor and in late 2002 he had a meeting with another oligarch, Mikhail Khodorkovsky, the owner of Yukos Oil. Khodorkovsky guaranteed there would be no interference in the station's editorial policy and Yukos became Afontovo's majority shareholder.

Any relief was short-lived.

In October 2003, Mikhail Khodorkovsky, viewed by Putin as a political threat, was arrested and charged with tax fraud. (He would spend a decade in prison.) Yukos shares were frozen and the company collapsed. As had happened with Media-Most, Karpov once again managed to buy back the Afontovo shares before the axe fell.

Meanwhile, a no less serious threat, the television landscape itself was changing. As Karpov describes it, 'News consumption in Russia was turning to the "scandal-gossip-rumour" format while avoiding criticism of the authorities, whether national or local'. Afontovo lost its first place in the ratings of local news channels to a station called TV-K. The battle for viewers even caught the attention of the *New York Times*,[1] believing it to be symptomatic of the state of Russian media. In contrast to Afontovo's traditional and rather worthy format, TV-K had adopted a brash tabloid style which, judging by the swing in the figures, appealed to a lot of viewers. Typical of the station's buccaneering spirit, the *New York Times* noted, was how it illustrated the corruption it claimed was endemic in the local administration by keeping a running tally of the number of different fur coats worn by one of the female deputy governors.

All this time, while striving to keep his station afloat, Karpov had been living under the crushing psychological burden of a personal tragedy. In August 2000, his wife and daughter had been killed in a car accident. The depth of his depression was such that he decided the only way to start a new life was to leave Krasnoyarsk. In early 2003, he handed over day-to-day management of Afontovo to its co-founder and moved to Moscow to join Russia's largest advertising company while remaining nominally chairman of Afontovo's board of directors. Four years later, he would sell his Afontovo shares and become CEO of the Moscow-based entertainment network, TV3.

By 2010, following a boardroom coup and a still sluggish economy, Afontovo was in a parlous state; there were layoffs and presenters and producers were jumping from what was by now a doomed ship, holed below the profit line. The station finally sank in 2011. The next year, remarried with three children and believing that Russia was heading for the abyss, Alexander Karpov exiled himself and family to Spain.

Like many other stations, Afontovo had failed to move with

the times and duly suffered when pitted against a more populist rival. Which is true across the broadcasting world, East and West. Viewers, irrespective of nationality, have to be wooed and won – and even then, they can be promiscuous. Given a choice between a quiz show and a regional news bulletin, they can't be counted on to choose the latter out of channel loyalty or a civic duty to keep themselves informed. Believe that and you're in danger of falling into the delusional mindset of the defeated politician who declares, 'The voters have disappointed us.'

But Afontovo's failure to move with the times is too simplistic an explanation of its demise. Those times were determined 4000 kilometres west in Moscow. The tactics of Vladimir Putin's regional supporters toward the media could be both brutal and subtle. Rather than their licences being revoked or not renewed, the stations that failed to self-censor in the Kremlin's favour would come under pressure to sell themselves to a pro-Putin individual or company. Failure to comply would typically result in death by financial strangulation as the station's revenue sources were cut off. It required little effort, for example, to 'persuade' advertisers to boycott the targeted station. When it eventually went under, the cause of death could reasonably be attributed to commercial failure. The result: no autopsy and not even an identifiable crime scene.

I did sometimes wonder what advice I would have given Karpov if I had been called in a year or two later when Afontovo was losing viewers to the populist TV-K. It's easy in this situation to take the high-minded line of the BBC's first Director General, Lord Reith, about dumbing down. His observation, 'He who prides himself on giving what he thinks the public wants is often creating a fictitious demand for lower standards which he will then satisfy', is fine and dandy, but what if that demand is real? Karpov's own retrospective judgement was, 'With the strengthening of Putin's dictatorship, Afontovo would either have been closed by the authorities or it would have become another propaganda channel proclaiming the "successes" of the Mafia government headed by Godfather Putin – which I would never have agreed to'.

There was little that I, as a visiting consultant spending barely a week with each station, could do about the wider politics and pressures, apart from sympathise. My job was to help ensure, within the limited time available, that a station's output was as close as possible to Western best practice. Accuracy, impartiality, balance, fairness.

And therein lay the miscalculation to which any Western adviser is prone when working in a foreign land: the unconscious assumption that the consumers of the client's service or product – in this case the viewers – are also Western in their tastes and preferences. On occasions when focusing on the job in hand, it is even possible to forget that there *are* consumers. Which is why the Morgan Motor case should be required reading for every consultant, irrespective of specialism.

+ ———— +

Sir John Harvey-Jones was a former chairman of the industrial conglomerate, Imperial Chemical Industries – aka ICI – which for much of its history was the largest manufacturer in Britain. In 1989, the BBC persuaded Sir John to front a television series called *Troubleshooter*. Acting as a high-powered business consultant, Sir John was sent around the country to look at failing companies and tell them, in his blunt but jovial way, what they needed to do to turn their businesses around. It made for compelling viewing, not just because of the squirming directors and managers trying to excuse their failures, but because Sir John's analysis was as quick and to the point as a rapier thrust. Often eviscerating, and always right.

Almost always. Sadly, the program for which the series will be best remembered is the episode in which Sir John got it wrong.

The company in question was the Morgan Motor Company. Although it wasn't failing, it recognised it was at a crossroads and might benefit from Sir John's expert advice. Based in rural Worcestershire, between the Malvern Hills and the Cotswolds, it had started out in 1909 making motorised three-wheelers. Eighty years on, it was producing made-to-order four-wheeled sports cars which, with their swooping front-wings and wide running boards, looked as though they had been driven straight out of the 1930s. Amazingly, the body frames were built of 100-year-old ash wood, while the metal panels were knocked into shape by chaps wielding hammers or, no exaggeration, pushing sheets of aluminium through a large, hand-cranked mangle to achieve the correct curvature of the bonnet. With the company turning out just nine cars a week, the delivery time was *six years.*[2]

Sir John was appalled and recommended the company should double production and, to enlarge and update the plant, jack up the price.

Morgan's directors politely demurred, rejected the advice and, as events would prove, they were right to do so. Five years after the broadcast, the company was motoring along nicely, having ridden out the 1990–91 recession without so much as a bump in the road while other manufacturers had ended up in the ditch. The long wait for delivery had worked to Morgan's advantage; demand being so far ahead of supply, the good times had cancelled out the bad.

So, what was it that Sir John had failed to factor into his expert analysis?

Answer: the people who bought the car, *the customers*, those who would ultimately determine the success or failure of the company. Indeed, of any company. Morgan buyers were prepared to wait years for their dream car precisely because it was coach-built by horny-handed craftsmen rather than assembled by machines or, worse, by robots. They were thrilled that their bonnets had been 'hand-mangled' and, like a Trivial Pursuit nerd, would bore rigid with technical details any passer-by who paused to admire the vehicle. The years-long wait was testimony not just to the care and skill required in the car's construction but to its exclusivity. It added to the cachet. In sum, the past which Sir John had been so keen to sweep away ensured both the company's present and its future.

Sir John's mistake, which he readily acknowledged, is a salutary lesson for all troubleshooters. Never forget the customers – the viewers – was a lesson I learnt only belatedly. No less important than not forgetting, don't assume. As I was to discover, Russian viewers have a wholly different take on life from that of their Western counterparts. Read on . . .

17.

US AND THEM

In my early consultancy days on the road, I was frequently shocked by what appeared on screen in Russia. I saw material that would either never have been shown on British or Australian news or, if shown, would have been blurred or otherwise sanitised in line with a voluntary code that required a warning: *Some viewers may find the following report confronting.* An interesting use of the English language since 'confronting' originally meant, 'creating thought or discussion'. Heaven forfend that a news report should do any such thing!

Waking up in a Russian hotel, in the Urals, Siberia or on the cusp of the Arctic Circle, I would fumble for the TV remote and select one of the many Western-inspired studio-based breakfast shows with titles such as *Good Morning, Xxxxgrad* or *Coffee with Xxxxxxxx.* In addition to regular news updates, they typically strung together interviews, video inserts, cartoons, cooking demonstrations and lasted two or more hours. (On one occasion I even found myself on air at 7 am being quizzed about my work in Russia. Unfortunately, the interviewer had decided beforehand not only on her questions but my answers. When these didn't accord with her mental clipboard, she blithely ignored the discontinuity and ploughed on regardless. The irony that we were discussing the importance of training for television journalists was, I fear, lost on her.)

The shows were particularly attractive for city stations because, although copying *Good Morning America* and the UK's *Big Breakfast*, the format was so loose that, unlike a quiz show, it required no licence to produce a Russian variant. There would be the bright set painted in sunrise colours (or, latterly, a more subtle pastel palette), an impressionistic kitchen-cum-living-room, along with comfy sofas where the perfectly primped presenters – one male, one female – would conduct pat-a-cake interviews with guests who had seemingly dropped in from next door, while coffee percolated merrily in the background.

In the middle of this homely family-fest and without a word of warning, one of the presenters would segue into a pull-together of the overnight murders and road accidents around the region, shot by a video-journalist who had spent the previous eight hours following the local police (still referred to by the Soviet-era term *militsiya*) on his motorbike, or even riding pillion on one of theirs. No stabbed, shot, strangled, splayed, twisted or maimed body was left unturned for the benefit of the camera. And this at an hour when children would be getting ready for school.

When working with some of these stations, I would ask them about the reaction of their viewers to such a brutal intrusion into their living-rooms at such an early hour. As often as not, my query would be met by expressions of incomprehension as if I had questioned the need for a weather forecast.[1]

Russians have a view of life that, to those of us in the risk-averse, playground-matted, death-denying West, can make them seem not just fatalistic but reckless in their smoking, drinking and driving. There is an immediacy about their lives, a need – for once the cliché applies – to 'live in the moment'. History, confirmed by the turmoil of both the twentieth and twenty-first centuries, has taught them that life is unpredictable; that it can be snuffed out in the bat of an eye. So, whatever you're thinking of doing, don't think . . . *Do!*

During my time in Moscow, Russian colleagues would frequently suggest around nine or ten in the evening that we should go and see Sasha (or Ivan or Yuri), sometimes phoning beforehand, more often not. Along the way we would stop to buy beer, vodka, bread, *Vobla* dried fish, salami and cheese and, twenty minutes later, pitch up on Sasha's doorstep. Sasha would invariably be delighted, buzz us in and up to his apartment.[2] When comestibles and conversation were exhausted, we would stagger out around two in the morning. Acts of such spontaneity were regarded not as an intrusion but as a mark of true friendship. For me it was like being a student again, only now I was more than twice the age with half the physical capacity to handle it.

The TV breakfast segments I mentioned might be dismissed as voyeuristic, but they reflected reality. I don't know whether they gave viewers a sense of schadenfreude . . . there but for the grace of God . . . or whether they were intended as a reminder, a memento mori, of the sort of daily horrors that in the West would have been tucked out of sight down the back of the studio sofa. The only thing I *did* know was that I had been viewing the program through my eyes, not theirs.

＋━━━━＋

The difference between us and them goes deeper, to our very different perspectives on comparatively recent history. It's a difference which feeds into present-day relations between Russia and the West that, when not recognised, can lead to misunderstandings at every level.

'History is written by the victors', a quote often attributed to Churchill, was in fact uttered and possibly coined in 1891 by American senator George Graham Vest, who tellingly added, '. . . and framed according to the prejudices and bias existing on their side'. During my time in Russia, I came to realise that Vest's quote required a further twist – that victors on the same side in the same conflict write their *own* histories according to their prejudices and bias.

It's impossible to understand the Russians of today, why they distrust us in the West, without an awareness of their view of two relatively recent and hugely significant events: the Second World War and the expansion of the North Atlantic Treaty Organisation (NATO) after the end of the Cold War.

Starting with the Second World War or, as the Russians call it, the Great Patriotic War, the narrative in the West dating from the birth of my baby-boomer generation is that Nazi Germany was defeated by the joint forces of America, Britain, countries of the British Empire (notably the Indian sub-continent, Canada, Australia, New Zealand and South Africa) and partisans in Nazi-occupied countries. The Soviet Union too, but way out on the Eastern Front. It was one arm of the pincer movement that would eventually meet Western forces in Berlin during the final phase of the war.

The reason that Russia is accorded less than equal status on the victory podium is its collaboration with Nazi Germany at the start of the war. The Molotov-Ribbentrop non-aggression pact not only saw Russia get the Baltic states of Estonia, Latvia and Lithuania, but conveniently kept it out of the conflict while Hitler expended his efforts and armaments attacking his European neighbours to the west and north, Britain included. The pact lasted nearly two years until Hitler launched Operation Barbarossa against the Soviet Union in June 1941, leaving Stalin no choice but to switch sides.

Images, both still and moving, have played their part. The drama of the D-Day landings, including Steven Spielberg's 'immersive' recreation of them in *Saving Private Ryan*, has eclipsed the hard slog of the Battle of Stalingrad, arguably the bloodiest and fiercest battle of the war, grinding on for more than six months before the Germans capitulated.

The Russian narrative, by contrast, is that it was the Soviet Union which ultimately defeated Nazi Germany; that the Western Allies held back the invasion of the European mainland so that Hitler's army would be weakened by its engagements on the Eastern Front, fully aware of the cost in Soviet lives – up to twenty-seven million, civilian and military – more than suffered by any other combatant in the conflict. (Stalin's own son, Yakov, was among them. After his capture at the Battle of Smolensk in June 1941, Stalin refused to trade him for a German general. Yakov died in the Sachsenhausen concentration camp in April 1943.)

As for the Molotov-Ribbentrop pact, Russia, so the narrative goes, had no choice because, in Vladimir Putin's words, '... the USSR sought not to provoke the potential aggressor until the very end by refraining or postponing the most urgent and obvious preparations it had to make to defend itself from an imminent attack'.[3]

It's a version of events that is chiselled in the Russian consciousness and which I heard from all generations. The counter claims of Western historians that Russian/Soviet losses were in part due to Stalin's incompetence as a wartime leader – his misplaced trust in Hitler, failure to rearm in time and, not least, the prewar purge of his own best military commanders (executing more than three-quarters of his generals and admirals) – count for nought in the greater scheme of things. Even those Russians critical of the Soviet Union and glad to see its collapse, hold to the line that Russia gave the blood of her children to save the civilised world. It's a sacrifice they feel the West has never acknowledged and, eighty years on, our failure to do so remains an enduring, suppurating grievance.

Now add to this what happened after the end of the Cold War when NATO doubled its membership from sixteen in 1990 to thirty-two at the time of writing, including every one of the former Warsaw Pact members.

Looked at from the Russian perspective, this represents the demolition of the bulwark that formerly protected them from the West – notably, from their historic and now reunified enemy, Germany. In the north, following the accession of Estonia, Latvia, Lithuania and, most recently, Sweden and Finland, NATO is lapping at Russia's border. Moving south, with Ukraine now in the Western camp even if not in NATO, only Belarus, and in the deep south Georgia and Azerbaijan, stand between Russia and the West.

Viewed objectively, one may argue the change was an inevitable outcome of the collapse of the Soviet Union. The West had no need to seduce the former Warsaw Pact countries or the Baltic states. Trapped for decades in an abusive relationship (the Kremlin-ordered invasions of Hungary in 1956 and Czechoslovakia in 1968), they had long been ripe for political adultery, looking west and wondering how soft the bed would be. As former US Ambassador to Russia John J. Sullivan remarks in his 2024 memoir, *Midnight in Moscow*, 'What Russia truly feared was not an attack by NATO eastward, but the sovereign, democratic decision of Russia's neighbours to look westward – to NATO and the European Union (EU) – for their future'.

But in addition to the injury, there is the insult. The wholesale recruitment, as Russians see it, of these new NATO members is contrary to what was agreed when the West promised Mikhail

Gorbachev there would be no eastwards expansion of NATO in return for his agreeing to the reunification of Germany in 1990. In short, the West broke its word. Russia, acting in good faith, was duped.

It's a tricky one. The West's counterargument is that any non-expansion assurances were made in respect *only* of East Germany, nothing wider. Equally relevant is that Gorbachev was President of the Soviet Union at the time. Fifteen months on, neither the office nor the entity existed. So, even if the Russians had believed the agreement to be wider, any such promise, actual or assumed, would no longer have held. The context, the circumstances and the world had changed.

Once the Soviet Union fragmented, its former republics, along with the Warsaw Pact states that made up its defensive wall against the West, were free to make their own decisions and take advantage of NATO's open door policy which, according to Article 10, allows its members to invite any similarly security-conscious European state into the club.

For the Russians, such an argument is disingenuous. As they see it, the West took advantage of the country's post-Soviet weakness and internal divisions and, believing that Russian concerns about their border security could be ignored, hung a huge, flashing WELCOME sign on the door.

In the end, this isn't a question of who said what and when, whether correctly understood or wrongly assumed. It's about *perception* and, in this case, Russia's perception of its vulnerability.

What we in the West see is an aggressive, re-energised Russia, the cartoon caricature of the lumbering bear trampling across the Northern Hemisphere, rather than a Russia that has good historical reason (Napoleon June 1812, Hitler June 1941) to feel threatened and that, in the case of its invasion of Ukraine, sees attack as the best form of defence. In addition to the demolition of its western bulwark, 7600 kilometres of its southern flank borders the predominantly Muslim state of Kazakhstan while, going further east, another 4200 kilometres borders an unpredictable China.

It's generally assumed that the nations that develop a fortress mentality are small – Israel and Taiwan being obvious examples. Not exclusively so. Paradoxically, the larger you are, the greater can be the concern about your ability or, rather, inability to defend your borders.

Working with television journalists in Yerevan, Armenia, 2002.

Multi-camera recording of *Jarayon*, Internews Uzbekistan's
ambitious retrial program. Author's composite image.

(pp. 283–284)

Bishkek, Kyrgyzstan: ritual crowning of a somewhat wary 'honoured guest'.

The making of a dynasty. Election poster, 2003, showing outgoing president of Azerbaijan, Heydar Aliyev, next to his chosen successor, his son Ilham Aliyev.

(pg. 342)

A teenage Lenin outside Kazan University
from which he was expelled for anti-tsarist activities.

(pg. 114)

The Internews office, Moscow, reputedly one of the poet Pushkin's
many love-nests, showing the chill-out terrace at the back.

(pg. 12)

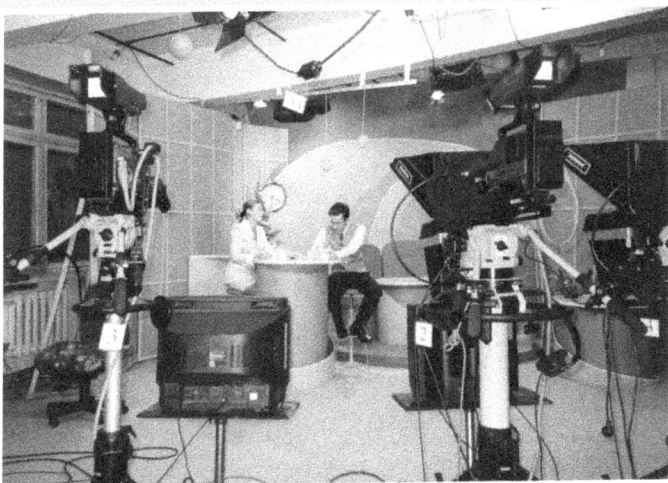

Ten minutes to transmission of *Morning Coffee*
with Afontovo, Krasnoyarsk, Siberia.

(pg. 169)

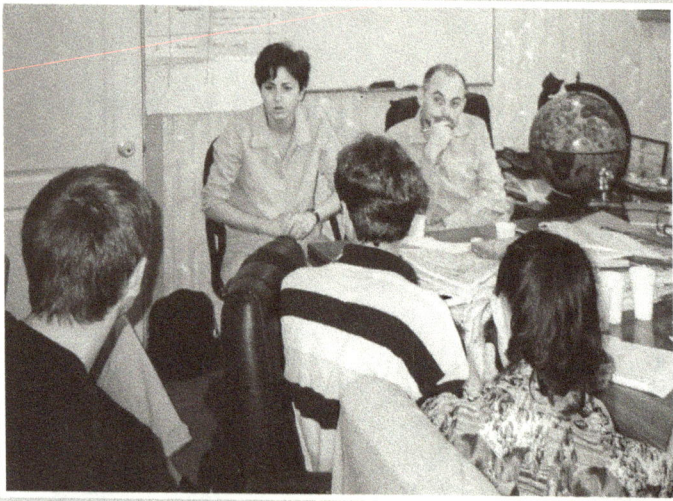

Yulia and Victor Muchnik, presenter/producer
and editor-in-chief of TV2, Tomsk, Siberia.

(pp. 67, 287–288, 337–340)

Veteran human rights campaigner Alexey Simonov
at Siberian TV Forum, Novosibirsk, March 2003.

(pp. 41–45)

In-depth research by workshop participants in Novosibirsk, Siberia.

Director of Internews Russia, the late Manana Aslamazian:
the 'Godmother of Russian regional television'.

(pp. 287–288)

Putin's media minister, Mikhail Lesin, in stripped-down mode
at a barbecue for foreign journalists, Moscow, May 2002.
(pp. 148–150)

Television Centre, Biysk, Siberia, close to Russia's
border with Kazakhstan and Mongolia.
(pg. 20)

UN armoured personnel carriers in western Georgia on stand-by
to lead convoys into the break-away state of Abkhazia.
(pg. 103)

Dilapidated Soviet-era factories, with every window broken, Georgia.
(pg. 125)

A typical bleak Soviet-era housing block in southern Georgia.

The Dry Bridge Market, Tbilisi, Georgia, a mecca
for those seeking authentic Soviet bric-a-brac.

(pg. 91)

Jano Zhvania, my Georgian karate black-belt bodyguard,
ensuring I won't be mugged after changing currency.
(pp. 99, 124–126)

Stalin's death mask, the Joseph Stalin Museum, Gori, Georgia.

(pg. 128)

Consultant's cap hanging on one of the 'historical nails'
personally hammered in by Stalin. Likani Palace, Georgia.

(pp. 123–124)

Mze TV, Tbilisi, Georgia – 'a four-storey mausoleum of a building'
during conversion, 2002.

(pp. 299–300)

News anchor Irakli Imnaishvili in Mze TV studio, Tbilisi, Georgia, 2002.
(pp. 299–300)

Picnic in Georgia's Pankisi Gorge, an active conflict zone on the border with Russia, protected by the long arm of the law.

(pp. 164–165)

Suburban housing estate in Georgia's second city, Kutaisi, 1999.
Note the tilting trolley-bus poles stripped of their copper wire.
(pg. 96)

18.

KNOWING ME . . . KNOWING YOU . . .

ABBA weren't alone in wanting to understand each other. There was one question I would always ask those I worked with in the post-Soviets: *What are your earliest memories of the West?*

During the Cold War, there was an assumption that those on the other side of the Iron Curtain were not just curious about our side but that they envied us, our freedoms and our capitalist, consumer lifestyle. There were the oft-repeated stories about jeans being a particularly sought-after commodity, about visiting foreigners being stopped in the street and asked if they would trade or sell the ones they were wearing, there and then.[1] Similarly, records by The Beatles and The Rolling Stones, along with VHS cassettes of Hollywood blockbusters, were supposedly the hottest items on the Soviet black market. The truth, I discovered, was infinitely more revealing.

Western music certainly made the most immediate and emotional impact. Oleg Dmitriev, my friend, fixer and interpreter in Moscow's Internews office, was only thirteen in 1981 when he managed to acquire, heaven knows how, a short-wave radio. The BBC's Russian Service, broadcasting from Bush House in London, was regularly jammed but just occasionally on Saturday evenings Oleg managed to pick up a program presented by a man who is half-jokingly described as 'the disk-jockey who brought down the Soviet Union'.

For thirty-eight years, starting in 1977, Seva Novgorodsev hosted a chat show with music. At its peak in the 1980s, when my friend Oleg was among Seva's devotees, it is reckoned to have reached at least 20 million Russians. Seva himself brushes off the suggestion that he was responsible for the collapse of communism but, as he told the BBC World Service, he believes in communication between not just people but peoples, plural, 'to provide a human element of intellect, of talent – inject some spark – because people are starving for human information, for something that will make their life lighter, easier. And by changing people from inside, we will change the society. I think it's the only way'.[2]

For Oleg, Seva's program was all about the music – an introduction to Pink Floyd, Nazareth, Deep Purple and The Eagles. A record of The Eagles' *Hotel California* was to become his most treasured window on the West. It is hard for those of us who have always had music pretty well on demand, whether vinyl, tape, CD, MP3 or Spotify, to understand what such glimpses of the lives of others meant to young Russians and to what lengths they would go to secure these objects of such desire. Thanks to some precious seconds in the clear between jamming (or, better still, by identifying the bandwidth which the KGB had left open to monitor the broadcast), though more often through a fog of static, Oleg and his friends would catch a few bars of a Western pop song and then spend weeks and months trying to track down a recording.

Imagine yourself in the nineteenth century attending a performance of music by Beethoven or Mendelssohn and being deeply affected by a particular sonata, concerto or symphony. As you listen, you are aware that it might be the only time you will ever hear it in your lifetime unless you are lucky enough to catch another performance or, second best, if you have the means to perform a small-scale version at home thanks perhaps to a Liszt piano transcription.

Sometimes Oleg and his generation struck lucky, chancing upon an original recording, typically one of the many vinyl records that were smuggled into the Soviet Union through the port of Leningrad by foreign crews looking for easy money. Or, failing an original, a bootleg copy, sometimes known as 'bone music'. In Russian, *roentgenizdat*. It was Oleg who introduced me to the expression, 'to record on the bones' and explained its origin.

During the Cold War, starting in the late 1940s, when Western music was banned, those operating in the underground music world were able to make a copy of a Western disc by means of specialist lathes which could duplicate – that is, re-cut – the grooves of the original on to a blank disc. But, although they had the equipment, they lacked the raw material: a vinyl-like substance from which to make the blanks. Until someone discovered that the photographic sheets used for medical X-rays had exactly the right combination of rigidity and surface 'give'.

Hospitals were only too happy to off-load them; if allowed to build up, they became a fire risk. In many cases the skulls, rib cages and knee joints remained visible on the bootleg discs. Hence the expression, 'to record on the bones'. A clandestine industry – a musical version of *samizdat* literature – was born, thrived and survived until the mid-1960s when tape recorders became available in the Soviet Union. Today bones records have become collectors' items, as sought after as the Western originals were in Soviet times.

+ —— +

Zurab Khrikadze was one of the coordinators in Internews' office in the Georgian capital, Tbilisi. When he was seven, a teacher asked his class what they would do if given a million roubles. The girl next to Zurab, being of a generous disposition, said she would give it to the poor, only to be scolded by the teacher. 'There are no poor in the Soviet Union!' she declared. But most telling, Zurab says, was that everybody knew the teacher was lying, and they knew that *she* knew.

Another teacher explained to Zurab and his classmates that, when socialism finally developed into communism and took over the world, there would be no states, no money and a single universal language. Even for a class of seven-year-olds still happily ignorant of Marx's dialectical materialism, this seemed wildly improbable. One of them asked mischievously which of the world's many languages this might be. After a few moments' thought, the teacher replied that it had yet to be invented. (There is seemingly no end to the lengths or lunacy to which authoritarian regimes will go to indoctrinate children. When I was working in the Middle East, Libyan journalists who had grown up under Muammar Gaddafi told me how they had been taught that every historical figure of note had Libyan ancestry. Thus, Shakespeare had been born 'Sheikh-speare'.)

Zurab's hapless teacher might have benefited from a chat with the country's leader at the time, First Secretary of the Georgian Communist Party, Eduard Shevardnadze. In 1978, Moscow tried to give Russian equal status with Georgian as the republic's official language. To his enduring credit, Shevardnadze stood up to the Kremlin, and won. Georgian remained the sole state language.

Zurab's most prized Western item, accessed rather than possessed, was a book that revealed an episode of his country's history which the Kremlin had for decades tried to expunge. By 1983, Zurab was a student at Moscow's Medeleyev Institute of Chemical Technology, which gave him access to the Lenin Library. The library's history books were restricted but, for whatever reason, reference books were not, including foreign ones. By now Zurab had learnt English and it was while browsing through the *Encyclopaedia Britannica* that he discovered that for nearly three years, starting in May 1918, Georgia had been an independent republic with a genuinely democratic multi-party system until 1921 when it was forced to become a Soviet republic. Why, you may ask, would the Lenin Library want a copy of the *Encyclopaedia Britannica*? Perhaps it was a case of know the enemy. It still seems a remarkable lapse on the part of the Soviet censors not to restrict its readership.

＋————＋

I was surprised how often a window on the West was opened by what to us would be an unremarkable, even disposable, object. Sometimes it was a set of West German coloured pencils, other times a stars-and-stripes lapel pin, a glossy brochure for an Italian car or just a bubble-gum wrapper. Why did they hold such power? An answer was provided by my Azerbaijani interpreter Ibrahim:

> Because we were always being told, and had to pretend to believe, that Soviet-made objects were, by definition, the best in the world . . . that we lived in the best, the happiest country on earth. This was proof, tangible proof, of the lie.

For Ibrahim, the Western object of greatest desire was a stapler that a schoolmate took into his class one day in 1980. The boy's father had brought it back from a business trip to Japan. Ibrahim was captivated by its totemic power. He recalls coveting the stapler like no other object he had ever come across.

> It was so neat and pretty that I wanted it, and I said, 'Oh, I wish I have it some day; it would be my best, the happiest day in my life!' Not because I had any use for a stapler but because it was a piece of somebody's life that we don't know and want to know.

The traffic between the Soviet republics and Japan was not exclusively one way. More than once I heard that during Soviet times Japanese visitors would buy Russian-made Zenit cameras, unscrew the lens and dump the body in the nearest bin. Allegedly, the Russian lenses were as good, or almost, as their Japanese counterparts and, even after paying for the entire camera, they worked out at a fraction of the price.

I was initially suspicious of the story. For a start, how many of the Russian lenses would fit the Japanese bodies? But photographer friends tell me it could well be true. As part of the reparations following the Second World War, the Russians got access to the designs and equipment of Germany's Carl Zeiss plants and proceeded to make surprisingly good copies (some of them of German Leica cameras). Soviet-made lenses therefore fitted many, probably most, Western cameras, Japanese included. As to why the Soviet-made cameras and lenses were so cheap, their price was massively subsidised by the Soviet authorities to bring in foreign currency.

+ —— +

Not surprisingly, the final days of the Soviet Union featured large in the memories of my post-Soviet colleagues.

For Internews' David Aslanyan in Armenia it was television that signalled the end – not what was on the screen but what was *not*. From as far back as anyone could remember, the Russian nightly news bulletin, *VREMYA* (Time), had been broadcast out of Moscow across all fifteen republics of the Union and, on the Kremlin's orders, every channel in every republic was required to clear the airwaves to transmit it at 9 pm Moscow time. Armenia boasted four state-run television channels. Then, one evening, for the first time ever, as David recalls, *VREMYA* didn't appear. Instead, the Armenian channels all continued with their own domestic programs. In political terms, it was the equivalent of the sun not rising.

Viewers started phoning each other, wondering whether their sets had gone rogue. Who, in normal circumstances, would dare to go against Moscow's orders? But it was true, the first indisputable proof that Russia had lost its grip on the republics. The empire was collapsing. The decision, it later turned out, had been taken by the Armenian minister of communications. A brave man who reportedly survived to tell the tale.

+ ———— +

Then there was Elena.

Elena acted as my interpreter for a brief stint I did in Nizhny Novgorod. Strictly speaking, she was a student who, as I quickly discovered, spoke English as well as any of the professional interpreters I had used. At twenty-two, she was of an age where half her life had been spent under communism, half under capitalism, or at least Gorbachev's and Yeltsin's version of it. When I asked her my routine question about her earliest memory of the West, she immediately responded, 'Bananas!' She explained:

They were difficult to get and you had to queue for two, maybe three hours. And sometimes they were so green that you had to put them in a warm place for several days. But my sister and I were children and we wanted to eat them straight away, right now.

This triggered a memory of my own from the early 1980s when I had spent some time in communist Bulgaria to research a spy novel. Walking around the capital Sofia, two things had struck me: men with windscreen wipers sticking out of their breast pockets because, if left on the car, they'd be filched, and Bulgarians bearing bananas, held out at arm's length with the proprietorial pride of a Rolex-wearer.[3]

During our off-duty chats over coffee, I was surprised to find that Elena knew my capital city almost as well as I did.

'So, when were you last in London?' I asked.

'I've never been out of Russia,' she replied.

On the spot, I invited her to spend a few weeks in Oxford that summer, subject obviously to her getting a visa.

The Russian authorities were happy to let her out. The problem was the British Embassy in Moscow. Someone had evidently decided that this was a classic case of the 'Olga Syndrome': middle-aged Western male working in Russia is captivated by attractive young Russian woman, tells himself they are in love and vows to take her away from all this. Back in the UK, they marry and within weeks of her getting her UK nationality, she leaves him. But not the country. It was a fairly common occurrence. I personally knew of two such cases involving fellow consultants. (In one case it was happy ever after but less so in the other when, after securing her British passport, the Olga in question ran off with a Romanian footballer.)

Elena was duly summoned to Moscow by the British Embassy for a grilling. What proof could she offer that she was going to return to Russia and not disappear once in the UK? She produced some pay slips and documentation showing an apartment in her name. Not enough. 'I have a boyfriend,' she added. 'My life is here in Russia.' Still not enough. Finally, she blurted, 'If I stayed in the UK, who would walk my dog?' Visa granted.

At the same time, the embassy required me to fax them a handwritten declaration, countersigned by my wife, that I was a happily married man who wanted only to give a young Russian a glimpse of life in the UK. This was accompanied by my personal undertaking that Elena would be on such-and-such a flight back to Moscow on such-and-such a date. I've often wondered what would have happened if she had missed the return flight. Might I have been charged with people smuggling?

+ —— +

'I think I'm dreaming,' were Elena's first words as Anni and I met her at Heathrow's Terminal 2. For the next three weeks we were to witness the dream play out: Elena's daily reaction to life in the West. It would have been hard to devise a better social experiment. Here was a young, hyper-perceptive foreigner seeing the reality of a world she 'knew' at one level but had never directly experienced. It was to be an education – as much for us as for her. She picked up on everything; mostly things that we had come to accept as perfectly normal. Sometimes she was amazed, other times amused. It was the proverbial Martian's view of life on earth.

It started within an hour of our driving back to Oxford. Since it was a Friday, we dropped into a large Sainsbury's to do some shopping for the weekend. By this time, 1998, the big Russian cities had supermarkets although some of the other former republics were slow to get the hang of them. Standing out as a Westerner, you would be followed around the store by a member of staff, leaving you wondering whether they were your personal shopper or a store detective. But there were still many shops which operated the old Soviet system. It was strictly choreographed. The customer goes to a counter, points to an item and is given a slip of paper with the price on it, then takes the slip to a central cashier, pays for it, and finally returns to the counter where, in return for the slip (now stamped), the item is handed over. And at each of the three stages, there will of course be a queue.

Comparing this rigmarole with the Sainsbury's experience, Elena was incredulous:

> But it's so easy! You don't have to ask to see. You're absolutely free to pick things up, read what's on the label and it takes so little time! In Russia I would spend several hours to buy all the necessary things. Here it would take me ten or fifteen minutes.

Sainsbury's practice of letting customers weigh and tag their own fruit and veg baffled Elena. 'What's to stop someone picking the most expensive apples but pressing the button for the cheapest?'

I had forgotten that in Soviet, and still in *post*-Soviet Russia, cheating the system was regarded as a national sport. (As was lying to officials; the rationale being that the system itself was a lie.) The answer to Elena's question according to the deputy manager was 'Nothing', unless you were unlucky enough to be caught by a very occasional spot check. Even then, I imagine you would have got off by pleading human error. 'Sorry, forgot my specs!'

Elena was equally bemused by the friendliness of Oxford's city centre shop assistants. 'Not only do they say "Hello", but they apologise if they don't have in stock what you want!' (In Russia, as I could confirm, shop assistants could be stunningly offhand; in fact downright rude.) She couldn't believe it when the Oxford branch of NEXT offered to get her size in the jeans she wanted from one of their other stores. This, I tried to explain, was customer service; a not entirely altruistic concept because yes, they wanted you to be happy but they also wanted to take your money and ensure your continued custom.

As for apologising, Elena reckoned we Brits had raised the practice to an art form. Seeing a sign 'regretting the inconvenience' of road works, she declared it to be beyond parody. 'They apologise that you queue – but still you have to queue!'

It has to be said that Elena's favourable reactions might have been coloured by her visit coinciding with a patch of glorious weather that bathed Middle England in an untypical golden glow. Time and again, as we passed through yet another honey-coloured, rose-festooned, postcard-perfect Cotswold village, I would threaten her with a wet Wednesday in Doncaster.

At the end of the first week, I asked Elena to list her first impressions before they faded. They were: a) men and women in the UK looked a decade younger than those in Russia, b) unlike Russians, Brits seldom dressed up in public, c) English gardens had so many flowers and so few vegetables, d) Brits didn't take off their shoes in the house and e) because the UK was so compact, we could visit friends and relations without crossing time-zones.

And yet, Elena noted, for all that we had only one time zone, we planned our social engagements like military campaigns. One evening she listened in disbelief as I phoned friends to invite them for dinner in a fortnight's time. In Russia, she declared, because of the instability and unpredictability of daily life, people were more spontaneous. 'We very seldom plan our time for even a week in advance,' she said. 'Anything may happen. If we telephone, it is to say we're on our way.'

Before coming, Elena had been told that in the West we ate only pre-prepared convenience food. It came as a surprise therefore to find that we, Anni in truth, didn't only cook but would regularly try out new recipes with different herbs and spices – Italian one night and Indian or Chinese the next.

But Elena's appreciation was not without the occasional critical edge. She picked up on something I had never considered; that spices disguise natural flavour rather than enhance it. 'Although they are grown naturally, they are artificial,' she observed. 'Your dishes smell so because of the spices. Russian dishes consist of simple ingredients but they are combined in such a way that they smell and taste delicious – without adding spices.'

She also wondered whether we had gone gadget crazy. 'You are so funny you foreigners,' she giggled. 'Even if it is much easier to do something with your hands, you use machines to make it more complicated!' Nor, as she discovered, was Britain without its own Soviet-style queues – for the women's toilets in museums, art galleries and even in that temple of capitalism, Selfridge's. 'You call this a market economy – and yet it is so difficult to spend a penny!'

Again, she questioned why, in some of our kitchens and bathrooms, we still had separate taps rather than modern mixers? Why were our theatre tickets so expensive? And how come our local deli had marinated herrings but not salted ones?

But, on balance, Elena counted these as mere irritants compared with so many positive points: the comfort and cleanliness of our coaches (particularly the Oxford–London ones), Regent's Park, the Hard Rock Cafe, Marks & Spencer, the *Carry On* films . . . and Marmite.

Sadly, there was a rather sour postscript to the visit. Elena wanted desperately to come back for six months as an au pair. But the British Government at the time didn't issue au pair visas to Russians. When I phoned a Home Office press contact for an explanation, I was told that Russia was not classified as a West European country. Yet, bizarrely, if she had come from Bosnia, Croatia, Hungary, the Czech Republic, Slovenia or Macedonia, there would have been no bar. I was tempted to suggest the Home Office should borrow a map from the Foreign Office.

In the end, the UK's loss was France's gain. Within a year of her return to Russia, Elena got a job as a nanny in France. After studying at the Sorbonne, she went on to marry a Frenchman, have two daughters and now works as a senior policy expert for the International Energy Agency in Paris.

19.

OF ADJECTIVES AND ADVERBS

My father Jack, an avid watcher of television and TV news in particular, thought I had the jammiest job in the world. 'You're on screen for a couple of minutes a week,' he used to say when I was a BBC correspondent. 'What the hell do you do the rest of the time?' When I moved into current affairs and reported for a half-hour program maybe once *a month*, his incredulity knew no bounds. I suspect he was not alone. So, it's time to reveal the secret life of the television journalist.

Television journalism is different. It is different from radio journalism and in many respects it is the antithesis of print journalism (including print online).

Strangely, the BBC, whose pioneering *Television Newsreel* was launched in 1948, didn't take this fundamental fact on board till the early 1970s. Up until then, its default policy had been to employ actors or 'chaps with a posh voice' to read the news, and former newspaper journalists to report it. This was notably the case with specialist and foreign correspondents where experience in the field trumped an ability to adapt to the new medium. The thinking was that you could take a newspaper journalist and he (in those days it invariably was) would pick up television by the process of osmosis, from the camera crews, picture-editors or newsroom colleagues. Rather like sitting next to Nellie in a nineteenth century cotton mill.

What BBC management failed to appreciate was that the 'column inch' of the print journalist bears no relation to the 'broadcast second' of the television journalist.

The corporate mindset finally changed in 1970 with the launch of the BBC Graduate News Trainee Scheme. It represented a reversal of more than two decades' practice and at the time was viewed as a brave, possibly risky, experiment. Instead of taking print journalists and hoping they could master television, the strategy was to take half-a-dozen university graduates a year (though heaven knows why such a narrow stipulation), most of whom would have no background in journalism. Only after they had been taught 'the grammar of television' would the journalism be leaked in with some classroom theory followed by secondments to the national newsrooms at Broadcasting House and Television Centre. Finally, they would be sent off to a BBC regional newsroom for several months where, like orphaned ferrets reared in captivity, they would be released into the wild, reporting on the ground for both radio and television. In fact, many of those who went through the scheme found their eventual home in radio, not television.

And there was one other requirement. Candidates for the scheme had to have spent a couple of years after leaving university working in the 'real world'.

I was lucky enough to be one of the first ferrets. Since leaving Durham University, I had spent two years teaching English to adults at the British Institute in Florence, although the BBC selection board seemed more impressed by the labouring I had done laying gas mains during my university vacs.

What I haven't mentioned is that this training, including secondments, lasted *two years*. Nearly thirty years later, the training that I and my fellow media missionaries were attempting in the post-

Soviets typically lasted *five days*, often working with the rawest of raw material. I should add that the formal training courses conducted on Internews premises with dedicated facilities, could last up to six weeks. Certainly better, but still little more than a primer.

+ ———— +

The first thing to note when comparing print with television is that in the case of a newspaper article (or such an article on a news website), the reader is in complete control. Whether fast or slow, you decide the pace. By contrast, when viewing the same story on a television news bulletin, you have to absorb the information at the speed determined by the reporter. This was certainly the case back in the early 2000s. Today, if watching a video report online, you can of course stop, start and rewind. But the truth is that, unless the story is of compelling interest, most of us don't, and today's TV reporter must bear this in mind.

No less relevant is that a television news report lasts, on average, just one-and-a-half minutes. Imagine, in a conversation over coffee with a friend, having to explain what might be a complex, nuanced, multi-viewpoint subject within 90 seconds.

But perhaps the most salient point, so obvious that it is easily overlooked, is that television is a visual medium. *It's the pictures that tell the story* – a mantra which television news trainers repeat till they are hoarse. Of course, there is the reporter's voice-over commentary, but its primary function is to complement the images on the screen. In a news report, the script is forever the bridesmaid at the service of the pictures. (Some purists go so far as to argue that the test of a good news report is to see whether it still makes sense with the sound off.) This is why novice TV reporters are told to think in pictures, not words, and that's the crux of why the transition from print to television can be so hard.

A print reporter may write about thousands taking part in a demonstration, knowing that the words will conjure up the scene in the reader's mind. But if you put the same line over an image of a dozen people standing on a street corner (perhaps because the cameraman arrived late), there is a howling mismatch between words and pictures. It doesn't work. The script doesn't have to slavishly match the pictures, frame by frame, but – the golden rule – it must never contradict them.

Now add to this the requirement, the discipline, to write 'to the broadcast second'.

A print journalist writes 'to the column inch' which, despite the term, is more often between one-and-a-half and two inches wide and accommodates between six and eight words. Roughly. The more important figure is the total word count that the news editor will have stipulated: 500, 800, 1000 . . . maybe even 2000. So long as the reporter's 'copy' is within that limit, it will fit the space allocated to it.

Compare this with how the television journalist writes a voice-over commentary.

On average, three spoken words consume one second of airtime, at least in English. In other languages it can be as little as two words to the second. Scripts must be timed literally to the second. One second over and your commentary will crash into the upcoming interview clip. One second under, OK; but two or three seconds under and the picture-editor will have to raise the level of the ambient sound to fill the silence.

Added to this, there can be other complications, both cultural and political. Working in Azerbaijan, I was helping a reporter in a regional station put together a video package with the voice-over in his native Azeri. The pictures, including a couple of interview clips, had been edited in a logical sequence but, despite our best combined efforts, we couldn't fit the half dozen blocks of the voice-over into their allotted spaces along the timeline. Every block was at least five seconds over, which is a huge amount. I asked the interpreter to go through the script again. Still, the words overran. It was only when I got him to go through it literally word-by-word that the problem revealed itself.

Two problems in fact. First, the reporter had introduced each block with the words, 'Dear and respected viewer'. Second, whenever President Heydar Aliyev was mentioned, which he was, repeatedly, he was accorded his full title with all the trimmings. I assume that at the time this was standard practice on Azerbaijani television.

+———+

Because every second counts, a television news script must be pared to the verbal bone. (I'm talking about *news* scripts, not documentaries, which can adopt a more relaxed style.) The first things to go are subordinate clauses. Single, discrete sentences are the order of the day and, additionally, are truer to conversational speech.

Next to go are adjectives and adverbs because the pictures are already doing their job. You, the reporter, don't need to tell me the president's limo is big, black and moving slowly. It's there on screen. Nor, for the same reason, do you have to tell me it's flanked by half a dozen motorcycle outriders. In short – mantra alert – 'Don't tell me *what* I can see; tell me *why* I'm seeing it' (Frank Ash, BBC Academy). In this case, you might explain that it's the first time the president has been seen in public since his recent illness, something the viewer cannot tell from the pictures.

On occasions, the pictures may be so self-explanatory as not to need any script. As the former BBC war reporter Martin Bell advised, television journalists should learn to 'write silence'.

And now the kicker.

It's a sad truth that the ability to write well, as the best print journalists do, employing the full figurative arsenal of idiom, simile and metaphor, can be a handicap rather than an asset when switching to television. The TV news script must be self-effacing; words that draw attention to themselves detract from the pictures. Similes are taboo because they create a mental image which the screen doesn't show. If, for example, you say, 'The aircraft fell to earth like a plummeting meteor', you are asking viewers to hold two images in their heads simultaneously: the actual one they can see before them and the metaphorical one you're comparing it to. But when viewers can see the actuality, they don't need the metaphorical. It may work on the printed page but in television it's unnecessary baggage; distracting at best, confusing at worst.

＊━━━＊

The fact that many of those I was training in the post-Soviets – in Azerbaijan, Tajikistan, Uzbekistan and Kyrgyzstan – were culturally or religiously Muslim presented an additional challenge. The reporters often saw themselves less as conveyors of information, more as poet-philosophers, much given to dispensing utterances of cosmic significance. One Azerbaijani reporter concluded her report about children in an orphanage with the line, 'Our report won't change anything. They'll continue to live as they do. The only thing to be said is that someday they'll ask the question, who am I?' (Perhaps I shouldn't be so snarky. I can recall a BBC reporter signing off his piece with the words, 'Whether the future will tell remains to be seen. But one thing is certain . . . Bolton will never be the same again.')

The Muslim journalist's attachment to the word is wholly understandable, given the supreme importance which Islam attaches to it. It is, after all, 'The Word of Allah' as revealed to the Prophet Muhammad, which in written form became the Quran. And it explains why calligraphy is the highest form of visual art in the Islamic world. But, when it comes to writing a television news script, this reverence can result in a reluctance – sometimes insurmountable – to strip away the finery and make the word, even with a small 'w', subordinate to the picture.

But, you may well counter, the Christian West also attaches importance to the word. 'In the beginning was the word' (John 1:1). True, but in its preaching and proselytising Christianity has traditionally made as much use of the image. In the early centuries, its adherents were mostly illiterate and 'the word', being in Latin, was the preserve of the clergy. For these reasons indoctrination in its non-pejorative sense was as often visual as verbal. Hence all those paintings, frescos and illuminations of the Annunciation, the Nativity, the Crucifixion, the Deposition, the Resurrection, the Transfiguration, the Assumption of the Virgin – not to mention the Orthodox icons of Jesus, Mary, the saints, prophets and the heavenly host of angels. (One of my own earliest memories is of Sunday school, of having to stick stamps of the life of Jesus into a picture book and then being told off because I'd got them in the wrong order – what later in life I would call 'editing'. Perhaps the Jesuits are right. Give me the child for the first seven years and I'll give you the man.) All of which makes it that much easier for the Western – more accurately non-Muslim – television journalist to accept the demotion of word to picture.

＋——————＋

Of course there are exceptions, but they are few and invariably one-liners. One such is BBC reporter Brian Hanrahan's line during the 1982 Falklands War when having to abide by the rules of censorship. 'I'm not allowed to say how many planes joined the raid,' he declared. 'But I counted them all out, and I counted them all back.' Another contender would be the opening line of Michael Buerk's coverage of the 1984 famine in Ethiopia; his reference to 'A Biblical famine, *now*, in the twentieth century'. Buerk's story was one of the very few instances of a TV news report making a difference. After airing on BBC news, it was rebroadcast by 425 television stations across the globe and famously prompted Bob Geldof to launch Live Aid.

Because there have been so many subsequent pictures of starving, dying and dead children, the report's images, so shocking at the time, have I suspect become generic in most people's memories. Except possibly for one shot: that of a body wrapped in a blanket with another smaller bundle laid not at, but on its feet. Its heart-rending contents are revealed by Buerk's voice-over: 'This mother and the baby she bore two months ago wrapped together in death.' It's a classic example of stripped-back text adding the necessary context to the all-important image. No adjectives, no adverbs.

Often, scenes of mass death and destruction are, without wishing to diminish the cameraman's skill and sensitivity, a grotesque case of point and shoot. It is in these situations that the so-called 'symbolic shot' assumes paramount importance. This is the single picture, typically edited to no longer than five seconds, that manages to encapsulate the enormity of the situation. Such as the Ethiopian mother and her baby. It has also been called 'the iconic image', as when referring to the 2003 toppling of the statue of Saddam Hussein in central Baghdad which, given the subsequent claims of orchestration, manages to be one of the most interesting examples but perhaps not the most helpful.

+————+

In May 1976, producer David Hanington and I were in Rome making a BBC current affairs report about the Italian election to be held the next month. We had pretty well wrapped when we got a flash message from London, telling us to drive immediately north to the Friuli region just beyond Venice which had been devastated overnight by a 6.4 magnitude earthquake. (According to the final tally, nearly a thousand people died, up to 3000 were injured and at least 150,000 were left homeless.)

David was one of those maverick producers who had moments of off-the-wall brilliance, and this was one of them. He declared that we needed not just any old hire car to take us north but, very specifically, a large white Mercedes limousine with tinted windows (which in Rome with its red-carpet movie community was surprisingly easy to find). While David sorted out the car hire, I scoured the stalls of the souvenir vendors around the Vatican for a white-and-yellow pennant bearing the crossed keys of St Peter. This was in the days when cars still had radio aerials that rose like mini periscopes from the bodywork and to which, if so minded, one could attach a small flag.

And it worked. At every roadblock we encountered on reaching the earthquake zone, the way was instantly cleared for our papal motorcade, no questions asked, no documents demanded, even though said motorcade amounted to a single vehicle. As a result, we beat the rest of the media pack to the epicentre of the quake where the rescue workers were still digging in the rubble. Since David was directing the camera crew, my job was to scan the shattered landscape for the all-important symbolic shots. I would identify three.

The first was an elderly man sitting on top of the chimney of his former home, frozen in bewilderment as he contemplated the devastation all around. What made it striking, apart from the image of a man sitting on a chimney, was that the chimney was less than a metre above the ground. The walls of the building had burst uniformly outwards, causing the entire roof to drop three metres, perfectly intact.

The second symbolic shot was one I would rather forget, since it's an example of how one can become so engaged in getting the story, that one forgets the respect and sensitivity due to one's fellow humans in such dire circumstances.

Unlike the house mentioned above, this one had been reduced to the proverbial pile of rubble. While volunteers dug, professional emergency workers were extricating bodies – whether dead or alive, there was no telling. Suddenly there appeared a chirping canary, saved by the fact that it was in a cage. It was the ultimate symbolic shot; the wretched bird had survived while its owners had likely not. Nothing so starkly, so poignantly, illustrated the randomness of Fate. I shouted to the cameraman to get his attention, pointing to one of the emergency workers as he crossed the rubble, holding high the cage and its still chirping occupant. My voice gave me away and there was an eruption of fury from volunteers and professionals alike. I knew what they were thinking: typical bloody animal-loving English and, worse, a sensation-mongering television hack, more concerned with the survival of a single bird than the likely death of an entire family! I thought I was going to be lynched, and frankly my widow couldn't have complained. What saved me was my knowledge of Italian from my days teaching English in Florence. The depth of my vocabulary expressing remorse knew no bounds. None of which was sufficient to wipe away the shame then, or its memory now.

And the third symbolic shot? It came three days later, by when the dead, at least those that had been identified, were being readied for burial. Because of their rapidly increasing number and the risk of cholera, many were having to be interred in mass graves. The body bags were laid out, row upon row, in a field. And there in the middle of them, sitting at a small kitchen table, was a single uniformed official, typing death certificates on his Olivetti Lettera portable, his peaked cap next to it, removed as a mark of respect. It wasn't just the incongruous image that struck. No less haunting was the sound – the only sound that day – of the peck, peck, peck, as the metal fonts hit the paper. The scene required minimal scripting – a reference, as I recall, to the official 'tapping out a requiem', followed by several seconds of actuality audio as the camera tracked along the lines of body bags . . . peck, peck, peck.

+———+

Training Slavic journalists, notably Russians, threw up a challenge that was less about the content of their scripts than the delivery. For reasons I could never fathom, many Russian reporters regarded the microphone as an item of military hardware. Every script was voiced in rapid machine-gun bursts – 'Kalashnikov commentary', as I dubbed it. I would point out that when someone had something important to impart, they generally *slowed down*; that urgency was more about tone than speed. But to little avail.

I had a particular problem with an experienced Armenian reporter (not Slavic but, a legacy of Soviet times, Russian-speaking) who was very aware of her public profile and, as I soon learnt, hypersensitive to criticism. Although her delivery was less rat-a-tat-tat, she left no gaps between her sentences, no pause for the viewer to digest her words. The result was the television equivalent of a stream of consciousness. Virginia Woolf on steroids. When I tried, tactfully, to take her to task, her response was, 'That's the way my viewers like it'. I don't know how many of them she had polled but I could see I wasn't going to win.

And there was one other challenge – a form of political correctness (in its literal sense) that could render futile an entire week's training.

Old journalistic habits die hard, and in many newsrooms the news editor, whether multiskilling as the old Soviet censor or just not trusting his own staff, would demand to see the reporter's script *before* the pictures were edited, before the words were adjusted to complement them. Once signed off, there could be no changes. Not a single word.

As a result, picture-editors who had been introduced to the professional practice of marrying the words to the pictures – a process that over the course of the edit could reduce the text by a third and change the word, sentence or paragraph order of much that remained – would revert to the bad old Soviet ways. Instead of leaving the recording of the reporter's much amended commentary to the end of the session, they would get the reporter to record it straight from the news editor's hand. Since it couldn't be changed, why not? Then, as if pegging washing out on a line, they would lay the pictures over it. The pictures were cut to fit the words instead of the words cut to fit the pictures; the reverse of best practice. The sole advantage of the procedure was speed. A one-and-a-half-minute report that would take up to one-and-a-half hours to edit professionally with the script being 'written to picture', could be thrown together in twenty minutes or less. This was hack and slash, and it showed.

+ ———— +

The bottom line of the above observations is that, even when best practice is followed, television compresses content. There is no denying it. The viewer gets what the viewer demands: the news of the day – regional, national, global – in a neat half-hour package. Forty minutes if the weather and sport are included. An obvious, albeit simplistic, comparison is to food: print journalism is wholesome and slowly digested, whereas television journalism is processed junk – quickly consumed, of little nutritional value and with an excess of salt and sugar to make it tasty. Which prompts a question that is both uncomfortable and unavoidable. Can we – *should* we – trust television as a news medium?

My answer is qualified. When opening a workshop or training course, I often observe that television, being essentially superficial and screen-deep, is arguably the worst medium for conveying information. But, because of the unique impact of moving pictures, television is the most effective tool at our disposal. It is still the one that most people in most countries choose as their primary source of news, whichever screen they may use, whether in the corner of the living room, on the laptop, iPad or smartphone. We therefore have to learn to use it as best we can. Responsibly.

This requires that the selected shots, *snapshots* in truth, and the way they are edited, should reflect the situation on the ground as honestly and accurately as humanly possible, while allowing for the visual grammar of the medium. You don't have to be familiar with the minutiae of television production to know how easy it is to take selective shots of a city's worst features – a rundown housing estate, a boarded-up shop bearing a TO LET sign, a slumped drunk begging on the street, a queue at the employment agency (with no indication that those in line are waiting for it to open) – string them together and give a totally distorted picture of what in every other respect may be a thriving and caring community.

And that is why television training is so important. It's as much about truth and ethics as about focus and exposure.

＋——————＋

One final thought: television can be cruelly discriminatory when it comes to the recruitment of those who appear on screen. Not just because it favours the photogenic but because it excludes, for whatever reason – an incurable stutter, an inability to 'act oneself' before camera, or just a nervous disposition – many of those who have genuine talent. It's got better over the years. These days, you can have both a beard *and* a regional accent and still get on screen.

When I started in 1970, the bar was higher. I was lucky in being able to disguise a speech impediment: an inability to pronounce the letter 'r'. It became evident when recorded, by which time it was too late for the BBC to throw me out. Even so, during my training secondment to the Manchester newsroom, the sub who wrote the nightly news update got much pleasure selecting the stories when he knew I'd be reading them. On one occasion he managed a hat trick: a story about the Wiver Wibble (River Ribble) bursting its banks, followed by one about the Dwoylsden Pony Twotting Twack (Droylsden Pony Trotting Track) facing closure and, the coup-de-grace, a fire in a Wawwington Bwewewy (Warrington Brewery). Years later when reporting from the Middle East, my producer asked me to change every mention of the 'Iswaeli pwoblem' to the 'Jewish dilemma'. (If you wish more of the same, I recommend the section in Angus Roxburgh's excellent memoir *Moscow Calling* where he describes his personal transition from print to television; how he learnt the importance of pictures and how to give gravitas to his 'reedy, weedy' voice.[1])

20.

THE INCREDIBLE SHRINKING
CAMERA CREW

Editorial considerations aside, the twin guiding principles of television newsgathering are speed and cost. In this respect, the technological revolution of the late twentieth and early twenty-first centuries has served broadcasters well. Most often cited is the switch from analogue to digital, particularly the resulting uptake in the 1990s of computerised 'non-linear' editing which, as the name suggests, enabled picture-editors to shuffle and reshuffle the shots of a news report or documentary as many times as required with a few mouse-clicks or keystrokes and, crucially, with no loss of picture quality. It was the equivalent of the move from the typewriter to the word processor in print journalism. (Some picture editors would likely add one downside: that it afforded the journalists they worked with far too many opportunities to faff and fiddle.)

For those of us working on the road as reporters or producers, no less consequential was the earlier switch from film to video during the 1980s. It's often been described as a step-change. In truth, it was an entire new staircase.

First, to the delight of station bosses, it meant a rapid reduction in the size of crews, and therefore costs. When I started as a BBC news trainee in the early 1970s, it was normal to work with a four-person crew: cameraman, assistant cameraman, sound engineer, lighting man (aka 'sparks'). The most important part of the assistant's job during a shoot was to ensure there was always a magazine of unexposed film to hand, so the cameraman could keep rolling with only minimal interruption. The assistant did this by placing the camera mag of exposed film in a light-proof bag on his knee, removing the film, canning it and re-loading the mag with fresh stock ready to replace the one currently in use the moment the cameraman asked for it. All of this was done purely by feel – a process that the best could accomplish in under five minutes. The assistant was also the one who would sit in the passenger seat of the crew-car with a satisfied grin as he assiduously recorded the penalty payments for missed meals and overtime. Being typically young and muscular, he usually got the girls too.

When video cameras came in, their tape cassettes soon made the assistant redundant, at least for news; the cameraman just took a new or recycled cassette from the box and slotted it in, ready to go.

The lighting man quickly followed because video cameras, being hyper-sensitive to light, can shoot and record in low-level situations where film can't or requires the type and speed to be specially selected. Not that cameramen didn't occasionally use lights. They now carried their own lighting kits which they would mostly use for set-piece interviews to give the scene a three-dimensional effect and 'sculpt' the human features.

Finally, the sound engineer would also be deemed superfluous because, in theory, the cameraman could now adjust the audio levels through the camera . . . always assuming that, like the former sound engineer, he wore headphones. (More about this in the next chapter.)

And there was one other change: an addition, not a subtraction. Although it's seldom remarked upon and measures only about 10 x 5 x 1 centimetres, its significance cannot be overstated.

In the days of film, when working as a reporter or producer, you could never be sure what the cameraman had shot until the exposed footage had been through 'the soup' – that is, processed – and you could view the rushes back at base on an editing machine. This could be hours, sometimes days, later. If you were filming abroad, it could be *weeks*. Sometimes, when required to send back a can of exposed but unprocessed film from a far-flung foreign location, along with a recorded voice-over and suggested cutting order, you never saw the rushes; only the edited and transmitted report when you got back.

This meant you could spend days working with an incompetent cameraman without knowing it. You could see where he was pointing the camera. You could tell whether he was tracking, panning, tilting or (sparingly, one hoped) zooming. But, when it came to the technical stuff – focus, exposure and white-balance – you had to cross your fingers. In effect, you were directing blind; or, at least, on trust.

And there was something else: something that had nothing to do with technicalities but everything to do with aesthetics.

One of the most important skills a cameraman has to master is the *framing* of the shots, particularly when required to shoot handheld off the tripod when an intuitive sixth sense, an uncanny ability to anticipate which way people are going to move, kicks in. We're talking about composition, the way the elements within the frame are balanced without, for example, leaving large areas of 'dead' screen. With a stills photographer, it's a given. Indeed some of the best make it a point of professional honour not to allow their shots to be cropped. In one respect, the television cameraman is also a stills cameraman in that he is taking a minimum twenty-four still shots – frames – a second. Often more, depending on the camera, special requirements and whether shooting film or video.

In the days of film you had no means of knowing the quality of the cameraman's framing. The exception was the one-on-one interview, when you could ask if you might 'check the frame' before the camera rolled, to ensure for example that the leaves of a pot plant in the background weren't sprouting out of the interviewee's head or that a glass-fronted cabinet wasn't reflecting camera, crew and reporter. (Backgrounds are always a danger zone. On one occasion, after I had unwisely pressured my cameraman to shoot an interviewee before a fish tank, its sole occupant entered one ear before emerging two seconds later from the other. Nobody remembered a word of the interview). The best film cameramen in my experience were all too happy to allow a second eye to squint through the viewfinder and, if there was the likelihood of zooming in for a close-up, show that framing too. Not so the less secure and less-competent ones, who would interpret such a request as a lack of trust and make their resentment clear.

Video changed everything. Not all video cameras had them but the introduction on many professional models of an LCD flip-out monitor (the aforementioned addition), duplicating the image in the viewfinder, meant that for the first time the reporter or producer could see the same image the cameraman was seeing by standing just behind him. Some of the best freelance crews would even offer you a hand-held wireless monitor, the size of a book, which meant that, like a big-time Hollywood movie director, you could watch the pictures in real time from several metres away.

Failing a monitor, you could always ask the video cameraman to rewind and replay the tape for you to double-check the shot or sequence through the viewfinder. (Impossible with film of course.) Again, some cameramen were reluctant, but this time with good reason. It could be a risky practice.

In the early 1990s when shooting a documentary in the depths of the Amazon rainforest, we lost my key, one-take piece-to-camera because the cameraman, having rewound and replayed the tape for the producer, thought I too might like to check it and so ran it back a second time. Trusting my producer's judgement, I said there was no need but the cameraman forgot to run the tape forward again to the point where he had stopped recording. As a result, the entire take of me striding fearlessly through a tangle of lianas and epiphytes, declaiming to camera while illuminated by shafts of light through the canopy thirty metres above, was wiped minutes later when he recorded the next shots over it – something we discovered only when viewing the rushes back at base.

The documentary, about a repentant logger who was using a native tribe to replant the thousands of mahoganies he had cut down over a decade, was memorable for other reasons. When, having got access to a helicopter, we suggested videoing the tribe at work, we were told they hadn't been checking their answering machine. It wasn't a joke. The Brazilian authorities, it turned out, had provided the indigenous population with 'communication posts' throughout the rainforest. I tried to imagine the recorded message: 'Thank you for calling the Kaributapúk. We are out at the moment but if you would like to leave your name, number and ethnicity . . .' It will probably come as no surprise that the documentary went from production to archive without so much as a flicker of transmission in between.

＋————＋

For the hundreds of broadcast pioneers in the dying years of Gorbachev's Soviet Union, it was an exceptionally lucky coincidence that relatively cheap lightweight video cameras were replacing the bulky old film cameras just when they were setting up their news operations. From what I saw, the early models were VHS, soon followed by S-VHS. Conveniently, the full-size VHS cassettes which most of them recorded on could be slotted straight into a VCR recorder/player for editing. (In fact, the process required *a pair* of VCRs lashed together. A second blank cassette would record selected shots and interview clips from the original to build up a sequential compilation – in effect, an edit.) The picture quality was consumer-grade and, because VHS was analogue, some resolution was lost in the editing and with every subsequent copy. But, for news reporting, VHS did the job in so far as content was generally more important than quality. And of course, unlike film, there was no processing – a huge saving in speed and cost. Had video camcorders not appeared on the scene when they did, in the mid-1980s, it's hard to see how the countless late-Soviet and early post-Soviet independent stations could have ever got into newsgathering. The costs would have been prohibitive. The only pool from which future television journalists (and cameramen) could have emerged would have been the network channels, state and commercial, and possibly the larger regional ones.

What often gets lost in discussion of television's technological revolution is the human element; how the progressive reduction in the size of both crews and equipment impacted those who were left. And it continues to do so.

TV news reporting (when the reporter is doubling as a producer) has always been a demanding, multi-skilled profession: directing a cameraman, conducting an interview, turning bald facts into a compelling visual narrative and just keeping going, frequently late into the night and at weekends. When talking to those at the start of their careers, or even considering whether television reporting is for them, I tell them bluntly they will need the leadership qualities of a general, the quick-wittedness of a lawyer, the creativity of a dramatist, and the stamina of a marathon runner.

Since 2010 when Apple launched its iPhone 4 with HD video and iMovie editing, I have had to add something else: that they may on occasions find themselves working alone, *totally* alone, in the field, while required to produce a news video package with a smartphone as their only item of equipment. Although still paid for one job, they will be doing four: camera-operator, sound-engineer, picture editor and of course, still and most importantly, journalist (so, a voice-over script, interviews and, if needed, an audio-visual selfie, aka a piece-to-camera).

To be clear, I am no Luddite. I've never used a smartphone for news but a few years back, an American colleague, Clint Dougherty, and I co-produced a twenty-minute mini-documentary about a medieval village in France where we were both living. The mayor, who commissioned it, thought it might attract tourists. It helped that Clint had been a Hollywood cameraman. He suggested that, rather than using conventional video cameras, we should – as an exercise – shoot with our smartphones attached to gimbal stabilisers (a highly sophisticated bit of kit bought online for a mere 130 euros). The quality, stability and fluidity of the result, as good as that produced by a Steadicam costing thousands of euros, was a revelation. It was *so* good that a UK network production company making one of the countless *Plucky Brits Abroad* series asked if it could plunder our rushes. I became an instant convert.

There is no question that mobile journalism – Mojo, as it's called – has a place in modern newsgathering and is becoming more sophisticated by the day. In addition to a smartphone, the latest Mojo kit comes with an external microphone, mini-light, stabiliser, tripod and peripherals; all in a standard backpack. And no problem getting the finished video package back to base, irrespective of distance. Just go on to a file-transfer website and click, UPLOAD.[1]

Today's smartphones have the potential to revolutionise reporting not just at the local level in the form of Mojo-trained regional journalists (the television equivalent of local radio reporters wielding audio-recorders) but across the globe in those locations, such as conflict zones, where the priority is to be as nimble and unobtrusive as possible. Even more so when phone and drone are combined, as in Ukraine.

Yet snobbery persists. 'Even though mobile technology, particularly with the iPhone, has surpassed traditional broadcast standards, there is a perception that smaller mobile setups are inherently unprofessional.' These are the words of Dublin-based broadcast consultant Glen Mulcahy, a man who has done more than anyone to promote Mojo, including organising regular international conferences. Big, he says, is still seen by many as beautiful.

The attitude doesn't surprise me. I can recall the reaction of some old school cameramen when Sony introduced a range of news cameras that were half the size of their conventional workhorses. These were men who had been used to the crowds parting when they entered a venue, the camera mounted bazooka-style on their shoulder, followed by an assistant (or, in the absence of such, the reporter) bearing a tripod the size of a small tree. Now nobody moved. One of them confided that, after a professional lifetime wielding a bloody great shovel, he felt he was having to make do with a spoon. What he failed to add was that, technically, the spoon was not just the equal of the shovel but in some respects superior.

The reaction was often mirrored by those on the other side of the camera. Captains of industry who had visibly glowed when their PA announced, 'There's a BBC camera crew in Reception, Sir Ian', were dismayed to be interviewed before what looked like a Fisher-Price version of the real thing, with the 'crew' reduced to a single operator.

Arguably Mojo's most important role is how it's contributing to media freedom. Glen Mulcahy cites the situation in Israel/Palestine. Mainstream media, he points out, have to submit their reports to the Israeli authorities for pre-broadcast review, which he says results in a clear pro-Israel bias. 'Meanwhile,' he adds, 'freelance Palestinian journalists in Gaza have shared raw, visceral content shot on their smartphones that has profoundly moved the world. This is testament to Mojo's founding principle: giving a voice to the voiceless.' On the flip side, Mulcahy acknowledges that the most incendiary content can be stripped of context and weaponised for propaganda purposes.

Mulcahy's current concern is the impact of AI: 'The future of news is at stake. Traditional journalism is shrinking, revenue is flowing to tech giants and AI is upending everything. What happens when fake AI-generated influencers are more trusted than real journalists? That's the crisis we need to confront.'

In this respect, television's technological revolution is no different from its political counterpart. Once unleashed, there is no directing its path or determining its end. As Mulcahy frankly admits, 'AI terrifies me.'

21.

A MONTH IN THE BALKANS

The Balkans get a bad press. Mention the name and what comes to most people's minds is ethnic division, political turmoil and regular eruptions of factional violence. The list seems endless: the assassination of Archduke Franz Ferdinand in Sarajevo that started the First World War, the atrocities committed during the Second by the Nazi-allied Ustasha movement in Croatia, the massacre of 8000 Muslim men and boys in Srebrenica in 1995, Serbia's ethnic cleansing of Kosovar Albanians in the late 1990s.[1]

It's hard to think of any other area of the globe that has given rise to its own verb, and a pejorative one at that – to balkanise, meaning, 'to divide a region into smaller mutually hostile states'.

All six republics of the former Yugoslavia fell within the Balkans. Though not strictly post-Soviet, they had still been subject to a form of communism-lite under the 35-year rule of Marshal Josip Broz Tito.

My first contact with Tito's Yugoslavia came when a student back in 1966. Driving north through Croatia, a university mate and I were passing through the outskirts of Slavonski Brod when we were stopped by a policeman. He pointed to a sign indicating that this particular strip of road became a pedestrian zone after 7 pm. It was by now 7.20. With a wag of the finger, he issued an on-the-spot fine and made a closer inspection of our beat-up Mini. It was then he noticed the GB sticker on the back. In halting English, he explained that he had thought we were German. (The Croatians blamed the Germans for giving them a bad name during the war.) Aware now that we were Brits – the good guys – he insisted that, to make amends, we stayed the night at his mother's house.

Next morning, his mother offered to make us what she insisted was the traditional English breakfast of 'Hamanex'. I scanned the supermarket shelves of my memory for a cereal with a name even vaguely similar. Weetabix, Frosties, Rice Krispies? Nothing suggested itself. It turned out to be the best ham and eggs I had ever tasted.

※

In the early 2000s, the Thomson Foundation had a long-term cooperation agreement with the national broadcaster of one of the former Yugo-republics and in late 2004 they asked if I would spend a month working with it. For reasons that will become clear, I'll give the former republic the generic name, 'Slavia'.

The only thing that caused me pause for thought was a lengthy phone call with Thomson's Head of Regional Partnerships, Russell Lyne, who had himself spent two years with Slavian National Television (SNTV), acting as Thomson's embedded project manager. He explained that SNTV's Documentary Department needed not just an update but a thorough shake-up. Money was tight, morale was rock-bottom and there were 'issues'. After a back-and-forth discussion, we agreed that injecting a current affairs ethos might be the answer. Building on the idea, I suggested we should persuade SNTV management to introduce a regular once-a-week half-hour current affairs slot into their schedule. Or perhaps, more realistically, every other week. But the first requirement would be a couple of weeks' training to introduce the doco team to the new, sharper style of film-making. Then, breaking them into three-person production units (producer, reporter, cameraman), send them off to make 10-minute video reports about contemporary issues and see what they brought back.

Russell didn't demur but there was something in his tone that suggested it wasn't going to be that simple. Normally during such calls, he would sell the assignment. 'A great opportunity . . . working with fantastic people . . . an invaluable contribution to . . .' and so on. This time we seemed to be having a two-track conversation. What I heard between the lines was, 'I'll fully understand if you turn this down', which by the end of the call had become, 'If I were you, I'd certainly turn it down!'

But the challenge attracted me. This was not so much stand-up training as hands-on doing: bringing an entire department of a former communist state broadcaster into the sunlit democratic uplands of the twenty-first century. That had to be worth a go. And, since my last post with the BBC had been as deputy editor of a weekly half-hour current affairs program, I felt more than qualified. It was also comforting to learn that we had our own Thomson man already there – acting project manager 'Craig' who had taken over from Russell. But the clincher was the funder: the OSCE, the Organisation for Security and Cooperation in Europe. This was a serious assignment with serious backing.

I accepted. All experiences, I told myself, the bad as well as the good, were valuable in the end. What I forgot to add was, even if painful at the time.

My first impressions of Slavia's capital were entirely positive. Casting off the grey garb of socialism, its shopfronts and advertising hoardings shouted their Western credentials to every passing consumer. One bank of the river that bisected the city was home to a flourishing cafe society which could stand comparison with Paris. Yes, there was the ubiquitous McDonald's but in the Old City on the opposite bank it was complemented by restaurants serving traditional Balkan fare. And, the ultimate proof of Western assimilation, it boasted an Irish pub, probably the only one in the world that didn't serve Guinness. (Western-style theme pubs and eateries in the post-communist world frequently missed the mark. In Yerevan, the capital of Armenia, the signature deerstalkers worn by the staff of the Sherlock Holmes Cafe-Restaurant were somewhat undermined by their Scottish tartans.)

In contrast to the bridges and boulevards of the city centre, the state broadcaster had been relegated to a depressing cluster of grey, brown and beige blockhouses that could have doubled for Gotham City. It needed no sun to cast a shadow over the surrounding park. As I approached on my first day, I decided it was so depressing in its twenty shades of sludge that it was worth a photo. A state security officer came bounding across the grass like an over-excited gundog. The building, he made clear by pointing and crossing his arms in a repeated scissor action, was not a tourist attraction. For want of any alternative identification, I produced the Internews press card I used in Russia. Although he didn't understand a word it said, it was enough to satisfy him that I was 'on official business'. Grudgingly, he let me proceed, forgetting to demand the digital deletion of what was evidently a hush-hush government facility – the national broadcaster.

Presenting myself at Reception, the first thing I saw was a notice advising that guns were not allowed in the building. My interpreter was summoned from an upper floor. As I waited, I watched a group of workmen whose job, it seemed, was to split the foyer into two separate entrances. (I learned later that this was a money-raising exercise to help balance the broadcaster's budget; half the building was being hived off as office units for rent.) They lifted one of the huge, heavy glass doors off its hinges and, shuffling sideways, edged it toward a flight of marble stairs when a corner clipped the bottom step. Made of toughened glass, the door exploded in a shower of crystals. For several seconds, stunned, the workmen maintained their stances like a troupe of mime artists, with one of them left holding only the handle. This was followed by a voluble outburst that I took to be the full repertoire of national profanities, sacred and secular, ancient and modern.

Seconds later, my interpreter 'Hana' appeared, totally unfazed by the drama as though such things were an everyday occurrence. I guessed she was in her late twenties or early thirties. Her English was both fluent and idiomatic, and I instantly felt I was in safe hands. There was also an impishness about her that I liked. We took the lift up.

As the doors wheezed open on the floor that housed the television division, we were hit by a tsunami of cigarette smoke. Fortunately, having worked in dozens of post-Soviet TV stations, I was inured not only to the all-pervasive reek of stale tobacco but also to the fresh exhalations. (In Moscow I took to task, in a fatherly way, a chain-smoking reporter. Why didn't she quit, I asked, if only for the sake of her two young children. 'Because, Michael,' she responded, 'it's one of the few pleasures I have left in life.' I was to get an even more poignant answer from one of SNTV's own female producers: 'It's the only thing that hasn't let me down.')

Hana suggested we go to the Tea Bar. It turned out to be Ciggy Central. Staff sat, puffed and coughed beneath framed photos of

SNTV in its glory days when there was money, job security and, I suspected, less cause to bituminise their lungs.

Thomson's acting project manager, Craig, arrived. With his spiky hair and heavy-duty boots, he could have passed for a Glaswegian bovver-boy, which would prove very handy over the next month. In securing the equipment we needed from SNTV'S Tech Department, he managed to terrify even the Slavians.

As we talked about the day's schedule, one thing quickly became clear. There was to be no formal welcome and introduction by a senior member of SNTV staff. The normal protocol on these occasions, and still true today, is that either the managing director or at least the head of the News Division or, in this case, the head of the Documentary Department, introduces the trainer/consultant to the troops. (In Malawi, the minister of communications, no less, performed the role.) The introduction usually consists of a couple of words of welcome, followed by an explanation of why the trainer/consultant has been called in and what is the intended outcome of the work they will be doing. This is not a matter of self-aggrandisement. It is a means of ensuring that the trainer/consultant gets the respect and attention they need for what lies ahead; to publicly confer on them the authority to do the job. But not at SNTV evidently.

With tea and passive smoke consumed, Hana led me to the office that had been assigned to us for the weeks ahead. It turned out to be a repurposed wardrobe cubicle, one up from a broom-cupboard and the size of a single-occupancy prison cell. The rails were still in place but at least the hangers had been removed. There was no window and only a stuttering strip-light overhead. Having already downgraded my expectations, I declared that I would use the cubicle for its original purpose and, laptop in hand, would hot-desk wherever in the building my mission took me.

By now, I was getting a queasy foreboding that my very presence in the building was problematic. Craig suggested that we go straight into the first training session. With him leading the way and interpreter Hana by my side, we entered a hall where members of SNTV's Documentary Department, about fifteen in all, were sitting half-a-dozen rows back from the front. An unmistakable cloud of surliness hung over them. The impression I was getting without a word being spoken was that they felt they had been dragged away from some far more important activity.

Sensing the unease, Craig stepped forward and did his best to introduce me, mentioning my years of experience working in the post-Soviets. But Craig was a Thomson colleague, my fixer and facilitator. He was one of us, not one of them. He couldn't give me the imprimatur that came from an endorsement by one of their own bosses.

I'd been in this situation before and recognised the knee jerk resistance to any outsider who believed he or she knew how to do the job better than they. I'd also seen it from their side – on those occasions when some well-meaning BBC apparatchik thought we could all benefit from a bit of outside scrutiny. 'You know how it is, Michael . . . the guy on the terrace and all that . . . seeing more of the game than those on the pitch!' And yes, like those now before me, I too had bristled.

Winning hearts and minds, I reminded myself, was all part of the consultant's job. I looked around for that most indispensable item of the trainer's kit, the flipchart. It may not have been the most creative of icebreakers but at least I could write something – even if it was only my mobile and email details – to signal the opening of proceedings and, with luck, concentrate minds. I spotted an easel to one side but without a chart, still less any flip. Craig went off to hunt down the necessary.

While Hana and I waited, a member of the seated group detached himself and started addressing his colleagues. He was in his fifties with what would normally be called a chinstrap beard on account of there being no matching moustache, except that his was so thin it looked more like a chin fringe. I'll call him 'Andrej'. I assumed he was the head of the Documentary Department (at last), my partner in the joint project, and that even though he was addressing them not me, he was adding his own words of introduction.

I was wrong on both counts. Hana told me that he was not the head but the person who ran the department. The operational head, as opposed to the executive head. Whatever Andrej was or did, it was soon clear that I had been sadly deluded in thinking he and I might be partners.

I listened to Hana's translation in growing disbelief. Andrej was telling the group, his own staff, that he personally was opposed to my coming, that there was no need and nothing for them to learn from a Western consultant.

Right, understood. Great to be on board and thanks, Andrej, for the warm words.

Craig had returned with some paper for the flipchart, except it turned out to be an old calendar which fortuitously was large and printed on only one side so that, when reversed, it just about did the job. No economy had been spared.

I started, as usual on these occasions, with THE BIG PICTURE – the changing role of any state broadcaster in the post-communist world facing the challenge of transition. I then explained how the term 'documentary' had changed over the years with the introduction of digital equipment such as hand-held mini cameras and non-linear computerised editing, and the liberating effect that this had on technique and style.

Moving on to content, I described how news and documentaries, once at polar ends of the broadcasting spectrum, had been hybridised into the concept of 'current affairs', each borrowing from and contributing to the other.

As Hana wrote a translation of key words alongside my jottings, a truculent boredom washed back from the rows of folded arms. Nobody was even pretending to take notes. I sensed I was confirming Andrej's earlier declaration that SNTV had no need of Western consultants. I moved on.

Turning to more practical matters, I outlined, week by week, my proposed schedule for the month ahead – the classroom training followed by practical work on the road. By now, though, I was treading water. For all the reaction I was getting, I might as well have been explaining the Rosetta Stone to a group of Mongolian schoolchildren. I thanked my audience for their attention – Ha! – and closed the proceedings.

Before I could do any meaningful training, I needed to know what the hell was going on. I had assumed that, as was normally the case, time had been set aside in the staff's schedule for the first fortnight's workshops I was meant to be conducting; the number of hours a day along with start times and breaks. But the impression I was getting from the display of passive aggression before me was that nothing of the sort had been prepared.

Again, where was senior management in all this? My belief after talking to Russell back in the UK had been that they were fully on board, not just recognising a need for the refreshment of their Documentary Department but actively engaged in arranging whatever was required.

And now, most puzzling of all, there was Andrej's subversive little speech. More than an expression of scepticism, it was a declaration of war.

This was probably the moment when I should have asked Craig to book my return flight. I was tempted to bluff it to test the reaction of SNTV management, but there was then the danger of my bluff being called. I was also mindful that Thomson took the view that its consultants were like television producers: if something wasn't working, it was their job to make it work. That was why many of us consultants *were* producers.

Later that morning, Andrej and I had a second meeting – in his office. He was almost affable. So much so that I wondered whether Hana might have mistranslated his earlier comments or I had misunderstood her translation. But no. It was soon clear that Andrej's intention was to show me he was a man to be reckoned with. To this end, he paraded on the screen before us examples of the Documentary Department's output over the last couple of years. It came as no surprise that they were his own works as a director, or rather, auteur. He explained that the department was focused on art and culture. In short, it aspired to cinema rather than to journalism, which he clearly regarded as rough trade. He told me his documentaries had won prizes at the Berlin Film Festival and other prestigious venues.

I didn't doubt it. They were well-crafted, but conventional. And I didn't mean that disparagingly. There was a place for such work. But it was a million miles from the sort of gritty ten to twenty-minute films I had in mind about the social challenges, the daily struggles and frustrations of SNTV's viewers, the people of Slavia.

I noticed behind Andrej a picture of Marshal Tito. I would see more of the same in other offices in the building, always with the assurance that they were 'ironic'.[2] In Andrej's case, I wondered. I doubted he was a closet communist but professional life must have been so much easier under the old regime. So long as you did what was required of you – in his case, turning out cinematic gems extoling Slavia's rich culture and spiritual depth, a form of soft propaganda – you would be left alone to get on with it without interference from philistine foreigners. Part of me felt for the man. He was the long-serving curator of ceramics at the Victoria & Albert Museum being told to give over a section to Beatrix Potter figurines.

'So, how do you make your documentaries?' I asked. 'What's the process?'

Thinking I may yet be won over, Andrej stressed the importance of the screenplay. In other words, the entire documentary was structured and written before the filming started, with nothing left to chance. Like a Hollywood movie, every frame was 'shot to script'. Again, fine in the 1950s but the documentary world had moved on. The pre-production – research, recceing locations and setting up interviewees – still had to be done, but most of what goes into a current affairs film these days (also true back in 2004) happens on location with camera rolling; not at a table on which the producer/ director taps out a neatly formatted screenplay weeks before the shoot.

Andrej turned the conversation to his latest work. Even before Hana translated the title, I recognised the ominous word *dusha* – soul – on the cassette label because it was the same in Russian. He showed me a sample clip, telling me with pride that the entire project required six months of preparation and nine days of shooting (which, to be fair, is not excessive but of course everything had been pre-scripted and as good as set in stone).

'And the editing?'

Andrej was glad I asked. It was an indication that I recognised quality when I saw it.

'Twenty-five sessions . . . each lasting between seven and ten hours.'

That made a total of more than 200 hours if one took an average eight-and-a-half hours for each session. Thinking of the resources – human, hardware and logistical – tied up by this single production, I was struck dumb, but infinitely more enlightened. Andrej, it was now clear, had made the so-called Documentary Department his personal fiefdom, with a lion's share of the effort and money being channelled into his pet projects.

I now understood the reason for his earlier behaviour, the speech to his colleagues. My very presence was threatening everything he had built up over the years. He had no concept of the current affairs style of documentary making and even less interest. In his eyes, I had been brought in as a hatchet man to break up his empire and siphon off his budget. I was his nemesis.

In terms of strategy, this meant he was going to do everything in his power to sabotage my planned modernisation of the Documentary Department and, from what I'd already seen, I had no doubt that would include intimidating those under him. Any member of his staff who 'fraternised' would be branded a departmental traitor and suffer the consequences.

Thinking of those staff, at least the fifteen I'd met, I wondered what they did all day while Andrej concentrated on his award-winning masterpieces. To find the answer, I made a point of watching the Documentary Department's weekly output. I didn't know their budget but, judging by what appeared on screen and compared with Andrej's highly polished but occasional output, it had to be miniscule. One program stood out. Two explorers had recently returned from an expedition across China, during which they had shot some video footage. For over fifty minutes, they were interviewed before a bank of monitors in an editing suite (or studio gallery?) that showed us, the viewers, a succession of amateur and loosely edited wide-shots. These they introduced and talked over.

I was reminded of a 1960s slide evening back in the UK when friends of my parents would invite round the neighbours to show them colour transparencies, projected on to a metre-square screen, of their recent continental holiday. 'And here's another shot of Pam in front of Lake Garda but taken from a different angle.' When the lights were flicked back on, half the audience would wake with a start.

But among the dross there was the occasional human-interest story – about women in prison, the effect on villagers when their homes were flooded by a hydro-power scheme, and the psychological aftermath of ethnic conflict on children. The production values were low, presumably reflecting the budgets, and the films tended to be an emotional 'study of' rather than a rigorous 'enquiry into'. Even so, it was clear there were some among the documentary staff who had an inkling of what journalism was about. I was encouraged. It was just a matter of identifying them and then peeling them off from the Documentary Department.

Meanwhile, after the disastrous opening session, formal training had resumed, though it was better described as ad hoc. As with the flip-chart on the first day, everything had to be begged, borrowed, improvised or, in some cases, commandeered. Participants came and went, and generally treated the workshops as an optional sideshow for when they had nothing better to do. In the first three days, we managed a total of just six hours and most of those were wasted in argument and circular discussion. Given the dismissive attitude of their boss – the licence he had given them to ignore me – I accepted the situation was as good as it would get. In my six years as a Thomson consultant, I had never known an assignment like it. This was *guerrilla training*. How we were going to fill the remaining weeks, only God knew.

I was also aware that my professional reputation was on the line. A three-day workshop that 'didn't go so well' could be put down to unforeseen circumstances, but there was no such excuse for a failed month-long consultancy with the aim of overhauling an entire department. Beyond my relations with the Thomson Foundation, there was my standing with the funders, the Organisation for Security and Cooperation in Europe, whom I had worked with on several previous occasions.

And yet, as the days passed, there was a stirring of interest and even the occasional question. Among the ashes of indifference, I detected embers of curiosity. What those who dropped in were hearing and being shown was at some level getting through. Of course, they had seen much of the same on foreign news channels such as CNN and BBC World, but now they were being offered a chance to try it for themselves as producers and reporters. At the very least, it offered another string to their bows and an alternative to puffing and wheezing in a smoking corner.

Andrej, meanwhile, was spending most of his time cloistered in his handsome office while the department's producers and researchers worked in their own offices strung out down the corridor. No doubt he thought he had seen me off and that the department was back to alert level amber. This enabled me not only to avoid him but to chat and sip tepid tea in smoke-filled rooms with his staff. By such casual socialising, I got an insight into the dynamics of the department, the tensions and the cracks. It was as I suspected. There were the favoured few, Andrej's acolytes, and left out in the cold were those who didn't buy into, or hadn't been invited to share, his rarefied milieu of festivals and awards.

By the end of the second week, I had persuaded seven of the Documentary Department to break ranks, to work on three video reports to be produced in a current affairs style. Encouragingly, and surprisingly, they were not the twenty-somethings but those in their forties and fifties, perhaps because they were not part of Andrej's creative coterie or because they had been around long enough not to care what he thought. Or, most likely, felt they had nothing to lose. One of them, 'Bosco', was an experienced producer/director in his mid-fifties who, handily, also shot video with his own Sony 'pro' camera. I immediately recognised an ally of the same generation. And, with the help of Bosco and his half-dozen colleagues, I now saw a way forward.

'The Magnificent Seven' were going to be my shock troops. The idea that I had discussed with Russell back in the UK – the injection of a regular current affairs slot into the network schedule – suddenly looked viable. The three reports we were shooting would serve as content for a half-hour pilot program, linked by a studio presenter, to be shown to SNTV management at the end of the month. If it were deemed a success, the logical outcome would be a dedicated current affairs team with its own production office and facilities; a free-standing unit within the department. But that was for the future. More immediately, we had a chance to escape Gotham, get out and do some filming.

✦ ———— ✦

And the three video-reports?

The first was about icons. My heart had sunk when the subject had been suggested – more arty-farty! – but my assumption had been hasty. The focus was not on the icons but their theft. The producer had discovered that, to date, some 500 had been stolen, allegedly by organised gangs which had spirited them out of the country for sale abroad. Some dated from the thirteenth century; all were irreplaceable. The problem was that the churches housing them were typically in remote parts of the country and lacked the necessary security.

The second was about the education of disabled children. It was a year since a law had been passed giving their parents the right to decide whether they should attend a regular school, a special school or, in the case of those most afflicted, be given personal tuition. So, a year on, how well had the new law worked?

The last story was the one which, for me, offered the best opportunity for good pictures and strong voice-over. It was that curse of capitalism, the garbage produced by a consumer-oriented society. All that unnecessary packaging, most of it not to protect but to promote. The average Slavian citizen, official figures revealed, now produced 700 grams of household rubbish a day, well on the way to the kilo a day being produced by citizens of the EU. You had only to stand on the stone bridge in the city centre and count the bobbing plastic bottles as they passed beneath. But what to do with all this domestic detritus: burn or bury? Or there was the EU option: separate and recycle. There was a good meaty debate to be had and one that had resonance in every other post-communist country coming to grips with 'the price of capitalism'.

It was at this juncture that I had a scheduled meeting with OSCE's local media development officers who, since the OSCE was funding the project, were responsible for monitoring it. There were two of them, both women. They were young and conscientious. My initial thought had been that their sole interest would be in box-ticking.

But they had proved me wrong. The junior of the two had already sat in on one of the few training sessions and seen first-hand what I was up against. I now told her senior colleague, a Brit as it happened, of my hopes for the creation of a Current Affairs Unit, carved out of the present Documentary Department. She warmed to the idea and offered to fund some equipment, including a Matrox editing suite, if I could get the unit off the ground.

It was excellent and quite unexpected news. Taken together with our new production schedule, we seemed to have turned a corner.

✦———✦

My normal practice when it comes to filming is to send out the teams and stay back at base, like a spider at the centre of the web. This way, I can call on the appropriate authorities if any of the teams encounter a problem, such as the camera being seized by an over-zealous security guard. Additionally, the very presence of the consultant on location can have an inhibiting effect on team members, prompting the suspicion that they are being monitored or, worse, marked out of ten.

But this situation was different. For one thing, I had no idea about the skills level of the camera-operators or how they interacted with the other members of the team. Did they take direction from the producer or, as was often the case, direct themselves and leave it to the producer or reporter to put the pieces together back in the cutting room? In current affairs, it's essential that the producer takes the lead.

The first day of shooting got off to a bad start. I had joined the garbage team. The cameraman 'Luka', a nuggety little man in his fifties with a walrus moustache two sizes too big, was clearly in the

CONSULTANTS GO HOME camp. He was quick to let me know he had thirty years' experience. Since there was no sign of a sound engineer, I assumed he was responsible for both the visuals *and* the audio. Yet I saw no evidence of headphones, crucial during interviews when the audio-cameraman has to make a fine judgement whether or not to stop shooting if a wailing ambulance passes, a plane flies low overhead or a dog starts barking. I asked. No, he didn't carry headphones.

'Why not?'

'My job is to shoot the pictures.'

As a response, it was more blunt, and arguably more honest, than the usual one: 'I keep an eye on the meters'. True, the audio meters are useful indicators but crude instruments compared with the human ear. Watching the sound makes about as much sense as listening to the pictures.

But I had anticipated the situation and now reached into my breast pocket for a pair of ear-pods, the sort that plugged into an iPod (this was 2004). Not as good as a set of proper, professional Sennheiser headphones but better than what cameramen like Luka did – set the audio recording to AUTO and hope for the best, which it never was.

He refused the ear-pods. Why?

'I have a hearing problem.'

Great! And yet he had had no difficulty understanding Hana's translation.

I accepted I had lost the first round so we went into the second, the filming. More accurately, the *video*ing.

As I looked over Luka's shoulder at the flip-out monitor, I could see that this was a cameraman who knew his craft. Old school, yes, but none the worse for that. He may not have had an ear but he certainly had an eye. His framing of the shots was spot on and, the other sign of a good cameraman, he was prepared to 'look for the angle': high, low and anywhere in between. The lazy and incompetent operators shoot everything from eye-level on the spurious grounds, 'Well, that's how the viewer sees the world, innit?'

We took a coffee break at one of the riverside cafes. I told Luka that I could see he was a professional and I asked him about working for the national broadcaster. Sensing perhaps that I might after all serve a useful function in passing a message back to management, he opened up. There was a shortage of equipment. (No surprise there. Before leaving to shoot, we had had to beg for a single cassette because the camera hadn't been supplied with one.) His monthly salary of $250 was invariably paid late and, worst of all, there was no certainty he would have a job in six months' time.

To explain why Luka, along with most of those who worked for SNTV, feared for his future requires a paragraph of historical context.

Following the breakup of Yugoslavia in the early 1990s, the population of Slavia, along with some of the other former republics, was ethnically split with a majority of Slavic Christians and a minority of Muslims. (In both cases, we're talking religiously and/or culturally.) Grievances among the Muslims led to a face-off with government security forces which was defused only by international mediation. Part of the peace agreement required Slavia's state institutions to reflect, proportionally, the ethnic split in the make-up of their workforces. In the case of the national broadcaster, there were only two ways that the Muslims could be given their agreed percentage share of the jobs: either recruit more Muslims, which would have increased the workforce with disastrous budgetary consequences, or give them some of the Christians' jobs. The result: every Christian member of staff feared they might be laid off within a matter of months, while every Muslim knew they were virtually unsackable.

It's not hard to imagine the effect on labour relations between management who had to implement the decisions and the workers who would bear the consequences; and between the Christians and the Muslims working alongside each other. Which is why cameraman Luka, being a Slavic Christian, had good reason to be worried. I had been aware of the peace agreement at the time it was hammered out. What I hadn't anticipated was how, all this time later, it would impact my month's consultancy.

Shooting on our three video-reports was complete. Because of the time wasted at the start of the month and the minimal resources at our disposal, the time left for structuring, scripting and editing the reports, along with laying down the commentary and mixing the audio tracks, was so tight that another day lost – even half a day – would up-end the entire project.

It was at this point that politics collided head-on with production.

The picture-editor assigned to us was competent, reasonably responsive, and Muslim. Despite our agreeing at the end of every day on a time to start the next morning, he would wander in up to two hours late with no apology and no explanation because, to his way of thinking, none was needed. He was fireproof and he knew it. There was nothing his superiors would do to oblige him to work according to our production schedule. (Just to be clear: human nature being universal, I doubt that the situation would have been much different if the Christian/Muslim figures had been reversed and we had been assigned a Christian picture-editor.)

Despite this, we just about managed to cobble together our three video-reports, but I was aware they were closer to rough-cuts than final edits. As for having them linked in studio by a presenter as planned, there was not a hope. Even so, I remained confident that anyone who had spent time in television, when shown the reports along with the script for the presenter links, would be able to fill in the gaps and see that here was a viable model for a thirty-minute current affairs program. And I still believed this when we walked into the office of SNTV's managing director to show him the fruits of our month's labour. I was relieved to see that Andrej was not joining us. Instead, his boss, the executive head of the Documentary Department, was to share the viewing.

It was a situation I had been in countless times before and since – both as the reporter/producer submitting my work for the judgement of a superior and, swapping roles, as the executive producer who gives the imperial thumbs-up or -down. Body language is all and I knew before the last report had finished that we had failed to impress. It was evident that the MD had made no effort to 'fill in the gaps'. The impression I got was that, as with Andrej, current affairs was a genre alien to him.

But there was still the head of the Documentary Department. Although she was well known in the building for keeping her cards close to her chest so she could sense (mixed metaphor alert) which way the wind was blowing, I had hopes she might be on my side. If so, now was the time for her to reveal her support. She remained tight-lipped. To provoke a response, I suggested she might personally oversee the proposed Current Affairs Unit for the first few weeks to get it off the ground. Her reaction was instant. It was as though I had offered her a red-hot coal and invited her to take a bite. I was left under no illusions. (Talking to others later, I would discover that, far from her being at odds with Andrej, as I had thought, she had long been happy to take a back seat and let him get on with running the department.)

Those I felt sorry for – guilty about – were the seven I had lured away from the Documentary Department. Bosco would be OK – he had experience and confidence on his side (and indeed would continue with SNTV for another decade before moving to academia). The same, I assumed, would go for the two Muslims in the group, for reasons already mentioned. But I feared the remaining four Christians would now have their cards marked and become convenient casualties of 'the great cull' to meet the Muslim job quota.

The Friday arrived for my last meeting with Andrej. He knew he had won. Over the past month he had done his damnedest to scupper my plans, including, I had no doubt, playing office politics to get the MD on side. The one thing to his credit was that he had been open about his views from the start.

His empire secure, Andrej was gracious in victory. When I mentioned that my flight didn't leave till the Monday, he became positively hospitable.

'Excellent! This weekend, we – myself and some friends – we're going hunting. You must join us! It'll be a chance to get to know each other. . . I mean, *properly*. And you wouldn't believe the animals – wild boar, chamois goats, four species of deer . . .'

I was aware of interpreter Hana gripping my arm so tightly that I feared she might draw blood. She needn't have worried. No way was I game.

Postscript. After I left Slavia, the OSCE media officers did their best to salvage something of Delahaye's Grand Plan. As part of a package to fund digital cameras and editing suites, they persuaded SNTV to set up a 'Joint News & Current Affairs Digital Desk'. Members of the Documentary Department had access to it but I was told that, for reasons I didn't have to guess, their use of it didn't last.

Two years later there was a general election and, hoping to exploit the opportunity, the OSCE switched its focus from training and equipment to governance and restructuring. Post-election, however, the new government acted the same way as the outgoing, by regarding the national broadcaster as its own political property, its mouthpiece. It became clear that the equipment the OSCE had funded was going to serve the interests less of the viewing public than of whichever party or coalition was in power.

In the end, the organisation publicly withdrew its support, concluding there was no possibility of SNTV making the transition from a state broadcaster to a genuine public service operation. To quote an OSCE source, 'We eventually gave up trying to depoliticize the place'. Twenty years on, it is still regarded as work in progress.

In hindsight, I was naïve to think I could establish a Current Affairs Unit. News bulletins are tricky enough for a television management under government control but at least news is essentially reactive. Current affairs programs, by contrast, are proactive and occasionally investigative. It's the difference between a rabbit and a ferret. The last thing the managing director of SNTV would have wanted was a regular slot in his schedule that asked awkward questions while probing into failures, scandals and corruption. Far better to keep pumping out emollient documentaries about love, life and the soul. Old-fashioned maybe, but safe and soothing. (For the record, within a year of my visit, the MD was offered and accepted one of the most coveted foreign diplomatic postings in the gift of the Slavian Government.)

And there you have the problem. An organisation like the OSCE, well-resourced and well-intentioned as it is, can subtly pressurise or less subtly bribe a government ('You're serious about wanting to join the EU?') to accept its pro-democracy initiatives, but it cannot force it to implement them after the funding has been spent and the trainers and consultants have left. Without the political will, nothing happens.

My consultancy – my fee, flights, accommodation, meals, my interpreter's fees, administration costs and the like – would have amounted to tens of thousands of pounds. And the effect I had? Let's say, I very much doubt that it reflected value for money.

Unless there is a clear, agreed pathway to democracy and, in the case of the national broadcaster, to editorial detachment (independence may be too much to ask), there will always be a tendency for those governing former communist countries to use external funding for their own political ends. The temptation, the opportunity and the historical mindset are just too great.

As the next chapter will show, that raises some tough questions for the funders.

22.

THE FÜHRER'S FURBISHER

Broadly speaking, Internews' policy during the Yeltsin era and the Yeltsin/Putin transition was to concentrate its resources on those television stations out in the regions striving, often struggling, to be independent. If not commercially self-supporting, which was hard, then having a majority shareholder who respected their journalistic freedom. (As had been the case with Afontovo TV in Krasnoyarsk whose majority shareholders had been, successively, the oligarchs Vladimir Gusinsky and Mikhail Khodorkovsky.) The policy was applied across those post-Soviet countries in which Internews had a presence but particularly in Russia. It made sense. As, one after another, the Russian network broadcasters were taken over by the state or brought under its control, the best hope of promoting media freedom, along with the transmission of impartial news, lay with the hundreds of smaller regional broadcasters beyond Moscow. This way, there was the possibility of building a critical mass to counter the network news channels.

My other employer, the Thomson Foundation, adopted a more relaxed attitude and saw no bar to working with state-owned channels in the post-Soviets. This wasn't so much a difference of principle, as of strategy. Thomson took the view that the primary beneficiaries of media training were not the stations or channels, but the individual journalists. These, they argued, once they had been trained in the Western tenets of accuracy, impartiality, balance and fairness, would become the torchbearers, the long-term instruments of change; ready and primed to put their Thomson training to use when their country's authoritarian regime gave way to a democratic government (which, by implication, it inevitably would).

In the early days of working as a broadcast consultant, I subscribed to the Thomson view. In fact, I developed and in various reports propounded a variation on it: 'The Darwinian Theory of Journalist Training'. I posited that, like evolution, long-term change – the creation of new species – depended on a few exceptional mutations to jumpstart the process. Looking back at those I had trained, I reckoned that roughly one in ten stood out for their ability, intelligence and intellectual independence. These were the genetic mutations who would rise through the ranks to become the news editors, station managers, channel controllers and authoritative interviewers and anchors of the future; the new species that would spread Western enlightenment and eventually change the face of post-Soviet television journalism in both the private and public sectors.

As the evidence grew of clampdown on media freedom in the still authoritarian former Soviets, I was forced to question the analogy, and in doing so, re-examine the Thomson view of Western-trained journalists as individual torchbearers. In Georgia and Armenia there was a chance; but in Russia, Belarus and Uzbekistan, vanishingly little.

How were all these Western-trained journalists meant to implement their training while waiting for the dawn of democracy and the moment of their activation – maybe years, if not decades, in the future? If ever. Were we expecting them to be like the 'sleepers' of espionage legend; to carry on working as normal but, to extend the metaphor, 'undercover', harbouring and hiding their allegiance to Western-style journalism?

This seemed unfeasible. More likely was that, unable to implement Western ideals, they would put their training down to experience and, disillusioned, leave the profession. Alternatively, they would implement a key part of the training but, and herein lay the danger, not to the ends we had intended. Had we been merely imparting the lofty principles of Western journalism, fine. But, more than that, we were sharing the skills and techniques of our craft: film-making.

The camera, microphone and editing software are the tools of our trade; often used to perform the tricks of our trade. They are the essential means of conveying the journalism and therefore to be mastered. You can be a first-rate reporter, correspondent or producer, intellectually and ethically, but if you don't know how to channel your talent through the medium of film-making – performing, directing, shooting, scripting, editing – the impact of your journalism will be blunted proportionally. You are, after all, not just a journalist, but a *television* journalist.

It is relevant in passing to mention that one of the star trainees of Internews Russia in the early 2000s was a certain Margarita Simonyan. In 2005 – certainly with President Putin's approval, possibly on his initiative – Ms Simonyan was appointed editor-in-chief of the newly launched *Russia Today* (now *RT*), Russia's English language, Kremlin-backed, 24-hour satellite news channel, tasked with offering an 'alternative perspective on major global events'. *RT*'s perspective, it would be fair to say, consists in highlighting the problems of America and Europe and downplaying, or ignoring, those of Russia and its allies. But, while the selection of stories may be questionable, the reporting is thoroughly professional. Ms Simonyan clearly benefited from her USAID-funded training.

On the face of it, training in film-making may appear politically neutral, but that's not how it works in practice. While waiting for the moment of regime change, there is nothing to stop the state journalists we train using the film-making skills they have acquired in the service of their authoritarian governments. The result: reports that are not just 'better' in a general sense, but more engaging and more *persuasive*. Not to mince words, more effective as propaganda. That is the cause for concern.

And, if you want to put a name to that concern . . .

Leni Riefenstahl was the director who filmed – some would add orchestrated – Hitler's Nuremberg Rally in 1934. The result was the documentary for which she is still best remembered, *Triumph of the Will*, a chilling two-hour compilation of jackboots, flickering flambeaus and rippling swastikas, with a cast of thousands and some musical help from Richard Wagner. And in the lead role – who else? – Adolf Hitler in his finest demagogic form. With Heinrich Himmler, Joseph Goebbels, Hermann Göring and Rudolf Hess vying for the award of Best Supporting Nazi. Nearly a century on, it stands as the most effective expression of audio-visual propaganda in modern times.

What made the documentary so powerful – so *dangerous* – was Riefenstahl's mastery of the medium: her cinematic innovation, both artistic and technical. Her postwar critics accused her of having glorified the Third Reich and, in so doing, having promoted its evil cause. By extension, they argued, she bore some responsibility for all the horrors committed in its name, not least the Holocaust. Her response throughout the rest of her long life (she lived to 101) was that she had merely been doing her job, at which she happened to be rather good.

Now, it may seem a huge leap to go from Hitler's favourite film-maker to a lowly reporter in the newsroom of, say, Belteleradio, Belarus's state broadcaster. But not *so* far-fetched. Here's why.

After my stint in the post-Soviets finished in early 2004, I worked as a Thomson consultant with the Al Jazeera satellite channel in Qatar. One of the first courses I conducted at their Doha training centre, jointly with my Thomson colleague, camera-consultant Karol Cioma, was for a group of television journalists, cameramen and picture-editors, seventeen participants in total, who all turned out to be from Sudanese State Television. (I say 'turned out' because Karol and I discovered this only on our arrival in Doha.)

The president of Sudan at the time was General Omar Al Bashir. Sounds familiar? The attacks by the Janjaweed Arab militia groups, which Al Bashir armed and encouraged, against the ethnic African pastoralists in the southern province of Darfur had been widely reported across all media, along with the appalling casualty figures. Nobody could claim ignorance. 'Darfur' had entered our collective lexicon alongside Rwanda and Srebrenica.

Karol and I found ourselves in a situation that was more than awkward. Over dinner the night before the start of the course, we debated whether to call it off in view of what was known about the Al Bashir regime and its reprehensible activities, and the use to which we feared our training could be put back in Khartoum. That is, to sugar-coat, sanitise or, worse, to justify what was going on in Darfur. But, since we were working for the Thomson Foundation under contract, and this was part of its training agreement with Al Jazeera, we parked our consciences and in line with Thomson thinking that we were training individuals, not stations or channels, we carried on. Not without misgivings.

The Sudanese participants were receptive, charming and two of them, both women, outstanding. In every respect the course went well. Even so, at the end of the three weeks, we were left feeling grubby; that, however indirectly, we had been complicit with the Al Bashir regime.

In later years, following the 'success' of the Doha course, I would be repeatedly asked to conduct training for Sudanese State Television on its home ground in Khartoum. By then, Al Bashir had been indicted by the International Criminal Court, charged with crimes against humanity and war crimes relating to the conflict in Darfur, but was still in power. There was no need to re-examine my conscience; the ICC had made the decision for me.

This is why the Riefenstahl precedent is relevant. It illustrates how actions which may at the time seem harmless – 'just doing my job!' – can have wider, deleterious consequences down the line. There are countless ways the film-maker's skills can be used to unscrupulous ends. The effectiveness, for good or ill, of a regime's message – a message which is typically conveyed by the state broadcaster – is as much determined by the medium as by the message. (Marshall McLuhan was right, assuming that's what he meant. If not, I welcome emails.) The more adeptly the medium is handled, the more effectively the message is delivered.

When Leni Riefenstahl was asked how she saw her role as a film-maker, she responded that it was 'to allow the image to express itself more strongly than it did in reality'.[1] It's as good a definition of propaganda as you're likely to find.

✦ ——— ✦

No doubt, it will be said I'm exaggerating the dangers; that those governing Belarus, Azerbaijan, Uzbekistan – and of course Russia – have no shortage of homegrown film-makers who are more than proficient in the dark arts of propaganda.

True. But, first, should we be adding to the number? Second, is this how our funding should be used?

23.

MY OBJECTIVITY OR YOURS?

It's impossible to write a book about journalism without tackling the subject which everybody agrees is of fundamental importance but nobody seems able to define, at least not adequately. Objectivity. It's regarded as roughly synonymous with impartiality, neutrality, detachment, disinterest, independence; and, in adjectival form, with unbiased, unprejudiced and dispassionate. And, when all else fails, it is defined by referencing its antonym, subjectivity.

And yet, objectivity is the term which we – we journalists, at least – always come back to. There is, it seems, a totemic quality about the word which sets it apart.

So, let's start with a statement which, depending on your viewpoint, is either contentious or blindingly obvious: no human being with a discernible pulse can be completely objective. Whether consciously or unconsciously, we are all influenced by the circumstances of our birth, ethnicity, upbringing, education and the three 'c's: culture, class and creed. We are products of our prejudices. Is it then realistic to expect a journalist to put all that messy 'lived experience' in a box and close the lid? I don't believe so, any more than our readers, listeners or viewers are able to do so.

So, perhaps we should search for another word; one which accepts the reality of the human condition. The Middle East, an area noted for the extreme, divisive and violent views it so often elicits, is a good place to start.

As I have mentioned in the previous chapter, when my stint in the former Soviets came to an end in early 2004, the Thomson Foundation asked if I would work with the Al Jazeera Satellite Channel in Qatar, with which it had just signed a training agreement. The channel was particularly keen that its new generation of foreign correspondents should be formally trained, a task that would entail a succession of courses, sometimes back-to-back, over two years.

At the time, there was still a lot of hypocritical prejudice against Al Jazeera with talk of its being 'Osama bin Laden's mouthpiece.'[1] True, it had obtained the first verified post-9/11 video statement by Bin Laden, pre-recorded 'to camera', which it had aired within hours of America and Britain launching their attack on Afghanistan. But why the expressions of outrage? Al Jazeera was an Arabic news channel broadcasting in Arabic to the Arab world. Of course Bin Laden would choose it as an outlet and of course it would transmit his views about 9/11. (Without claiming responsibility, he expressed support for those who carried out the attacks.) It was news. As proof – and here's the hypocrisy – all those Western TV networks which either cut across to Al Jazeera live, or *rebroadcast* the tape later without always crediting Al Jazeera as the source.

What most people don't know about Al Jazeera is that its roots are in the BBC.[2] In 1994, the corporation got into bed with a Saudi prince who owned a satellite TV company called Orbit. The deal was that the BBC would provide Orbit's channels with an Arabic version of its news service on the understanding that the bulletins would observe the same editorial policy as the rest of the BBC's World Service. Since they were to be broadcast from the corporation's studios in West London, the BBC set about recruiting and training some

250 Arab journalists and administrative staff. Predictably perhaps, it wasn't long before the Saudis tried to censor unflattering news about Saudi Arabia and within eighteen months the partnership had ended in tears.

Coincidentally – we are now in 1996 – the then Emir of Qatar, Sheikh Hamad bin Khalifa Al Thani, was adding a satellite television news channel to his portfolio of interests. It would be called Al Jazeera – which translates as 'The Peninsula', one of the names by which Qatar itself is known. And it needed journalists. No doubt with huge relief, 120 of the BBC-trained, now redundant, Arab journalists signed up with Al Jazeera and swapped a damp, chilly London for Qatar's thrusting young capital, Doha. They would form the editorial bedrock of the Emir's new channel.

Once Al Jazeera had secured a satellite slot that enabled reception by a standard domestic dish, the impact of its broadcasts was more than far-reaching; it was seismic. For the first time, the Arabic-speaking nations of the Middle East were not dependent on their various state broadcasters for news of what was going on in the world. Al Jazeera gave its viewers a window not just beyond their borders but also *within* their borders, in their own language and free; a view that was often at odds with what their state broadcasters had been force-feeding them for decades. All they had to do was point a satellite dish at the right corner of the sky. And there was little their governments could do apart from ban the sale of dishes, jam the signal (difficult with satellite transmissions) or, as many of them did, close down the local Al Jazeera bureau. The effect of this last measure was only to enhance the channel's reputation because it was proof that its journalism was hitting home. It was the equivalent of a campaign medal, and in its early years Al Jazeera collected many.

At the time I started working with the channel in spring 2004, its managing director was Wadah Khanfar. A Palestinian by birth, worldly and inquisitive by nature, Khanfar had worked in the field, first as Al Jazeera's correspondent in South Africa, then as its bureau chief in Afghanistan and Iraq. From our discussions, it was clear that one of the reasons for bringing in former BBC reporters and news managers as trainers was to tap into the channel's roots. In developing its journalistic credentials, Khanfar recognised that there was a need to fix its editorial values.

Al Jazeera had already taken as its motto 'The Opinion and the Other Opinion.' It was a declaration less of objectivity than of balance; a commitment to presenting both sides of any argument which, particularly in its studio-based interview and discussion programs, it pursued with enthusiasm, even gusto. In some respects it was an abuse of balance in that it provided a platform for extreme Islamic views and offered the channel's many critics an all-too-easy target.

And objectivity?

Significantly perhaps, the word doesn't get a mention in the BBC's charter, which prefers 'impartiality', 'independence' and 'fairness'. The sole and only mention of the notion, in its adverbial form, comes in the last paragraph: that the charter itself should be 'interpreted objectively'. Make of that what you will.

For its part back in 2004, Al Jazeera's Code of Ethics had raided the thesaurus in an attempt to cover all the bases, referring to the channel's, quote, 'Adherence to the journalistic values of honesty, courage, fairness, balance, independence, credibility and diversity' which reads like, 'If you don't like our values, we've got others . . .'. But there is no mention, you will note, of objectivity.

It was a word that Khanfar admitted to finding problematic, as did many of us. If one accepts that our world views are determined by our very different experiences of that world, it follows that my objectivity can, and very likely will, be different from your objectivity, which makes a nonsense of the term. (Although we didn't know it at the time, there was a parallel here with the dispute in 2017 over the number of those who attended Donald Trump's first inauguration and the infamous comment by Kellyanne Conway, Counsellor to the President, that it came down to, 'alternative facts'. In other words, there could be *my* facts and *your* facts.)

Khanfar favoured what I thought was a reasonable substitute: *perspective*. Addressing the World Electronic Media Forum in December 2003, he observed, 'Our [Al Jazeera's] cultural perspective is different from that of the West. We see things from a different world view, because we are Arabs and Muslims – not the BBC in London or CNN in Atlanta.'

This is self-evidently true in so far as Al Jazeera, the BBC and CNN select the stories that are most relevant to the lives of their viewers. Not exclusively but predominantly. Indeed, this is the case with any news outlet, whether local, regional, national or global.

The more pertinent test is how each channel reports the *same* story; whether it cherry-picks the facts of the story favourable to its own cultural and geo-political perspective while conveniently ignoring the rest. If so, can their reports still be regarded as objective, impartial, unbiased – whatever term you care to use – even if the filtered facts, taken individually, are true? Or is it indeed a case of 'my objectivity' and 'your objectivity', of telling the truth but not the whole truth?

In 1998, a new element was added to the debate by the former BBC war correspondent, Martin Bell. Based primarily on his experience of reporting from Bosnia in the early 1990s, Bell not only rejected objectivity but heretically suggested a degree of *sub*jectivity might on occasions be appropriate. He called it 'the journalism of attachment', describing it as 'a journalism . . . that cares as well as knows, and that will not stand neutrally between good and evil, the victim and the oppressor'. Journalists, he argued, should not just bear witness to acts of inhumanity and horror, but should call out governments' indifference and/or inaction; that on such occasions they should be free to, in effect, editorialise.[3]

Bell's suggestion split the journalistic community and it continues to provoke reaction and counter-reaction to this day. Loath as I am to disagree with the secular saint of television journalism, my own view is that, while Bell himself may know where the line is, his suggestion risks blurring the distinction between the journalist and the campaigner, activist and agitator – allowing the latter three to falsely claim the status of 'journalist'.

The debate over objectivity is the proverbial rabbit hole; go down it and you may never re-emerge. It is, however, possible to fix the word in its practical application, in what is termed, 'the journalism of objective method' or simply, the 'objectivity of method'. It was Walter Lippmann, the great American reporter and political commentator of the 1920s, who put it most succinctly, arguing that 'the method is objective, not the journalist' and that method is the discipline of the craft.

When you think about it, there is nothing revolutionary about the concept; other professions and trades employ it all the time. A surgeon operating on a patient makes no distinction between a philanthropist and a mass-murderer. A female barrister assigned 'off the rank' to defend an alleged rapist does the job, not necessarily irrespective of her personal feelings but by assiduously following her professional code and according to the law. A scientist conducting research may have a desired result in mind, a hypothesis, but will apply the so-called 'scientific method' to determine the actual result, whether it is the desired one or not. Even a staunchly left-wing house builder is quite capable of putting up a top quality residence for a client he regards as a fascist bastard by following the tried-and-tested techniques of his trade. The motivation may be pride in his work, but no problem with that.

So, if a surgeon, a lawyer, a scientist and a builder can do it, why not a journalist? And the fact is that the best of them do. One of the criteria by which those broadcast journalists who regularly interview politicians are judged is whether their on-air exchanges afford the listener or viewer an insight into which way they vote. Taking those who work for the BBC and its Australian counterpart, the ABC – the ones I watch and listen to most often – I would say the overwhelming majority pass the test.

So, what does 'objectivity of method' look like in action? The simple answer is that it is not so different from the researcher's scientific method.

By no means comprehensive but roughly in order: the reporter would identify and note the most reliable sources; interview those who best represent their respective corners, not just some opinionated 'Johnny off the street'; consider and ask the toughest questions of each side (in the manner of a Devil's Advocate); select each side's strongest answers when editing their interviews while giving each adequate time to make its case.

And one other thing – the voice-over text. Objectivity of method requires that the television reporter stick to a neutral vocabulary, studiously avoiding emotive and partisan terms such as *terrorist, freedom-fighter* and more recently, *martyr.* Few of us realise just how slanted language can be, how loaded and reflective of our personal world views are the words we use unthinkingly every day. When

I was trained by the BBC decades ago, it took a wise old (or so he seemed to my 24-year-old self) former news editor called John McKinnon to make me question why trade unions always 'demand', with its hint of menace, rather than 'want' or 'ask for'; how the verb 'claim' carries the suggestion of untested and possibly untrue, while 'point out' assumes what follows to be agreed fact. Most times, 'say' is not just the least judgemental word but the most accurate.

Mind you, this was the same John McKinnon who advised that, when broadcasting, the title 'Mr' should be accorded 'anyone commanding respect, including American politicians', but that it could be dropped 'in the case of convicted criminals and sportsmen'. To put McKinnon's remarks in context, this would have been 1972 – the year of the BBC's 50th anniversary. As one wag scrawled on the back of a toilet door in Broadcasting House: 'The BBC has always been fifty.'

NEVER MIND THE QUALITY, FEEL THE BANDWIDTH

In an ideal world, broadcasters would concentrate on 'lighting the fire', offering their audience programs that would engage, inspire and stimulate. But for most television stations in the post-Soviets, economic reality dictated that it was more about 'filling the pot', keeping the schedule topped up with whatever was available, (almost) irrespective of quality.

One way of doing this, notably for the medium-sized city stations, was to sign up with a content provider – one of the Moscow-based companies that would provide the station with a stream of movies, soaps, talk shows, documentaries, sport and quizzes for a fee or a share of its equity.

Then there were the big boys with the big budgets: the network channels, whether state-owned or, in the early days under Yeltsin, still independent. For them, a guaranteed audience-puller was one of the Western quiz shows. They could buy the format and produce their own national version under licence. The most phenomenally successful was, and remains, the British creation, *Who Wants to be a Millionaire?* It has been adapted and aired in around 160 countries. No matter what hotel you're staying in, no matter where in the world, if you click through the channels on your TV remote, chances are you'll come across a version of *Millionaire*.

To date, nationally modified clones of the show have been produced and broadcast in eleven of the fifteen former Soviet republics and in all of the half-dozen satellite states that made up the old Eastern Bloc (including both Slovakia and the Czech Republic, carved out of the former Czechoslovakia).

Why is *Millionaire* so successful? Apart from the program's format and dramatic staging (Lights! Music! Action!), there is the drawing power of the title itself and its shameless appeal to that most universal of human passions, *greed*.

And something else that is not often appreciated: the convenient fact that, when translated into different currencies, the totemic 'million' still holds its value, proportionally. In the UK, the million pound top prize is a big deal, a potential life-changer. But in Russia too, a million roubles – even though the sterling equivalent was £24,000 (roughly $35,000) at the time the state channel ORT acquired the show in early 2001 – was still a substantial amount in terms of its buying power because the Russian cost of living was a fraction of the UK's. So the top prize retained its mesmeric status without breaking the program's budget. The same held true, to a more or less extent, for the currencies of Estonia, Lithuania, Kyrgyzstan, Moldova and Ukraine.

That left the smaller regional stations, too cash-strapped to pay for a content provider, still less to buy the licence for a Western quiz show. Many would revert to the practice of the earlier, buccaneering days when broadcast entrepreneurs were transmitting from apartment blocks: buy some dodgy VHS tapes of Hollywood movies from an underpass kiosk and slap them on screen. Copyright? What copyright? In fact what *was* copyright? Many believed that, having bought the cassette, they had also bought the right to do whatever they wished with the contents. As a media consultant preaching

Western values and practices, I would regularly, and forcefully, point out to station bosses that, aside from the international illegality of their actions, this was people's livelihoods they were stealing; that, even in the free-wheeling market economy they were so enthusiastically embracing, workers were entitled to their due remuneration, whether in California or the Caucasus. I got nowhere.

More than twenty years on and based in Australia, I am regularly, and embarrassingly, reminded of my pious tirades when friends, doctors and lawyers among them, offer me flash-drives of the latest hot TV series they've ripped off their subscription-only streaming services in what the BBC's Huw Wheldon once described as 'the piracy of their own homes'. History makes hypocrites of us all. Or, as the American designer Jim Fiebig put it, 'If you can look back on your life with contentment, you have one of man's most precious gifts – a selective memory'.

Aware of their affiliated stations' need of content, Internews Russia came up with a novel, and legal, alternative. It was called *Provintsia* (Provinces) and was a form of barter – not of physical goods but of stories.[1] As already noted, Russia is vast, more than twice as big as Australia, encompassing both Europe in the west and, on the other side of the Urals, Asia in the east. At the time, again as noted, it could boast about *600* regional television stations.

Provintsia created a closed market where human-interest stories could be traded electronically for stories from other regions. Every month, Internews-affiliated stations, not just in Russia but the other post-Soviets too, would send Internews' Moscow office their best video packages. There, the project's manager, my colleague Oleg Dmitriev, would select the best of the best and redistribute them to all members of the group, to broadcast as and when they wished. And for no charge.

Provintsia was launched in late 1999 and initially attracted twenty-three participating stations; by mid-2004, the number had more than tripled to 74, with up to a hundred stories being offered every month. A bonus side-effect of the exchange was an improvement in the quality of output as stations realised that their video packages had to stand comparison with those of other stations and would be judged accordingly.

The stories were as wide-ranging as the former Soviet territory. Among the most memorable were those that challenged stereotypes. One told how nuns at a convent near Ekaterinburg were using computers to create and maintain their website, communicate with other seminaries via email and electronically design nuns' clothing and icons. Another focused on a Muslim farmer in the Kzyl-Orda region of Kazakhstan who was risking community disapproval by raising pigs; his justification being that he wasn't eating them himself but selling them to non-believers so his family could eat.

Apropos, farmers played a crucial role in the history of communism as the providers of wheat and meat. Perhaps because of that, they have featured in many stories, both Soviet and post-Soviet. The hero of my all-time favourite – turned into 'a short' by Sverdlov Films in 1990 – was Vasili Filipovich Filipov, aka *The Night Reaper*. Blind since the age of five, Vasili lived alone on a remote farm in the Urals. Since night and day were alike to him, he would scythe his crops at a time and temperature of his choosing – regularly, and all too literally, scaring the living daylights out of any passing motorists who caught him in their headlights.

At the height of the exchange program, *Provintsia's* reports had a potential audience of more than thirty million Russians as well as another potential thirty million viewers in seven of the other former Soviet republics. (I readily concede that 'potential' is a weasel word but, from what I saw on the ground, the project was having a significant impact.) *Provintsia* reports were even broadcast by a channel which served the Russian community in New York.

One of the reasons for the project's success was that it gave small regional stations a national dimension. For many Russian viewers, it opened a window on to the entire federation from St Petersburg to Vladivostok. As a station in Khabarovsk (a few degrees further east than even Vladivostok) reported: 'Those of us who live in the Far East are locked in our corner. Because of the cost, we rarely travel west.' For this station and all the others on the fringes of the federation, *Provintsia* brought the rest of the country to them.

Thanks to this nationwide reach, *Provintsia* also helped coordinate the observance of significant dates in the national calendar. In 2001, to mark the 60th anniversary of the start of The Great Patriotic War, affiliated stations recorded and exchanged more than 60 clips of people sharing their memories of 22 June 1941 when Hitler invaded the USSR.

By steering clear of politics, none of the material that *Provintsia* was distributing, from the folksy (culture) to the pharmaceutical (health), was of a sort to cause the authorities concern. On the contrary, it was a unifying force, bringing the country together by showing it to itself.

But, as the next chapter will show, it wasn't the stories that worried the authorities. It was the fact that those enabling their transmission and exchange were financed by the West.

25.

HUMAN RIGHTS AND HORRIFIC WRONGS

In 1997, shortly after Tony Blair's New Labour party came to power in the UK, the Foreign Secretary, Robin Cook, made a statement which still reverberates nearly thirty years later:

> Our foreign policy must have an ethical dimension and must support the demands of other peoples for the democratic rights on which we insist for ourselves. The Labour Government will put human rights at the heart of our foreign policy.

The fact that such a morally indisputable declaration was regarded as controversial is indicative of the gap that had grown between cynical reality and what was regarded as impossible idealism. Human rights (HR) had long been in the TOO HARD tray, not just in the UK but in almost every other major Western country. Of course, we deplored the extra-judicial actions of the world's nastier regimes – the kidnappings, beatings, rapes, torture and executions – but we had to live in the real world if we wanted not just diplomatic relations but, no less important, trade relations with these countries, while not forgetting their support on the international stage when we needed it. So, shake the hand, pat the back and sign the deal . . . all the while holding the nose.

The Labour Government's new world view gave birth to a new entity – the Department for International Development, or 'DfID' as it was usually abbreviated. And, lest anyone doubted its importance, the formidable Clare Short was appointed its Secretary of State (that is, chief minister), along with a seat at the Cabinet table.

The first reaction of British non-profit organisations involved in journalist training, like my employers the Thomson Foundation, was that the increased focus on international development had to be good news. But, a year into the new department's life, there were concerns that journalist training was slipping down the agenda. There was a new toughness at the top, characterised by the minister's ill-judged comment that the Caribbean island of Monserrat, appealing for aid after a devastating volcanic eruption, would be 'wanting golden elephants next'. Journalist training had had a good run for the government's money, but it was now viewed as expensive and its effectiveness hard, if not impossible, to quantify.

The latter has always been true. Journalist training isn't like any other training. In a factory you can judge the effectiveness of training just by looking at the production line: one person not up to speed and the whole line slows down. Even teacher training, a close comparison to journalist training, is measurable in so far as teachers are assessed by inspectors and, less directly but no less brutally, by the exam results of their pupils. But when it comes to journalist training, it's a sad truth that one of the few, perhaps the only way its effectiveness can be measured is by counting the number of journalists who are locked up in those parts of the world where they and the training are most needed. Or worse than locked up.

It was at this moment of potential crisis, mid-1998, that the Director of the Thomson Foundation, Gareth Price, a wily, smooth-talking former controller of BBC Wales with excellent government contacts, had an inspired idea. Mindful of the Blair government's commitment to an ethical foreign policy, he overnight rebadged 'Journalist Training' as 'Human Rights Training'. The necessary reorientation was frankly minimal; most journalism worthy of the name seeks to cast a light on a human right that has been denied, delayed, ignored or generally trampled upon. But this was about packaging rather than product. Although very little had changed under the bonnet, the addition of a couple of speed-stripes and an HR-READY sticker on the back bumper enabled Thomson to offer what looked like a whole new, client-oriented, suite of courses, workshops and consultancies. And it worked.

There was, though, a downside: Thomson consultants now had to openly acknowledge and discuss abuses of human rights in countries where the very mention of the words could excite suspicion. Given that the new courses and workshops had the words 'human rights' in their titles, there was no hiding their true nature. As a result, we consultants now found ourselves in the same boat as all those British diplomats who, following the Foreign Secretary's speech, were having to implement his 'ethical dimension'. If the injunction were interpreted literally, it meant they were obliged to call out abuses of human rights when brought to their attention. Not easy in the former Soviets.

+———+

In those states like Georgia, looking west and openly discussing human rights, along with the reforms needed for their implementation, there was usually no problem. But it wasn't long before I was asked to do an HR course in a former Soviet republic under autocratic rule and renowned for its brutal clampdown on dissidents. A couple of days before the start, I sought out our on-site British ambassador to get his perspective. How had he managed the change?

The ambassador in question was one of the new generation of Blair government appointees, still in his forties and with a reputation for being not just unstuffy, but something of a joker. One of his female colleagues told me how on one occasion returning to the embassy, situated at a busy intersection of the capital, she had looked up to see her boss standing at the window of his upper floor office. Spotting her below, he pulled up his shirt to expose and pat his bare tummy, presumably betting that nobody would know he was Her Britannic Majesty's most senior diplomatic representative.

The morning we met, such jokey gestures were far from His Excellency's mind. When I asked how he was handling the HR issue, he crossed to his desk, opened a drawer and, without a word, handed me a letter. Written in ungrammatical English, it was from a father whose son had been arrested. The police had contacted him to say that, if he wanted to see his son alive again, he would have to pay $3000. A police car would stop at a certain corner at a certain time, with the kerb-side window open. He was to throw the money on to the seat. The father said he had raised the money and followed the instructions. The next day, he got a call from the mortuary to collect his son's body.

Pushing back his chair, the ambassador splayed his hands. 'So, as the representative of Her Majesty's Government, accountable to a minister who says we must put human rights at the heart of our foreign policy, what am I to do?'

The answer, it turned out, was nothing – at least not immediately or even soon – because, as the ambassador explained, anything he did do, any protest he made at whatever level, would be counterproductive. One of his EU counterparts had decided to go public about the country's widespread abuse of human rights and had been diplomatically ostracised. For all the influence he now had, he might as well have been running a flower shop.

I flicked the letter. 'So what's going to be your response?'

He sighed. 'The one we have always given – not protest but pressure. The only way to effect long-term change in these countries is by applying quiet and discreet pressure.'

Not all British diplomats agreed.

In October 2002, Her Majesty's ambassador to Uzbekistan, Craig Murray, broke one of the cardinal rules of diplomatic protocol: he made a speech in which he publicly criticised his host country; specifically, the government of President Islam Karimov for its widespread breaches of human rights, citing the 'apparent' boiling to death of two Muslim dissidents.[1] Strangely, the greatest fury came not from the British Foreign Office but from the Americans who regarded Karimov as a key ally in the 'war on terror', the more so for his having allowed a US airbase in the country as part of the 2001 invasion of Afghanistan.

The rogue ambassador (who, to be clear, had merely given voice to his government's ethical dimension) was recalled to London, rapped over the knuckles, had a breakdown, recovered and returned to Tashkent . . . to continue his campaign. All the while, salacious details of his alleged lifestyle were being leaked, resulting in the breakup of his marriage. The whole episode was a diplomatic disaster, threatening to poison Britain's relations with both the Uzbekistani and American governments.

Just weeks after Ambassador Murray's inflammatory speech, with the subsequent bruhaha showing no signs of abating, an odd thing happened. The Thomson Foundation asked me to conduct a human rights course in, of all places, Uzbekistan. Stranger still, it was to be funded by the British Embassy in Tashkent – Craig Murray's embassy – and facilitated by Internews Uzbekistan. Everything about the proposed course was puzzling: the subject, the venue, the involvement of both the Brits and the Americans and, not least, the timing. It was like flicking a lighted match into a petrol spill.

Could the timing be a coincidence? It seemed unlikely. My conclusion was that doing such a course at such a time in such a place had to be calculated. A deliberate provocation perhaps?

If so, who was the provocateur?

The American involvement, although strange in the circumstances, could be explained by the fact that the Thomson Foundation and Internews routinely worked together in the post-Soviets. Thomson provided the consultant/trainer while Internews arranged the equipment, facilities and logistics. It was a long-standing arrangement.

Then there was the British involvement. I assumed the funding had come out of the personal pot that every British ambassador and high commissioner has at their disposal for local projects of their choosing. But if this was Ambassador Murray's continuation of his personal campaign by other means, why had his bosses in the Foreign Office not intervened and cancelled the course? Had he not already caused enough trouble?

Or could it be that the Foreign Office itself, in continuation of its own HR mission, wanted to send Karimov a message: 'We may have issues with the way our ambassador has been conducting himself but, be assured, human rights remain at the heart of our foreign policy'?[2]

Whoever the sender, it seemed I was to be the messenger.

It's easy to become paranoid in these situations. I arrived in the Uzbekistani capital Tashkent in early January 2003, courtesy of Uzbekistan Airways. My case didn't. It finally turned up three days later. I'm a methodical packer, particularly when working. Nothing was missing but it was clear someone had had a good rummage and, significantly, didn't care if it showed. I also noticed that a couple of the video cassettes had not been wound back to the start, as was my standard practice to avoid 'drop-outs' when replayed.

Not that I had any worries about what the rummager might have found. There were two rules I observed as a journalist when working in dodgy foreign parts that had been reinforced when starting out as a broadcast consultant in the post-Soviets: first, keep anything confidential or sensitive, particularly contact details, on an SD card (the size of a stamp and easily concealed or disposed of); and, second, never accept a letter from a stranger or even a slight acquaintance who asks for it to be posted outside the country you're working in, no matter how plausible or sympathetic they may seem. The letter, written by a government agent, would typically express support for a terrorist group – just the sort of material which, when 'discovered' on your way out of the country, could be used to trigger your arrest and detention.

The day before the course started, I was given the list of participants. There were twelve: six men, six women; seven journalists, five cameramen. The journalists were not trainees in the usual sense. They were all experienced, at least in years; four were news editors; three were reporters. All but one of the twelve worked for independent TV stations. The exception, not to my surprise, was a reporter for Uzbekistani state television. I suspected she had been planted to report back. If so, I reckoned that, for once, training a journalist who worked for the state broadcaster might serve a useful purpose. In the event, she was the most tenacious of all the participants. I flattered myself that I might even have turned her.

According to the schedule I had put together, the first three days of the course would focus on theory, including a day devoted to the history of human rights (I always knew that full-size copy of Magna Carta would come in useful). During the remaining days, the participants would work in teams to produce three-minute 'special reports' about a human rights issue of their choosing but subject to my veto.

We got off to a good start. The group was attentive and, the journalists at least, were keen to ask questions. It was clear that the notion that humans, all humans, irrespective of gender, country, colour or creed, were born with certain inalienable rights was something not often discussed in either their homes or their workplaces. (Yes, I chickened out of sexual orientation. The very mention of homosexuality can be a flashpoint in Muslim countries, and I couldn't risk cratering the course on its first day.) That these rights had been specified and spelt out in the 1948 UN Universal Declaration of Human Rights prompted lively discussion. I may have been kidding myself, but I sensed a window had been opened. With the theory done, we moved on to the practice.

It had been obvious from when the course was first mooted that any video reports resulting from it would have to be handled with care. In fact, it wasn't a course at all, nor even a workshop. Instead, more innocuously, we had described it as a seminar which enabled us to avoid the standard final ceremony to which local dignitaries are invited to hand out certificates and view the fruits of the participants' labours.

That still left one other potential issue. It was customary, at the end of any course involving practical training, for participants to take away with them a copy of the report they had worked on as an aide-memoire of what (we hoped) they had learned. I wasn't overly worried about the stations of these participants broadcasting their reports, since most stations balked at airing anything that might even remotely displease the authorities. The greater danger was that a copy would get into circulation, end up online – uploaded perhaps by a well-meaning NGO – and come back to bite those who had produced and reported it. In theory, I could have issued a ban on any video material leaving the building, but I knew from experience how easy it was for a picture editor to surreptitiously run off a copy on to a memory stick for the reporter or producer he was working alongside. I decided to leave the matter till the reports were finished and we could gauge their sensitivity.

'So . . . we need some subjects with a human rights theme!' I declared, standing at the whiteboard, marker in hand. 'Any ideas?'

I was gratified and horrified in equal measure. Gratified because of the participants' enthusiasm to embrace human rights reporting but horrified by their failure, despite their alleged experience, to see just how problematic were some of the reports they were proposing. Anything that directly, or even indirectly, criticised the authorities was asking for trouble, and yet they seemed oblivious to the risks. Perhaps during my standard talk on 'the role of the journalist in a functioning democracy', I should have underlined the last two words and stressed their aspirational nature. On the other hand, a talk about 'the role of the journalist in an absolute autocracy' wouldn't have got past the title. In a grim way, the bind in which I found myself reflected the challenge of doing any human rights training for journalists in such an oppressive socio-political environment.

A couple of the reporters, even though born post-Watergate, clearly saw themselves in the Woodward-Bernstein mould, fearlessly exposing corruption, abuse of power and political wrongdoing. The problem was that they didn't have the *Washington Post* behind them – or anything remotely like it. Internews was facilitating the course but, realistically, it couldn't offer cover if the proverbial hit the fan. As for the British Embassy which was funding the training, it was in too much turmoil to be relied upon and at the time without its ambassador. Equally unsupportive would be the Foreign Office in London; the last thing it would have wanted was another confrontation with the Karimov government. Which left me. Apart from having zero clout, I would be on the next plane back to the UK.

I spent an uncomfortable night working through what was both a dilemma and a paradox. It would be over-dramatising to say that I wrestled with my conscience, but there was a stark question to be addressed; indeed, one that should have been thought through when such training had been first suggested. What was the point of training journalists in human rights reporting if you didn't let them make reports about HR abuses of the most egregious kind on their own doorstep? For three days I had fired them up and now I was about to hose them down. My first duty, having trained them, was to protect them from the possible consequences of that training. It looked like an impossible circle to square.

The solution I arrived at was hardly a *Eureka!* moment but it did offer a way out, or rather, a reconciliation of conflicting pressures. I took another look at the UN Universal Declaration of Human Rights produced in the aftermath of the Second World War in the hope that such a global catastrophe would never be repeated. As I read through the thirty articles, it struck me that the specified rights neatly fell into two categories: soft and hard. The soft rights were the ones which even the most obdurate autocrat might be prepared to endorse, or at least be identified with in his role as 'Father of the People': the right to shelter, the right to education, the right to work and remuneration, the right to food and clothing, the right to health care. Even Islam Karimov, I felt, would go along with those.

At the other end of the scale were the far more contentious hard rights: the right to due process, not be grabbed off the street and locked up indefinitely without being charged (aka Habeas Corpus); the right to a public trial and presumption of innocence; the right not to be tortured or raped in custody (or dunked in a vat of boiling water); the right to freedom of speech, opinion and religion; the right to form a trade union or political party; the right, at the individual level, to have a say in the governance of one's country. That is, democracy and fair elections.

Even in the best-run, most humane societies, most rights are hopeful rather than actual, but I could see that if the hard rights were a bridge too far, then – pursuing the military metaphor – the soft rights might make an effective beachhead, enabling journalists to tackle the harder rights later. The strategy would be to first build a base, a succession of reports on soft rights that would be showcased in a regular television program with an innocuous title such as *You and Your Rights*, suggesting education rather than investigation. Internews Uzbekistan would be the obvious production house and, I envisioned, would seek videoed contributions from its many affiliated (that is, financially supported) regional TV stations. Once the program had attracted an audience, established its credentials and become part of the media landscape – the aforementioned beachhead – it could venture, tiptoeing through the political minefield, into the hard rights territory. It seemed like a plan.

And this was how we shaped – or, rather, reshaped – the so-called seminar. It became in effect a pilot for the proposed showcase program. The subjects we chose for the reports were all relevant to Uzbekistani society but fell into the soft rights category: domestic violence, the plight of AIDS sufferers and the denial of secondary education to children whose parents couldn't afford the books or clothes to send them to school. What was most revealing, and supportive of my thinking, was that the makers of the education report persuaded the relevant official at the Ministry of Education to give an on-screen interview.

Despite my earlier fears, I felt by the end of the week that we had arrived at a novel stratagem for the reporting of human rights. This was doable. More than that: it was replicable. As a model, it could be applied worldwide, from South America to East Asia. In short, I was pretty pleased with myself. I had accepted a seemingly impossible challenge and emerged with an innovative and workable template.

The course concluded, I sent Khalida Anarbaeva, the Managing Director of Internews Uzbekistan, and Marika Olsen, the Country Director of Internews Network in Uzbekistan, a detailed report of the soft/hard approach and how I thought Internews – possibly only Internews – could implement it. A copy also went to Chris Hirst, the Third Secretary at the British Embassy, whom I had met during the week but who would resign within the year, another casualty of the diplomatic debacle. And that, I thought, was the end of the story.

✦ ⸺ ✦

Six months after the so-called seminar, I was called back to Tashkent to work with Internews staff on a series called *Jarayon* (in English, 'Legal Process' or, more simply, 'Trial'). I was gratified to see it was the sort of program I had recommended; it turned out we had all been thinking along the same lines. If anything, *Jarayon* was more creative and ambitious than what I had had in mind – a case of journalism meets showbiz. The subject matter was teetering on the line between soft and hard rights but, since it was ostensibly educational, on the right side. Or so it seemed at the time.

Funded by USAID, the program was designed to show the workings of a fair and transparent legal system by retrying old cases in a mocked-up courtroom built in Internews' impressive central atrium, using real lawyers as defenders and prosecutors and a real, albeit retired, judge as – in both senses – the acting judge. And there would be a public gallery to accommodate a small studio audience of two dozen people. All to be recorded by multiple cameras positioned around and above the set. Imagine if you can a post-Soviet version of *Judge Judy*. There would also be a host/moderator to give explanations as required, together with a three-minute video dramatisation of the alleged crime, like those shown on the BBC's *Crimewatch* program.

This was to be a big production, and one which the Internews-affiliated stations around the country would be given free, to help fill their broadcast schedules, attract viewers and keep them on air. Beyond that, *Jarayon* was a commendable attempt to explain due process to an audience largely unfamiliar with the concept. A fine example indeed of human rights awareness in practice.

But it was more than that. Back in 1997, the Uzbekistani Government had launched, through parliament, the Oliy Majlis, a national program for 'Improving Legal Culture in Society'. Official quote: 'The activities of the mass media are of great importance in ensuring the legal literacy of the population. It is necessary to significantly increase their attention to legal topics, explaining on the pages of periodicals, *in television and radio broadcasts* those legal questions that arise among the population.' (My emphasis.)

Jarayon, it seemed, was made to measure. Its time had come. How could the authorities not welcome such an initiative?

Even so, while working with the production team in Tashkent, I learnt that some of the Internews-affiliated stations out in the regions had raised concerns, fearing that they were being offered not so much a schedule-filling gift as a slow-acting suicide pill. They had gone so far as to threaten not to transmit the program unless 'the judge' was not just a real judge but a *serving* one approved by the Ministry of Justice. It was a case of the tail trying to wag the dog and, if implemented, their demand would have amounted to a co-production, with Internews and the Uzbekistani Ministry of Justice working as partners – and little doubt who would be the senior partner. It was never going to happen.

<hr />

Although delayed by a few months, *Jarayon* eventually went to air in December 2003. It was broadcast monthly, ten programs in all, the last in September 2004. Despite the earlier reservations, all eighteen Internews-affiliated stations transmitted it.

As originally proposed, the judge was a real, but retired, judge. The defendants and accusers were the actual persons involved in the original cases but, significantly, most of *Jarayon's* reconstructed trials arrived at the *opposite* verdicts because, as was pointed out, the original judges had often failed to follow the law. The program's lawyers meanwhile became minor celebrities and Internews was swamped with requests to use their services, including from viewers who had themselves ended up in court. As a result of the advice they received, they appealed for a review of their cases, and many got what they regarded as successful outcomes.

In short, *Jarayon* more than fulfilled its objective. Not only did it contribute to the legal literacy of the population as intended but, unexpectedly, it effected real change in getting a number of verdicts overturned.

✦──────✦

In cynical hindsight, it might have been better if *Jarayon* had been *less* successful for, looked at in another light, the program embarrassed the Uzbekistani Ministry of Justice by exposing deficiencies in the country's legal system. There would be repercussions. In the same month as the last program was shown – September 2004 – Internews Uzbekistan found itself in the Karimov government's crosshairs.

First, it was subjected to a financial audit, a familiar tactic of oppressive governments, that resulted in its bank account being frozen. The next year, in August 2005, Internews' Managing Director, Khalida Anarbaeva, and its accountant were convicted of producing television programs without a licence. (Although spared jail under a presidential amnesty, they were left with criminal records.) One of the offences on the charge sheet was that Internews had used its logo without the prior permission of the Ministry of Justice. The judge claimed that it 'had begun to meddle in Uzbekistani politics and in the president's policies'. Five weeks later, the municipal court in Tashkent ordered the NGO's permanent closure.

Several factors contributed to the demise of Internews Uzbekistan. One was Internews' acceptance of a tiny grant from George Soros's foundation to reproduce pocket-sized copies of the country's constitution for the use of journalists. The Karimov government, it seems, had a particular concern about Soros' influence in the region, based on what was seen as the disruptive impact of his support for non-governmental organisations in other countries.

As for *Jarayon*, former Managing Director Khalida Anarbaeva has no doubt that 'the program was one of the reasons for Internews' closure'. She specifically recalls the government investigator accusing

Internews of 'wanting to reform the current judicial system'. In response, she says, she pointed out that the *Jarayon* project had been in line with the government's own 1997 national program to improve the legal literacy of the population. But to no effect.

The closure of Internews Uzbekistan was a harbinger of worse to come.

Eighteen months later in January 2007, Manana Aslamazian, Director of Internews Russia, was returning to Moscow after visiting friends in Paris. When filling out the obligatory forms as she went through the arrival process at Sheremetyevo Airport, she miscalculated the amount of foreign currency she was carrying on account of fluctuations in the exchange rate. Instead of her euros being worth less than the minimum number of US dollars that had to be declared on entry, they were more. Had she been anyone else, her failure to declare them would likely have been judged an 'administrative violation'. Instead, realising the big fish they had inadvertently netted, the authorities charged Aslamazian with the criminal offence of smuggling and, claiming to suspect wider financial improprieties, shut down the servers on which Internews Russia (or the Educated Media Foundation, as it had just been rebadged), depended.

It was the end of Internews' operations in Russia, the end of the *Provintsia* video-exchange scheme, and the end of an invaluable support resource for hundreds of independent regional television stations across the Russian Federation. During its fifteen years of activity, Internews Russia had trained nearly 20,000 television personnel – not just in journalism but in management, financing, advertising and media law.

Victor and Yulia Muchnik of Tomsk's highly successful TV2 station, saw a certain inevitability in its end. They wrote:

The Russian authorities perceived Internews as an enemy organization. This has a certain logic to it. The existence of a media business that strives to be professional, self-sustaining, and independent from the authorities, even on a local level, contradicts the whole system of 'vertical power' in Russia . . . We miss Internews very much. It was, among everything else, a place that regional media professionals could call 'home'. Coming to Moscow, we always knew that there was a place where you felt welcomed, where you could share your problems, and where you could always find help if you needed it.[3]

Victor Muchnik initiated a letter to President Putin – not a petition but a demand – to stop 'the murder of Internews'. Within days, two thousand regional and Moscow-based journalists had signed. This was an impressive act not just of bravery but of logistics when, in the days before the development of social networks in Russia, signatures had to be collected individually. There was no official response to the letter.

Tragically, Manana Aslamazian, 'the godmother of Russian regional television', died in August 2022, aged 70, after being hit by a car in Yerevan. But her legacy lives on. As a close colleague observed, 'There's a piece of her in thousands of folks, including many participating in the kind of "silent opposition" in Russia these days'.

And Ambassador Craig Murray? He and the Foreign Office parted company in 2005. Murray went on to become an author and human rights activist. There would also be a falling out between the Americans and their thuggish friend, Islam Karimov. Following the Andijan Massacre in May 2005 when Uzbekistani Government forces killed hundreds of unarmed protesters, Washington threatened to withhold millions of dollars of aid to the country. Karimov, deciding that Russia and China might be more useful best buddies, responded by giving the Americans six months to vacate the Karshi-Khanabad air base.

✦ ——— ✦

The fate of the Internews presences in Tashkent and Moscow should have come as no surprise. It would be simplistic to say that they were the victims of their own success. But the judge who accused Internews of meddling in Uzbekistani politics was correct in so far as those of us who worked for Internews – in Uzbekistan and the other post-Soviet republics – were training indigenous journalists to be independent and, when appropriate, to challenge those in authority, their governments included. A stand-off was inevitable.

But the resulting loss went well beyond media training and support. The Internews offices in Tashkent and Moscow were just two of hundreds, possibly thousands, of NGOs which would be shuttered across the former-Soviets over the following years. While Internews itself was not intended to be a source of news (although training and helping others to produce it), many other NGOs were. What made these non-governmental organisations so useful to journalists in the post-Soviet world was what made them so threatening to autocrats: that they were sources of *non-governmental information.*

Journalists in the West love NGOs, a term which covers most not-for-profits: charities, special interest groups like Greenpeace, consumer protection organisations and citizen advice bureaus (which in the UK are dependent on government funding but independent and often critical of government). And, of course, the likes of Amnesty International and Human Rights Watch – not always loved by politicians in the West but not to be ignored either.

NGOs perform a service for journalists similar to that of the proverbial, loquacious taxi driver, except that the information provided by NGOs is research-based and supported by facts and cases. And they are accessible – always ready to give a quote, put up a staffer for interview or suggest an appropriate victim or case to illustrate their cause. At the same time, in their attempt to reach the widest possible audience or at least not alienate sizeable sections of it, they generally strive to be non-partisan in the sense of not identifying with any political party. This – no small consideration – qualifies them as objective sources.

In authoritarian countries where the flow of information is controlled, one of NGOs' most useful functions is that they provide reliable statistics. These will typically have been drawn from a recent study or survey carried out on the ground, and in most cases they will be more up to date than the most recent government ones which will often be two, three or more years old and massaged to accord with official claims and avoid embarrassment. (It should be added that the figures of Western governments too are often several years old.)

So it was that in the early post-communist years, Western and Western-supported NGOs in the former Soviets fulfilled an invaluable function as information providers for the new generation of freshly trained, fact-and-figure-hungry journalists.

While working as a consultant/trainer in these countries, I would often ask a reporter, when viewing a rough cut of their video package, what the relevant government ministry had had to say, particularly in relation to statistics. How many cases of AIDS for example ... or the number of clinic-performed abortions? The journalist's usual response was not 'Don't know' but, more creatively, 'The press office people don't answer their phones'. Typical lazy journalism, I would think, a variation on, 'Sorry, Miss, the dog ate my homework'. But, most times, I would be proven wrong. A government department might claim to have a press office and list a phone number for it but nobody would pick up at the other end. They were 'Potemkin Press Offices'.

Compare this with the situation in the UK, then as now. Every government department has a press office, as does every major company. (Even medium-sized companies will have someone who handles the media. In a small one, it will typically be the boss.) They may not always be as informative as one would like but there is a mutual understanding that a failure to communicate or call back, and in a reasonable time, will have consequences and that the worst possible response is *No comment*.

The failure of a government department to answer a relevant media query can lead to a question in The House (that is, Parliament) and embarrassment for the minister concerned. When a company finds itself the centre of unwanted attention, its first recourse these days is to a crisis-management consultant to handle the media. An inept response to whatever has gone wrong can lead to a loss of customer confidence, a fall in sales, a revolt by shareholders or even a national boycott of its products, quite apart from resignations at the highest level. The media in the West have power, real power.

But in the late 1900s and early 2000s, most governments in the former Soviets saw no need to communicate with the media because they had no fear of it. Journalists were an irrelevance at best, an irritant at worst. Why, say, would someone in the Ministry of Health bother talking to a small independent TV station with an audience of maybe 30,000 about a failure of local medical care? So what if that night's news said the Ministry was unavailable for comment? It was the equivalent of the *Berkhamsted Bugle* at the height of the 1956 Suez Crisis running the headline 'WE WARN YOU, PRESIDENT NASSER'. And the same went for statistics. 'Don't know, don't care.'

Which was why under Boris Yeltsin's presidency of Russia (1991–1999), Western NGOs had been welcomed. They were seen as helping in the transition to democracy and capitalism, and in the case of NGOs such as Internews and the Thomson Foundation, training the journalists who would inform the electorate and monitor the elected. They were needed and appreciated.

But not for long. Under Vladimir Putin, the foreign-funded NGOs soon became more of a pain than an aid, a thorn in the side of the body politic. Also for Aleksandr Lukashenko in neighbouring Belarus and Islam Karimov in Uzbekistan. But how to rein them in or, better still, shut them down?

There was the oblique way: use the pretext of a financial irregularity to close the bank account or seize the office servers as was employed against the Internews presences in Tashkent and Moscow. Effective but, tackling one at a time, slow. And in terms of media coverage, messy.

Or there was the broad-sweep, catch-all, scythe of legislation . . .

In 2012, Putin pushed through a law requiring NGOs in receipt of foreign funds to register and, in subsequent amendments, to declare themselves as 'foreign agents' in any public communication, websites included. This had the advantage of seeding the suspicion in the population that they were Trojan horses, financed by shady foreign entities operating under cover of good works to undermine the state. The foreign agent branding was an eerie echo of the old Soviet practice of declaring dissidents to be 'enemies of the people'.

In October 2024, the European Court of Human Rights (ECtHR) in Strasbourg ruled in favour of 107 NGOs, media organisations and individuals. It deemed that Russia's foreign agent legislation was 'stigmatising, misleading and used in an overtly broad and unpredictable way'. Its purpose, the ECtHR concluded, was 'to punish and intimidate rather than to address any alleged need for transparency or legitimate concerns over national security'.[4]

Not that Putin would have worried a jot. His handling of foreign-funded NGOs had already attracted the admiring attention of his fellow autocrats. In November 2021, President Aleksandr Lukashenko was asked by the BBC's Steve Rosenberg about the 270 Belarussian NGOs he had closed in the previous four months. His response was characteristically restrained: 'We'll massacre all the scum that you [the West] have been financing. Oh, you're upset we've destroyed all your structures! Your NGOs, whatever they are, that you've been paying for . . .'[5]

Faced with such tactics, some NGOs sought to survive by breaking their links with Western funders and appealing to domestic donors to make good the loss of foreign support. With limited success. Even if the money were available, it was a brave donor who was prepared to risk the wrath of the authorities.

Belarus under Lukashenko and Russia under Putin are known quantities. In some respects more worrying, the government of Georgia, once regarded as the best hope for democracy in the Caucasus, progressive and media-tolerant, has introduced its own foreign agent law based, the opposition claims, on the Russian model. This has prompted mass demonstrations, fuelled by the fear that the new law could herald a crackdown not just on NGOs but on civil society generally, and ultimately threaten democracy itself.

Most recently in early 2025, Viktor Orban, the prime minister of Hungary – a member of both NATO and the EU – also signalled his intention to take legal action that will eliminate NGOs receiving foreign funding.[6]

But a pause for thought . . .

Looked at dispassionately, is requiring registration of foreign-funded organisations really so unreasonable? Many countries have foreign agent laws, including the United States.

Since 1938, the American Government has had its own *Foreign Agents Registration Act* (FARA), which requires those engaged in political, advocacy or lobbying work on behalf of foreign entities in the US to register with the Department of Justice and disclose their relationship, activities, receipts, and disbursements in support of their activities. The law was introduced in the run-up to the Second World War to identify German propaganda agents in the US, and it is still on the statute books. In 2017, Russia's RT channel was required to register after being judged to be 'Russia's state-run propaganda machine'.

The difference between FARA and Putin's law is that the US law doesn't specifically target NGOs or their financing. The focus, irrespective of the entity or the source of its funding, is on the nature of its activity. Quote: 'FARA requires individuals or organizations to register as foreign agents *only* if they engage in certain specified activities at the order, request, or under the direction or control, of a foreign principal – *not simply by receiving contributions from such an entity.*' (My emphasis.)[7]

This means you can be a foreign-funded NGO without the requirement to register with the Department of Justice. By comparison, in Russia, the mere fact of being foreign funded brings you within the foreign agent net with all the legal requirements and restrictions that follow.

Putin's suspicion of foreign-funded NGOs, bordering on obsession, long predates the 2012 law. He would have noted in November 2003 the significant part that Georgia's NGOs played during the Rose Revolution, both behind the scenes and on the street, in overthrowing then President Eduard Shevardnadze. But he articulated his concerns most clearly in his speech to the 2007 Munich Security Conference when, in the opinion of many, he revealed his true colours. This is the official, unedited, Kremlin translation:

> What bothers us? I can say and I think that it is clear for all, that when these non-governmental organisations are financed by foreign governments, we see them as an instrument that foreign states use to carry out their Russian policies. That is the first thing. The second. In every country there are certain rules for financing, shall we say, election campaigns. Financing from foreign governments, including within governmental campaigns, proceeds through non-governmental organisations. And who is happy about this? Is this normal democracy? It is secret financing. Hidden from society. Where is the democracy here? Can you tell me? No! You can't tell me and you never will be able to. Because there is no democracy here, there is simply one state exerting influence on another.[8]

A decade on, quite a few Hillary Clinton supporters would counter that Putin himself knows a thing or two about foreign interference in elections.

But the president had a point. NGOs, whether foreign-funded or not, can influence voting and therefore the outcome of elections. While they may try to avoid *party* politics, their aim, their raison d'être, is to increase awareness of the issues they champion. Put crudely, they are lobbyists – not for companies or countries but for causes. Those NGOs concerned with human rights, civil society, democracy and media freedom are hoping to raise public awareness. More than that: to mobilise public opinion. And what does mobilise mean in practice? It means, come the next election, encouraging individuals to vote for those parties and candidates which support those NGOs' agendas.

But Putin was also being disingenuous. His objection to the category of NGOs just mentioned is less that their funding is 'hidden from society' than that they represent a threat to his government's conduct and control.

It's a bit rich that, in making his argument against 'secret financing', Putin should invoke democracy, not once but three times in thirty seconds, and apparently with approval. Perhaps the translator should have made clear that the president's favoured version is '*managed democracy*' – the sort that requires institutions to cede their power and independence to the leader, rewrites the constitution to extend his term in office, restricts those who can stand for election and, not least, muzzles the media.[9]

26.

PRIME MINISTER,
THAT IS JUST NOT TRUE!

One of a media consultant/trainer's off-duty chores is to build a personal archive, a collection of video clips grabbed off news and current affairs programs that can be used to illustrate points you may wish to make during training sessions or on-site consultancies. Among such clips are interviews that show the interviewer holding an authority figure to account.

A clip I frequently use dates from February 2003 when my BBC colleague Jeremy Paxman, at the time Britain's most feared political interviewer, interrogated (not too strong a word) Prime Minister Tony Blair weeks before the UK and US invaded Iraq and toppled its leader, Saddam Hussein. Blair's justification was that Saddam was concealing weapons of mass destruction while preventing the United Nations inspectors from doing their work. The interview has barely begun before it turns into a verbal duel.[1]

> **BLAIR:** The truth is the inspectors were put out of Iraq so –
> **PAXMAN [interrupting]:** They were not 'put out of Iraq', Prime Minister, that is just not true. The weapons inspectors left Iraq after being told by the American government that bombs would be dropped on the country.
> **BLAIR:** I'm sorry, that is simply not right. What happened

is that the inspectors told us that they were unable to carry out their work, they couldn't do their work because they weren't being allowed access to the sites. They detailed that in the reports to the Security Council. On that basis, we said they should come out because they couldn't do their job properly.

PAXMAN: That wasn't what you said, you said they were 'thrown out of Iraq' –

BLAIR: Well, they were effectively because they couldn't do the work they were supposed to do.

PAXMAN: Effectively they were not 'thrown out of Iraq', they *withdrew*.

BLAIR: No, I'm sorry Jeremy, I'm not allowing you [to get] away with that. That is completely wrong. Let me just explain to you what happened.

PAXMAN: You've just said the decision was taken by the inspectors to leave the country. They were therefore *not* 'thrown out'.

BLAIR: They were effectively thrown out for the reason that I will give you . . .

On the face of it, it's a spat over semantics but it's important because it shows that Paxman has done his homework and he's going to call out any self-serving half-truths. But what marks the interview for broadcasting posterity is that Paxman is, as near as dammit, calling the British prime minister – *his* prime minister – a liar.

In confronting Blair in this way, Paxman knows he's not going to lose either his head or his job, nor be charged with criminal defamation, as might be the case in China, Thailand or the UAE. He has not only the BBC behind him but also a sizeable section of the British public as Blair is aware, which is why he addresses

Paxman matily as 'Jeremy'. The prime minister is acknowledging the rules of the game whereby politicians in the UK, even the highest, are expected to subject themselves and their decisions to public scrutiny. Paxman is representing not just the viewers but, no less important, the voters, those who have put Blair where he is and, by the same token, can remove him. The fact that such an interview can take place and be broadcast on national television is part of what constitutes a mature democracy.

But what happens when a journalist who has been trained in Western standards tries to apply them in their own less-than-democratic homeland? And what responsibility does the training organisation bear when that journalist finds themself in hot water?

✦———✦

Irakli Imnaishvili was a television journalist I trained in Georgia. We first met in November 2000 when Irakli was just 21 years old and about to join Georgian State Television as a reporter. He was one of a dozen participants on a six-week School of Journalism course I conducted in Tbilisi. Intelligent, personable, self-confident, humorous and mature beyond his years, Irakli was the stand-out participant. And, not unimportant in the superficial world of television, good-looking with it. In the end-of-course appraisal, I described him as having the potential to be 'one of the best Georgian television journalists of his generation'. A potential Paxman in fact.

Two years later, in 2002, our paths crossed again. I had been asked by the Thomson Foundation to lead a four-man consultancy team to help set up a privately financed Georgian television channel in the capital. Called Mze (Sun), it was to be housed in a new, four-storey mausoleum of a building, originally constructed for an insurance company that had decided it no longer suited its purpose.

Our job was to put together the station's news and current affairs department, which meant planning its newsroom, creating a day-by-day weekly broadcast schedule, training the necessary staff, both technical and journalistic, and signing off with an 'as live' dry run to prove we had done our jobs. All of this was to be accomplished between early September and mid-December.

We arrived to find that the building was not just unfurnished but unfinished and still being repurposed for its new function. There were no technical facilities, no landlines, no Internet and, as we discovered with the arrival of winter, the only heating was a couple of domestic electric radiators – little better than hand-warmers – that had to be trundled from room to room.

Yet there was no shortage of money. Working our way through the building, from ground to top floor, we opened doors to reveal boxes piled to the ceiling, labelled Sony, Panasonic and Sennheiser. Inside were top-of-the-range digital cameras, matching audio-gear, computerised editing stations and even a complete news server. It was like finding a trainset under the tree on Christmas morning.

Putting it all together was another matter. Before leaving the UK, I had been sent a plan of the ground floor, from which it was clear that the building's greatest asset was a vast open-plan foyer. I worked out that it could house a combined newsroom and studio (the newsroom, raised on a platform, acting as a backdrop behind the anchor's desk), with an area off to one side for a talk-show with host and three or four guests.

Bang in the middle of the foyer was a curiously dotted outline of a square which, for want of identification, I took to be a notional coffee table – a bit of draughtsman's whimsy. The three-dimensional reality that I and my team encountered a fortnight later turned out to be a stonking great, floor to ceiling, structural pillar. My colleague with responsibility for set design buried his head in his hands. In the end we flew in from the UK a studio designer who had recently worked on ITN's latest news set in London. His solution was simple: since the pillar couldn't be removed or disguised, make it a feature by hanging an equally stonking great monitor from it.

As for staffing, we had the best that our owners' thick chequebook could buy: fourteen journalists (reporters, presenters, producers), eight camera-operators and two graphics designers – cherry-picked from both state and commercial channels. Individually, they already had the skills: the priority was bonding and teamwork.

To our surprise, all the cameramen turned up with handguns; one even with a pair. This, they explained, was not for their protection, at least not primarily, but to deter anyone with an eye on their $30,000 cameras. Since Thomson had provided us with an armed guard, we left it to him to draw up a weapons protocol during training hours while being especially careful how we used the term 'shoot'.

One of those recruited – more accurately, commandeered – from Georgia's state channel was potential Paxman, Irakli Imnaishvili. Now twenty-three and with two more years' experience under his belt, he was even more impressive than previously. It was noticeable how those a decade older were deferring to him. Within a fortnight my colleague David Seymour and I had decided Irakli had the qualities to be the face of the new channel, its on-screen anchor.

✦ —— ✦

The channel's launch on 1 June 2003 was propitious. Within six months – November 2003 – the bloodless Rose Revolution would force President Eduard Shevardnadze to stand down and, in the election that followed, the pro-West opposition leader Mikheil Saakashvili would secure 96% of the votes. The atmosphere was euphoric. As the poet Wordsworth said of an earlier revolution, 'Bliss was it in that dawn to be alive, but to be young was very heaven!' Saakashvili, just thirty-six, was hailed internationally as the man who could carry through Georgia's transition to democracy. But any hopes of respect for media freedom were dashed when, sadly but predictably, his government started to exert its control over hitherto independent television news outlets. (That said, radio and online media outlets continued to operate without hinderance. The reason, it's speculated, is that Saakashvili doubted the influence of the Internet because its coverage was still limited and smartphones weren't yet widely available.)

First to be targeted was Georgia's most popular commercial channel, Rustavi-2, which had given a platform to Saakashvili and other opposition voices during Shevardnadze's presidency. Following a change of ownership (in effect a forced buy-out), it started to toe the new government's political line. Having supported Saakashvili when in opposition, it became his prisoner the moment he gained power. A cautionary tale for all broadcasters who get too close to politicians.[2]

It wasn't long before Mze, the station which my colleagues and I had helped to set up, came under similar pressure. Matters reached a head in February 2005 following the suspicious death of the Georgian prime minister, Zurab Zhvania. While other stations reported and followed the story, the editorial team of Mze's popular political talk show, *Archevanis Zgvarze* (On the Verge of Choice) launched an investigation. It was a brave decision. The show's host was our man Irakli Imnaishvili.

Zhvania, along with a deputy regional governor, Raul Usupov, had died in a rented apartment. According to the official version rushed out by the Ministry of Internal Affairs at 7 am after the early morning discovery of the bodies, the men had been killed by carbon monoxide from a faulty gas heater – which was odd because the first forensic results weren't available until mid-afternoon. Additionally, the CEO of the gas supply company claimed that, on account of technical problems with the pipeline, the supply had been off during the night.

As part of their investigation, Irakli and his team invited on to their program experts who pointedly failed to corroborate the official explanation of the PM's death. The government was furious and a few months later in early July the management of Mze took the program off air. (Mze was subsequently sold to a businessman with links to Saakashvili. Its editorial policy became more government-aligned before it was eventually stripped of all its news content.)

Irakli resigned from Mze, feeling he was unable to work as the professional journalist he had been trained to be. He was not just out of a job but regarded as so 'hot' as to be unemployable. He emailed me:

> I am on Saakashvili's blacklist. Every newsroom is closed to me. I have always kept the standards as I was taught by you. They could not make me change these rules. If I had made propaganda, my program would not have been closed. I have made my choice and I think it was the right decision.

There was nothing I could do by way of intervention (I was by now working with Al Jazeera in Qatar). But, as Irakli's trainer and mentor, I was aware of having a duty of care. Getting him out of Georgia till the dust settled looked like the most feasible plan. So, when he expressed interest in studying for a master's degree,

I readily supported his application for a Chevening Scholarship in the UK. I told the British Council representative in Tbilisi that I felt we – the Thomson Foundation and the British Government – had an obligation to support, morally and practically, those young Georgian journalists who had spearheaded the implementation of Western values and, as in Irakli's case, were now paying the price. I laid the emotional blackmail on with a trowel.

To her enduring credit, the British Council representative was sympathetic and all the indications were that, subject only to an interview which I was confident he would sail through, Irakli would be awarded the scholarship (for which, incidentally, he was eminently qualified). Within a few months, he would be out of the country. Job done, conscience salved. Or so I thought.

While the gears of bureaucracy turned, Irakli, now a free agent, decided to make a field trip at his own expense. His aim was to produce a media map of Georgia's regional environment, in particular clarifying the opaque issue of station ownership. It was timely, as by now Saakashvili had brought not only most of the national media outlets under government control but the regional ones too.

One of the stations on Irakli's list was Rioni TV based in Kutaisi, the capital of the Imereti region. While visiting the station, he was invited to take part in a televised debate about press freedom and soon got into a heated argument with Imereti's Saakashvili-appointed governor, Akaki Bobokhidze. The governor brought the debate to an early close by walking out, but the row overflowed into a corridor where Bobokhidze, aided by his bodyguard, expressed his dissatisfaction (or, as he subsequently put it, 'defended my and my family's dignity', a reference to an exchange about who had been better brought up) by breaking Irakli's nose.

A regional governor and friend of the president physically attacking a high-profile journalist was not a good look and that evening Bobokhidze resigned. He would, however, continue to be supported and even promoted by Saakashvili – and was never prosecuted because, it was said, the authorities deemed Irakli's injuries to have been very slight. That is not Irakli's recollection:

> I wish it was only my nose. I was severely beaten by the governor and his bodyguard. But when the state-controlled media reported it, they downplayed everything, saying only that he had broken my nose. In reality, the attack left me with fractured jawbones, a serious head injury, concussion, and critical blood loss. I was unconscious for several hours. No one dared to administer first aid to me – everyone was too afraid to put my name in official records. Even the ambulance service refused to transport me to Tbilisi. My fiancée managed to drive me at night from Kutaisi to Gori, a journey of eighty kilometres, even though it was only her second time driving a car. This is the miracle that I am alive today. It was a near-death experience. Recovery took me eighteen months and left several 'gifts' like chronic blood pathologies.

Back in the UK, I learnt about the attack from the Internet. The need to get Irakli out of Georgia assumed a new urgency. The incident had been an international embarrassment for the Saakashvili government and it wasn't long before Irakli received 'friendly' warnings, along with reminders of how dangerous winter roads could be. Accidents happened. Even so, he demanded and got a meeting with Georgia's Ombudsman who, Irakli says, 'simply nodded with a concerned expression . . . and did nothing'.

That Irakli was now in danger, mortal danger, I had no doubt. There was a precedent for the extra-judicial elimination of a vexatious talk-show host. I was familiar with it because I had been working in Tbilisi at the time. Giorgi Sanaia was the 26-year-old host of Rustavi-2's *Night Courier*, a news talk show noted for its incisive discussions. Early in the morning of 26 July 2001, Sanaia was shot dead in his apartment with a single 9mm bullet to the back of the head, execution-style. An estimated 30,000 mourners packed the streets of the capital on the day of his funeral.

But how to expedite Irakli's removal? Whatever clout I may have had previously was now 'residual'. The splendid Deborah Barnes-Jones, the British ambassador with whom I had had regular contact when working in Georgia, had moved on a year earlier. Meanwhile, Irakli still had a formal board interview to pass before his scholarship could be confirmed but was in no state, physical or psychological, to attend it. He could barely open his mouth, let alone engage his brain. Mercifully – for once in its literal sense – the British Council deferred the interview till March, by which time the University of Westminster had accepted him for an MA in Media Management.

Irakli finally arrived in London on 1 September 2006. Shortly after completing his MA the following year, he got a job with the BBC Russian Service. By 2014, he had risen to be an SBJ, a senior broadcast journalist. This would lead to his joining a team specifically created to counter Putin's propaganda machine, when he was tasked with recruiting (and protecting) producers and contributors for the BBC offices in Kyiv, Minsk, Riga, Jerusalem and, importantly, Moscow.

In September 2019, after twelve years with the BBC and Mikheil Saakashvili's presidency (almost) a distant memory, Irakli was persuaded by the Rustavi-2 channel to return to Georgia as their executive director in the hope of his being able to resolve its troubled internal politics and restore it to a position of editorial independence.

After three years with the channel, most of which coincided with the COVID lockdown, Irakli left for health reasons. Given his dual perspective of working as a journalist in both his native Georgia and the UK, I wondered how in hindsight he would assess his career. He replied:

> One of the biggest challenges for journalists trained to Western standards is the lack of a safety net. While the training provided valuable knowledge and principles, applying them in post-Soviet states can be life-threatening. We were taught what to do without being fully informed of 'the price'. The reality is that you are alone against the state and have to accept that the worst-case scenario might be something like the Georgian-Ukrainian journalist Georgiy Gongadze who was kidnapped in Kyiv and decapitated, or the human rights activist Anna Politkovskaya who was fatally shot in Moscow. I was naïve to think I could apply BBC standards while working in a Georgian private TV station. It was a lost battle from the start.

The words, 'We were taught what to do without being fully informed of "the price"' hit home. It was true. My assumption had always been that you didn't go into journalism, particularly television journalism which required you to be on site and in vision, without being aware of the risks. You had only to watch the nightly news to see reporters dodging bullets, diving into ditches and generally putting themselves in harm's way. Indeed, for many it was part of the appeal of the job.

My own training by the BBC – two years of it – supported this. The only safety advice that I recall came in the form of a fifteen-minute film of (never broadcast) out-takes of reporters and correspondents on location in potentially dangerous situations. I believe it was titled *What Would You Do?* The most shocking clip was of correspondent David Tindall – in Biafra, I think – intervening as a soldier is about to execute a captured rebel. After assuring Tindall, on camera, that he isn't going to harm the man, the soldier waits several seconds and, wrongly assuming the camera is no longer running, shoots him point-blank. This raised the question whether Tindall had been right to intervene, or whether he should have kept his distance as a neutral observer. And the answer? If there was one, I don't remember it.

In fact, everything I was ever told about safety was that my primary duty as a reporter or producer was to protect my cameraman (and/ or crew): from ensuring there was someone behind him to clear his path when walking backwards while filming to not putting him in an exposed position where his shoulder-mounted camera might be mistaken for a rocket-propelled grenade launcher. Both eminently sensible measures since the cameraman is more often the true hero in such situations. I mentioned earlier those pictures of reporters diving into ditches. Guess who is standing *above* the ditch to take them.[3]

As for the reporter's safety, I should add that, since the mid-1990s, the BBC has made safety training-and-awareness courses mandatory for its producers and reporters, along with the completion of hazard assessment forms. Even so, if these measures were to be copied and applied in the training of post-Soviet journalists, the one thing they cannot address is the safety of those journalists like Irakli, and before him Giorgi Sanaia, who find themselves alone against the state, *their* state, when the danger zone is as likely to be a television studio as the front line. Hosting a talk show in a lounge suit can prove as perilous as doing a piece-to-camera in a Kevlar vest. No hostile environment training can cover that sort of scenario.

Again, I tried to put myself in Irakli's position. With difficulty. Certainly, there had been times when British Government press officers and civil servants had tried to derail an investigation by denial or obfuscation. There had also been an occasion during a dockers' meeting on Liverpool Pier Head when a shady character with an unconvincing fox-terrier had hinted that my name was on a Special Branch file after I had refused to let my cameraman take close-up still photos of the strike leaders. But never, not even remotely, did I feel I might be under physical threat from my own government or its agencies.

'Alone against the state.' It's a chilling phrase, worthy of a thriller title. But how, realistically, could any Western organisation like Thomson or Internews provide a safety net for those we train? What would it even look like? As matters stand, the best we can do – and, as I type the words, I'm embarrassed by how limp they appear on screen – is to emphasise the importance of assessing the degree of protection their own station management will afford them if/when the authorities object to their output. Broadcast bosses always want their flagship programs to be 'hard-hitting' . . . until the hit ricochets. As a BBC colleague, a reporter who became a regional controller (the aforementioned David Seymour) once remarked, 'Management is lustful before the event . . . and virginal after it.'

Beyond this, every journalist must balance their personal safety, their lives even, against their professional role and the public's right to know. Nobody should be expected, in the old cliché, 'to go down for the program', even if there will always be those incredibly brave, mission-driven individuals who will be prepared to pay the price.

Not me. There's a difference between accepting a risk, such as boarding a flight knowing that civilian aircraft have been shot at as they come in to land, and consciously putting yourself, and those with you, in danger. It is ironic that the only time I have had to make that risk-versus-danger assessment, as against those instances of unanticipated danger when there's been no choice, has been not as a reporter but as a consultant, which takes us back to where this chapter started.

In March 2004, a year after the invasion of Saddam's Iraq, I was asked by USAID's Office of Transition Initiatives Iraq Program whether, given my experience in the post-Soviets and familiarity with the Muslim world, I would consider working on-site for them, training journalists employed by US-funded news outlets (after several days' safety training at a Texas military base). I was minded to accept, driven in part by the guilt of having supported the Iraq War based on my belief – more specifically, my prime minister's belief – that Saddam had weapons of mass destruction. Perhaps also by a rather self-aggrandising wish to atone. When I told an ex-Internews colleague, Dan Bolger, he urged me to get the Committee to Protect Journalists in New York to run a safety audit. He probably saved my life.

The CPJ auditor, Frank Smyth, a former war correspondent who had been imprisoned in Saddam's Iraq a decade earlier, pointed out something that should have been already obvious to me, that working directly for an occupying power was far riskier than reporting for an independent news organisation:

> Michael, I would NOT do it. I would not do it because the risk is extremely high, higher than any conflict in memory to date. It is high for Western journalists and Iraqis who work with them. It would be even higher for anyone directly working for

U.S. authorities, as you would be considered a target, as would anyone working with you. The question is, if you were to unfortunately end up maimed, paralyzed and/or disfigured, would you feel, looking back on it, that it was worth it. If not, don't do it.

It will come as no surprise that discretion trumped valour.

27.

BLESSED ARE THE FILM-MAKERS

How much influence does television have on events?

It's a question that has been endlessly debated, though with more speculation than proof, and without always asking the no less relevant follow-up, For better or worse?

Take Italy in the 1950s and 60s. One of the reasons for the mass migration of southern Italians to the north – tens of thousands found jobs with Fiat in Turin – has been ascribed to the postwar ubiquity of television sets in public bars. For much of the day, these would show soap operas which were mostly produced and set in the north. According to the theory, the impoverished southerners, leaning on the bar sipping their *espressi*, would watch them and think, If that's the way they live up north, I want a piece of it!

The phenomenon was repeated decades later, though this time better documented, in Albania on the other side of the Adriatic opposite the heel of Italy's boot. When communism collapsed there in the early 1990s, thousands of young Albanians who for years had been exposed to Italian television because of the countries' proximity, took to boats and rafts in search of a better life across the water.

Most famously, television has been given credit for helping to end the two-decade-long Vietnam War (1955–1975) by bringing the front line into the living rooms of the American people. No longer dependent on the black and white, censored, sanitised, morale-boosting cinema newsreels of the Second World War to learn what had been going on a week after the event, viewers could now watch the bloody conflict nightly and unfiltered, and latterly in colour. It should be said though, that if television did help end the Vietnam War, it took a remarkably long time. And it wasn't television that revealed the truth about the most shocking incident, the 1968 My Lai massacre by US soldiers, but a print journalist, Seymour Hersh.

More recently, and periodically, there has been the debate over dramatised violence on the small screen and whether it has not just inured the viewing public to such acts but promoted their imitation in real life. The jury remains out, but it's worth noting that a contrary theory was floated in 1994, in a paper for the US House of Representatives written by Internews researcher (as he then was), Eric S. Johnson, after visiting Tajikistan. While the Tajikistani Government claimed Western movies were corrupting its youth, the country's independent television stations cited in their defence statistics compiled by local police departments which showed that crime figures had *dropped* by around two-thirds when the movies were being shown. The implied explanation: that young people were inside watching rather than out on the street fighting, thieving and vandalising.[1]

✦————✦

The belief endures that television can change not just events but attitudes, and it's been the bedrock assumption of a number of 'reconciliation projects' during the early years of the twenty-first century. Television journalists, the theory goes, can play a part in bringing about peace between the warring factions of the post-Soviets, underpinning the efforts of diplomats and politicians.

The notion boils down to this: that if you take television journalists from the opposing sides and get them to work together on a documentary-style production about the conflict that divides their nations, they will recognise their common humanity and, through both the experience of working together and the resulting production with its balanced analysis of the conflict, they will enlighten their respective populations while personally setting an example of coexistence and cooperation.

Spelt out like that, in the manner of a proposal for a doctoral thesis, it looks like a very large slice of aerial pie, but it's the sort of left-field thinking that can appeal to those peace-promoting organisations with the resources to put it to the test. The more so in the context of the many so-called frozen conflicts across the post-Soviet world, where the absence of war is not peace but a state of perpetual tension and occasional flare-up. In short, it had to be worth a try.

At this point, it's worth stressing how radical the idea is. And therefore controversial. Any television journalist reporting a conflict in which their own people are involved naturally arrives with a bundle of loyalties and prejudices, conscious and unconscious. But, if scrupulously following the professional code, the journalist is required to put these aside and report the facts objectively, irrespective of the partisan narrative back home. Fine in theory, but to do so to the letter demands the sort of moral courage that risks being branded a fifth columnist . . . or, worse, a traitor.

The BBC's reporting of the Falklands War in 1982 after Argentina invaded and occupied two British dependent territories in the South Atlantic was, and remains, a textbook case. Its late evening *Newsnight* program decided to adopt the same even-handed approach to its reporting of the conflict as it would to any other despite its being an arm of the *British* Broadcasting Corporation. So, when presenter Peter Snow used phrases such as 'If we believe the British' and at more length declared, 'Until the British are demonstrated either to be deceiving us or to be concealing losses from us, we can only tend to give a lot more credence to the British version of events' (note the loaded qualifier, 'tend to'), the reaction was immediate and furious. Bernard Ingham, Prime Minister Margaret Thatcher's press secretary, spoke on behalf not just of the government but of the right-wing press and probably most patriotic Brits when he remarked, 'It is one thing to be objective. It is another thing to be objective in a nauseating way.'

The *Newsnight* program had scrupulously applied the BBC's own editorial principles and been rewarded with brickbats. What was now being proposed to thaw the post-Soviet frozen conflicts was a step even further, something beyond objectivity: *empathy*. Specifically, empathy with the enemy; attempting to see the situation from their viewpoint. Put in those terms, it sounds not just unfeasible but delusional. And yet . . .

In 2005, I conducted a workshop in the Middle East for Palestinian women TV journalists. One of the exercises I occasionally include on these occasions is called 'Hypotheticals'. I ask the participants what they would do, what decisions they would take, in a number of morally ambiguous situations which, though hypothetical, are realistic to their daily working lives. One of the questions on the Palestinian list was, 'Who would you inform if you learnt that a Palestinian group was planning an attack on an identified bar in Tel Aviv?'.

I was sure they wouldn't inform the Israeli authorities and thought the most likely response would be to pass on the information to a contact within their notional government, the

Palestinian Authority. By referring up in this way, both professional and patriotic duty would be done and personal conscience cleared. The answer surprised me. The consensus, after discussion, was that they would pass the details to one of their Israeli counterparts, a fellow journalist. What this suggests is that there is a 'confederacy of journalists' that binds even those who find themselves on opposing sides.

(It should be noted that this was of course before Hamas's October 2023 attack on Israel and the Gaza conflict that followed.)

So, getting journalists to work together, reporting a conflict that divides their nations is not such a wildly unreasonable objective. Yes, we are talking about that loaded word, 'collaboration'. But the connotations don't have to be exclusively negative when such collaboration is in the interests of peace and reconciliation.

The Organisation for Security and Cooperation in Europe (OSCE) took up the idea and developed it. A test case was chosen – in the South Caucasus – and other agencies recruited. Facilitated by Internews Georgia and funded by the British Embassy in Tbilisi, the exercise would focus on Georgia's conflict with its two breakaway regions of Abkhazia and South Ossetia. In terms of cracking nuts, they didn't come much tougher.

Since I was already working in the Caucasus at the time, it took little persuasion to get me on board. This was a truly innovative exercise. To be in from the start was both challenging and exciting.

First, though, we had to demonstrate that television journalists from opposing sides could work together, period. The chosen format was therefore a two-week workshop in which the participants, three Georgians, three Abkhazians and three South Ossetians, would be trained together, split into three-person *mixed* teams, and be required to make a news package of their choice but unrelated to the conflict. Bolted on to the front of the workshop, to launch it in the right direction, would be a two-day conference involving senior representatives of all three parties.

The format settled, there was the question of a venue. It was quickly realised that holding the conference and workshop in any of the three 'participating entities' (as they were delicately called) would involve political hurdles, not least arranging visas. Holding them in the Georgian capital, Tbilisi, for example, would require the Georgians to turn a blind eye to the fact that those governing Abkhazia and South Ossetia were not just secessionists but technically traitors. In the end, Moscow emerged as the favourite – easy to reach, no visa issues and with the advantage that Russian could serve as the common, neutral language for both the training and the video reports. As Britain has found, one of the advantages of having had an empire is that a common language outlasts both the rule and the responsibilities.

✦ —— ✦

On 9 June 2000, we – nine participants, two facilitators and myself as lead trainer – booked into a fifteen-storey concrete box off Moscow's Lenin Prospect, south of the river. There was no disguising the Hotel Akademicheskaya's Soviet pedigree. Despite my room looking out on a thirty-metre-high advert for Winston cigarettes, every item of furniture within bore an oval metal tag stamped with its ID number and the Cyrillic initials, CCCP.

The first days, once the conference was over and the real work began, were hardly auspicious. I had been doing the job long enough to recognise the signs. Only one of the journalists was taking notes, while the overlong coffee breaks seemed to be assuming more importance than the training sessions. But, I reminded myself, getting to know each other was part of the workshop's objective. So, perhaps the extended breaks could be serving a useful purpose. I then discovered that two of the participants had decided that the course would be a perfect opportunity for getting themselves baptised in Moscow. I was starting to think that Birmingham might have been a better venue.

By the half-way stage of the workshop, my Georgian coordinator, Zurab Khrikadze, and I were despairing. The dominant ethos among the participants was all too Soviet: avoid taking responsibility and let someone else do the work. My suspicion that the workshop was regarded as more of a holiday trip than a training opportunity was confirmed when, by chance, I bumped into one of the baptismal opportunists in Red Square with wife and children in tow. At least he had the grace to be embarrassed when I asked him whether the guidebook in his hand was proving useful.

For the second week – the production week – we put together the three teams, with a Georgian, Abkhazian and South Ossetian in each. This was to be the test of cooperation and productivity upon which the project had been predicated. Would it work? Would they bond and produce something that was more than the sum of its multi-ethnic parts? The whole exercise was taking on the scientific rigour of a laboratory experiment.

First, each team had to agree on a subject that could qualify as a news report. How hard could it be, with the entire capital of the former Soviet Union to plunder? After an eight-hour day for research, not one of our lab rats had come up with a single story. The three cameramen aside, the other six were all supposedly working journalists back home. One of them, a political reporter for Georgian State Television, whinged, 'The Russians won't talk to us because we're just little Georgians.' (Weeks later I would kick myself for not realising that 'A Moscow Baptism' would have made a perfect subject.)

As the teams struggled, one of them resorted to a refrain all too familiar during training courses when effort and initiative dry up: 'Why don't we make a story about ourselves?' As always, I resisted the idea as a lazy, incestuous cop-out but, reconsidering it, I decided it might be worth a shot if they were prepared to be totally honest about their differences and the way the workshop had changed their views of each other. I finally persuaded myself and my colleagues that, since journalism typically involved intrusion into other people's lives, thoughts and emotions, we should be equally capable of examining our own.

In the event, it turned out to be the best of the three video packages even if, technically, it wasn't a news report. It took the form of the two journalists, one male Abkhazian, the other female South Ossetian, filmed by their Georgian cameraman, taking in the sights of Moscow while discussing, with admirable candour, the changes in their perceptions of each other after a week of living, socialising and training together. It was precisely what the project had hoped to achieve and we were all struck by the video's raw honesty. Viewing it, I had that rare feeling, almost an epiphany: this madcap idea might just work! The video demonstrated that, at the level of the individual, connections could be made and reconciliation achieved. More subversively, it suggested that the problem might be the politicians. My colleagues were similarly impressed. Peter Šelepec, the OSCE's representative, felt the video, together with the other two packages (which had turned out better than expected), should be made into a compilation tape, not just as a record of the course but as a fundraising tool for future exercises with the same aim.

Just one problem. In some respects the perception changing package was *too* good. The Abkhazian journalist was worried. He reckoned that if the video were given a public airing, he would never be sent on another course; that voicing his favourable feelings about his Georgian cameraman might cause problems back home.

Had we perhaps, in our enthusiasm, miscalculated? Had we underestimated the very real security concerns for the individuals involved in our laboratory experiment, how difficult it might be for them to step out of line with their employer, their community . . . perhaps even their own family?

In the event, neither he, nor we, need have worried. None of the videos was ever shown on television, at a film festival or any other public screening. At the end of the opening conference it had been deemed significant, a breakthrough even, that the General Director of Abkhazian State Television had signed a 'Protocol of Intentions' which would facilitate an exchange of information between Abkhazian, South Ossetian and Georgian media outlets. Only weeks *after* the combined conference and workshop were the relevant questions asked: Did 'information' include video material? Did 'exchange' cover its possible broadcast? Frustratingly, I was back in the UK by the time these discussions took place but, in both cases, the answer was 'NO'. The Abkhazians, it seemed, feared that the broadcasting of the workshop's videos – whether on their own state channel or any other – could undermine the authority of their official negotiators in the peace process.

Technically, it would have been possible for Georgian State TV or Internews' affiliated stations to have aired the videos but that too ran the risk of ruffling diplomatic feathers. The depressing conclusion was that the more successful the exercise, the more likely it would be thwarted. Politics would trump journalism every time. The best we could argue was that we had proved our primary point: that television journalists from opposing sides were able to work together. It was just a pity that we couldn't show that proof to a wider, public audience.

However, the word, if not the picture, spread and two years later in 2002 the idea was picked up again by the London-based NGO, Conciliation Resources, which had been working with Abkhazian and Georgian journalists across the conflict divide since 1999. This time, the exercise was to be more focused, involve fewer people and – the big leap – the journalists would be reporting not on a news story of their choice but on the conflict in which their respective governments were combatants.

The plan was to take a pair of experienced Georgian film-makers and team them up with three Abkhazian TV journalists (one independent and two working for Abkhazian State TV) to form a single production unit. They would make two documentaries. One would be about those Georgians living in the disputed border region of Gali who, in the absence of a peace agreement, were regularly having to cross back and forth over the front line to maintain contact with friends and relatives. For the other report, complementing the first, it was decided to examine a parallel conflict that had been resolved by negotiation and send the team to Northern Ireland to see how the 1998 Good Friday Agreement between nationalists and loyalists had brought peace to the province after three decades of conflict and 3500 deaths. Among those they would interview was the Rev Ian Paisley, the leader of the Protestant Democratic Unionist Party.

This time, my role was one of oversight: regular email communication with the team, monitoring of the production process and a meeting in Oxford on their way home from Northern

Ireland so that I could view the Gali report in rough cut and the rushes of the Northern Ireland report. I had reason to be optimistic. The decision to see how peace had been achieved in Northern Ireland and ask what lessons might be applied to the Georgia/Abkhazia conflict was an astute one. Also, I had known both the Georgians, Mikheil Mirziashvili and Mamuka Kuparadze, for three years and respected their work as independent film-makers. They were professionals, had an impressive back catalogue in the reconciliation field and were in a different league from the teams we had taken to Moscow.

The end product was competent but, if I'm brutally honest, disappointing. There were two issues. First, on account of the shoestring budget – miniscule compared with a mainstream media budget – no time had been allowed for on-the-ground research. Instead, the team had researched as they went – a smash-and-grab operation. In news there is often no alternative but these were documentaries and if only one of the journalists had spent a few days on location prior to the filming, choosing the best families to focus on, it would have made a world of difference.

Second, there was no overall Producer with a capital 'P', because, in a spirit of equality between Georgians and Abkhazians, neither side wanted to assume the leadership role. Thus, the project became a victim of its own laudable sensitivity. No surprise then that the result resembled a work made by a committee – more of a camel than a horse. Understandable but regrettable.

Even so, two important messages came through: that journalists from opposing sides could work together in a respectful and productive partnership and, regarding the conflict itself, peace was possible when both sides were prepared to make concessions; that if the seemingly intractable 'troubles' in Northern Ireland could be resolved by negotiation and good will, there had to be hope for a similar resolution of the Georgia/Abkhazia conflict.

If the Moscow exercise had scored five out of ten, this was a clear seven. It was a stretch to claim the format had *proved* that journalists could make a meaningful contribution to peacemaking, but it showed the potential. The joint team also went on to make more films together, one in Abkhazia, the other in Georgia.

✦ ———— ✦

A couple of years later, in 2006, Conciliation Resources extended its interest to another regional conflict. The project was called *Dialogue Through Film* and involved partnerships with Internews' offices in Armenia and Azerbaijan, and the Stepanakert Press Club. Although I took no part, I naturally followed the exercise with interest.

The chosen zone this time was the Nagorno-Karabakh region that had been fought over by Armenia and Azerbaijan even when they were still members of the Soviet Union. Before it ended in 2023, an estimated 35,000 people would lose their lives.

The Nagorno-Karabakh enclave was internationally recognised as belonging to Azerbaijan but most of the population were ethnic Armenians who regarded it as *their* home. In January 1990, as the fatigue cracks opened in the Soviet system, the long-simmering dispute came to a head with what came to be called 'The Baku Pogrom'. Over seven days and nights, Armenians living in the Azerbaijani capital's Armenian Quarter were beaten – some of them murdered – and driven out of their homes as their Azerbaijani attackers, furnished with lists of addresses, went from apartment to apartment on a rampage of ethnic violence while the authorities stood by. There were reports of Armenians being thrown off rooftops, through windows, burned alive and literally torn to pieces. A decade later when working in Baku, I heard at first hand from one of those targeted – an Armenian woman, married to an Azerbaijani:

> When they came to our block, I had to hide in a cupboard. It was only thanks to my Azerbaijani neighbours that I survived. But my mother and other members of our family, along with many friends ... they all fled to Moscow. My mother never came back, not even for the funeral of my elder sister. The attacks stopped but not the hatred. I lost my job ... then, when our daughter's Azerbaijani boyfriend proposed to her, his father discovered I was Armenian and forbade the marriage.

The 2006 Conciliation Resources filming project followed the by-now established model. Television journalists were drawn from the opposing sides with an emphasis on youth, and this time including both press and radio journalists wishing to explore a new medium. Like the 2002 Georgia/Abkhazia co-production, they would make a documentary about 'the hopes, fears, sadness and humour' of those living in the region with the consequences of the conflict.

But with one difference. In a 180-degree reversal of previous projects, there would be no mixing of the two sides. Instead, each side would form its *own* team of its *own* people. Thus configured, the young Azerbaijanis would make three films reflecting the experience of the Azerbaijani population while, on the other side, the young Armenians would make three films reflecting the experience of their people. In other words, they would be working professionally from their different perspectives just as their countries had for years been confronting each other politically and militarily.

How anyone thought this might be a recipe for reconciliation, I couldn't begin to comprehend. Everything I had learnt about journalists' potential to contribute to peacemaking told me it made no sense at any level. It was like picking at a scab.

The completed films were given a public airing in September 2007 at the Institute of Contemporary Arts, the ICA, in London to which I was invited. Sitting on a stage at the front of the auditorium below the screen were a representative each of Armenia and Azerbaijan, with Jonathan Cohen, Conciliation Resources' Co-Director of their Caucasus Program, acting as moderator. The format of the evening was that the Azerbaijani and Armenian films would be projected alternately, followed by a Q&A session with those involved in the productions.

The result was a 'shouting-shop' as each side, when given the floor and sometimes when not, accused the other of lies and distortion, with members of the audience piling on. It was as though the entire Nagorno-Karabakh conflict were being re-enacted in a theatrical production. I saw no evidence of reconciliation, not even of an agreement to disagree.

When I recently put this to Cohen, now Conciliation Resources' Executive Director (we have remained on cordial terms over the intervening years), he preferred, 'A robust and even uncomfortable discussion – part of a peacebuilding process'. He described it as 'the start of a process . . . to enable the journalists to develop their film-making and narration experiences'. And he explained the reason for the policy reversal. While the Armenian authorities might have been open to persuasion, there had been no willingness by the Azerbaijani authorities to have mixed teams. In fact, neither side had allowed the other to cross the shared border to make films.

Cohen also suggested that the volatile atmosphere at the ICA could have been due to the presence of officials from the respective embassies. As a result, he said, 'journalists who can collaborate might not be at ease speaking in public about the collaboration because it exposes them in a different way, and to an extent they revert to antagonism as a way to protect themselves'. Welcome to the topsy-turvy world of peacemaking and reconciliation!

Given all of this – the inability to mix the teams and the probability of there being embassy staff in the audience – I was left wondering how anyone could have thought the ICA public screening was a good idea.

Fortunately, that wasn't the end of Conciliation Resources' involvement in the conflict. Thanks to some creative thinking, some of the later films in the *Dialogue Through Film* project did involve joint production. To get around the travel bans, the shooting was done separately in Armenia, Azerbaijan and Nagorno-Karabakh, but the journalists would come together for the edit and scripting in a neutral country, most conveniently neighbouring Georgia. The result was a number of genuinely collaborative productions. As one of the Azerbaijani scriptwriters, Nailya Babayeva, says of her experience working with her Armenian counterpart, Armine Martirosyan:

At the beginning of the project, there was a lot of suspicion on both sides. All the stereotypes in both our countries came to the fore. But if you have the will, with some trust and faith, it is possible to find a way out of the dead-end. And that's what happened with our Armenian colleagues. We didn't shy away from misunderstandings but at the same time we didn't let them turn into something more. Like normal people, we tried to find a solution which would suit us all. During the course of the project, I learned to listen and to give way. I'm not afraid to say that I made a good friend on the Armenian side. It's not right for peacebuilding projects to divide people into Armenians and Azerbaijanis. In projects like these it's not your nationality that is the main thing; it's your common cause and shared efforts.[2]

Most of the films have been broadcast on Armenian television, as well as in some Central Asian countries, though not in Azerbaijan. They are online and have been viewed by several thousand people at public outreach events where the showings were followed by discussion.

—◆———◆—

Arguably the most successful example of 'collaboration in conflict' to come out of the Nagorno-Karabakh conflict was a series of films made between 2012 and 2019. Again, thanks to the support of Conciliation Resources.

It was titled *Parts of a Circle* and was an attempt by many of those who had worked on the earlier films to produce a joint history of events up to 2016. (Proof, Cohen suggests, that relationships require time and patience to develop meaningful cooperation.) An agreed history would be to overstate the result because again events are seen from contrasting perspectives. But this time the exercise seems to have been a calmer, more cathartic one, perhaps because it was an effort to process the past, to see events in context, and in some cases, from a distance of twenty years. Each side still argues its case but now, significantly, the viewer is given a role: to 'triangulate' the opposing narratives.

In part, inevitably perhaps, it's a balancing act. Although, for example, the pogroms against the Armenians were widely reported at the time, the films acknowledge there were also pogroms against the Azerbaijanis which were less well covered. *Parts of a Circle* is an impressive and innovative exercise, quite apart from being an invaluable historical resource for future generations. It is also available online. It's not peacemaking as such but, in its own way, it's an act of reconciliation.

+———+

As matters turned out, the Nagorno-Karabakh conflict would be resolved by neither television nor reconciliation, but by force. In 2023, the Azerbaijanis blockaded the region and followed up with a military offensive which led to almost all of the region's 120,000 Armenian residents fleeing over the border into Armenia itself. Within days, Nagorno-Karabakh became *de facto* what it had long been *de jure*: part of Azerbaijan.

So, was the journalists' contribution to the peace process a waste of effort because the process itself ultimately failed? Far from it. The conflict may have been resolved militarily but the geography remains the same. Armenia and Azerbaijan are still neighbours, sharing a thousand-kilometre border. With the propensity for grievance on one side and triumphalism on the other, the need for reconciliation is arguably greater now than ever.

Jonathan Cohen is wary of claims that collaborative productions lead to reconciliation. Too big an ask, he reckons, when such small-scale films are up against the antagonistic rhetoric of state-controlled media. What they can do, he believes, is 'help keep the flame of an alternative perspective alive'. He remains, though, a realist. 'When I think of the resources invested in peacebuilding compared with the resources invested in militarisation, is it any wonder that the forces of war are often stronger?'

28.

THE LUXURY OF HINDSIGHT

One of those I asked to read a pre-publication draft of this book – an ex-BBC colleague who was once my editor – wondered why I had carried on working in the post-Soviets for so long, given all the frustrations and failures that I describe.

The first thing to say is that I plead guilty to the journalistic tendency to focus on cats that are lost rather than cats that are found. There will, I am sure, be those who will say the often-depressing picture I've painted is unrepresentative. In defence, I can only respond that this book is what it says on the cover, 'a foot-soldier's story' – told from the confines of the trenches, not from High Command with its sweep of the entire battlefield. It is for others – a general or field marshal – to paint the broader picture. (In fact, David Hoffman, one of the founders of Internews, did just that in his magisterial 2013 book, *Citizens Rising: Independent Journalism and the Spread of Democracy*. Time for an update, David?) What I have described is what I have seen and, in that respect, it is representative of my experience.

My former employers – Internews Network and the Thomson Foundation – do an extraordinary job and I would be the last person to suggest that their funders are wasting their money. What I do say is that the money doesn't always produce the hoped-for results. There will inevitably be an element of hit and miss when working in hostile political environments, sometimes actual conflict zones, trying to achieve what are frequently impossible ends. The fact that I have been involved with a disproportionate number of the misses may say more about me than about my employers. (I did wonder whether the book should be titled not *After the Fall* but, *Heading for a Fall*.) Alternatively, there is the medical analogy of the surgeon who has more patients expire on his operating table than his colleagues – not because he is less competent but because he has been given more complicated cases with less chance of a successful outcome. I'm just putting it out there.

As to why I carried on working in the post-Soviets, the short answer is that it became my job. It paid the bills. Working as a media consultant was a natural extension of my journalistic career, the next chapter. I was also aware that I had the luck, the privilege, to be a witness to one of the hinges of history. Anyone who had followed the transition from Gorbachev to Yeltsin knew the Putin era would be no less momentous.

It's tempting to add in these situations that one wanted to give something back and, although it wasn't the motivating factor, I was of course happy to do so. It's in the nature of training and consultancy, however, that one becomes aware of any good one might have done only years later, and often in a roundabout way.

In August 2007, a producer for the BBC Russian Service in London's Bush House made a call to Novosibirsk TV in Siberia to follow up a story about a woman who kept 160 cats in her small apartment. He talked to Elena. At the end of the call, Elena asked the producer if he knew Michael Delahaye, an ex-BBC TV reporter who had trained her a few years earlier. Doubtless with an indulgent sigh, the producer responded, 'You have to understand, the BBC is a massive organisation, employing over 20,000 people across hundreds of different buildings. We're just the Russian Service, a tiny cog in a huge machine, and it's highly unlikely that anyone here would know Michael Delahaye . . .'

Hearing her colleague mention my name, a Georgian producer on the other side of the room shouted that she too had been trained by Michael Delahaye, in Tbilisi in 2001 – and yes, she knew him!

That producer was Natia Abramia. Of the more than 500 post-Soviet journalists I must have trained or advised, Natia is one of those I recall with most pride. After working as a TV presenter and correspondent in her native Georgia where she attended one of my courses, she won a UK Foreign Office Chevening Scholarship to study for an MA in International Journalism at Cardiff University in Wales. She returned to join Georgia's premier independent TV station Rustavi-2 as a documentary producer but, a few years later, was back in the UK after being recruited by the BBC Russian Service. For over a decade she worked as a BJ, a broadcast journalist, for the BBC World Service News & Current Affairs Department before moving to the *Newsnight* television program as a producer. She currently works for the corporation's Strategy & Transformation Office, reporting to the Director General. (In 2012, Natia very nearly became Director General of Georgia's *own* public service broadcaster, the GPB. In the final shortlist of five candidates, she came runner-up.)

There is more. No matter how busy she is, Natia returns every year to her native Georgia to train mid-career journalists – a commitment which she generously attributes to the influence my training had on her back in 2001.

So, here we are, a quarter of a century later. After I trained Natia and her generation, she now trains the next generation of her compatriots. It's hard not to feel a satisfying circularity.

My personal motivation aside, there is a bigger, more pertinent, question. One of the dangers of giving a book a subtitle is that, even if the interrogative is only implied, it still requires an answer at some point. That point has arrived. So, 'The battle to save independent media in the post-Soviet world' . . . Did we win?

There is a poem by the Englishman Arthur Hugh Clough, much loved and often quoted by his fellow countrymen, which begins, 'Say not the struggle naught availeth'. It concludes, 'In front the sun climbs slow, how slowly! But westward, look, the land is bright!' The same might be said when rating media independence in the countries of the post-communist world thirty-five years since the fall of the Berlin Wall. The farther west you look, the brighter is the landscape.

We're talking broadly about three geopolitical entities: 1. Russia (more accurately, the vast Russian Federation); 2. the fourteen other Soviet republics that made up the Union; 3. the former Eastern Bloc comprising the six countries of the Warsaw Pact (excluding the defunct Soviet Union); along with the half-dozen republics of Yugoslavia which, though politically non-aligned, were notionally communist until their breakup in the early 1990s.

The Russian Federation: We lost. And our failure in Russia remains the biggest blot on our record. It is possible that we – the West, its leaders, journalist-training NGOs and those of us sent in as boots on the ground – could never have won. But it is also possible that we miscalculated.

When the Soviet Union collapsed, it was hard to repress the relief, elation even, that the ideology that had represented the greatest threat to our existence since the end of the Second World War had evaporated in a series of events no one could have imagined. For all the exhortations to avoid triumphalism, there was no denying that our twin ideologies, democracy and capitalism, had proved superior to theirs; no matter that communism had succumbed not after a head-to-head confrontation but beneath the weight of unrealised expectations. Such was the euphoria that there was even talk, serious talk, of disbanding NATO. With no longer an adversary, what was its point?

During the Yeltsin years (1991–1999), careful to cast ourselves now as benefactors rather than victors, we gifted democracy and capitalism to those who had lived under the failed system. The generosity was not entirely altruistic. Conversion to our way of thinking and governing made strategic sense, as it had in the case of Germany and Japan following their defeat in the Second World War. That aside, like most benefactors, we expected our gifts to be appreciated – or at least received uncritically.

Those of us who worked as consultants and trainers with the new generation of post-Soviet Russian journalists never doubted that democracy and the watchdog role it accords journalists was 'the true path'. To that extent, we were evangelists and, yes, proselytisers. I don't think we were ever condescending, certainly not arrogant, but we should perhaps have been more mindful of Russian sensitivities. The journalists I worked with were mostly in their twenties and thirties, their lives roughly split between communism and democracy/capitalism. I never detected any nostalgia for the old order, but that didn't mean they didn't still harbour feelings of patriotic pride – not for the Soviet Union but for their own now-former Soviet republic.

While communism may have been consigned to the scrapheap

of history, Russia remained – politically gutted, economically crippled and militarily weakened but with its past contribution and continuing relevance to the world undiminished. It was our failure to appreciate this which, I would argue, deprived us of foresight.

Russia's thousand-year timeline is studded with iconic figures – Ivan the Terrible, Peter the Great, Catherine the Great, Alexander II[1] and, no less, Vladimir Ilyich Ulyanov, aka Lenin. It has the distinction of having produced not one but *two* successive empires: the Russian Empire under the Romanovs, followed by the Soviet Union ruled from Moscow. During the nineteenth century it had also been a cultural beacon to the world in literature and music – Tolstoy and Tchaikovsky being just two of the greats it gave us. In the twentieth century too. Apart from the artists Chagall and Kandinsky and composers Shostakovich, Prokofiev and Rachmaninoff (who emigrated to the US after the October Revolution), Russians can rightly claim that in the 1920s the Soviet film-makers Eisenstein, Pudovkin and Kuleshov helped lay the foundations of world cinema. Other pioneering directors followed, even if sometimes like Andrei Tarkovsky in opposition to, rather than support of, the Soviet system.

In geopolitical terms, the events of 1991 were cataclysmic. With its former empire reduced by a quarter and no longer driven by an ideology, Russia lost its status as a superpower, leaving the field to America and China. As late as 2014, President Obama felt able to dismiss Russia as a regional power, arguing that Vladimir Putin's invasion of Crimea was an indication not of strength but of weakness.[2]

Obama's casual contempt for Putin was misplaced. What he, and we, didn't foresee was the ability of this slight figure, strutting like a wind-up toy and seemingly devoid of demagogic charisma (or, in Obama's words, 'looking like the bored kid in the back of the classroom')[3] to tap into his compatriots' crushed patriotism and project himself as the leader who would restore global respect for *Matushka Rossiya*, Mother Russia.

Angus Roxburgh, the BBC's Moscow correspondent in the 1990s, makes a similar point, arguing that the West conflated the ideology with the nation. While it was understandable that the other Soviet republics should regard their declarations of independence as liberation from Russian occupation, this obscured the fact that the Russian people too had been oppressed by communism and, with its collapse, saw themselves as no less liberated. According to Roxburgh, 'Russia needed our help even more than the Eastern Europeans did'. Instead, we in the West treated Russians as if they were still the enemy. Taking the other republics into the NATO fold made them feel unwanted and distrusted. Had the West not seeded this sense of rejection, Roxburgh argues, we might have been spared Vladimir Putin.[4]

Putin's belief that Russia had been not just disrespected but cheated was fuelled by a personal, enduring rancour. In February 2022, justifying the 'special military operation' against Ukraine, he felt obliged to deliver a history lesson, to remind his domestic audience how the West had exploited Russia's weakness:

> We lost confidence for only one moment, but it was enough to disrupt the balance of forces in the world . . . We saw a state of euphoria created by the feeling of absolute superiority, a kind of modern absolutism, coupled with the low cultural standards and arrogance of those who formulated and pushed through decisions that suited only themselves . . . They have deceived us, or, to put it simply, they have played us.[5]

While there were those like Obama who underestimated Putin, others misread him, continuing to believe he was a democrat at heart who favoured peace and cooperation with the West. As Yeltsin's chief of staff, Valentin Yumashev observed, 'Putin was like a blank canvas. Anybody's dream could be drawn on that canvas'.[6]

And yet the signs of Putin's autocratic streak were evident within months of his winning the presidential election in March 2000. One of his first acts was to place the country's 89 regional governors under the control of seven personally appointed 'super governors'. Then in late 2004, following the Beslan school siege, he signed into law a bill to cancel direct popular elections for the regional governors; the president would appoint them too, 'to improve national security'. From then on, they would all be the 'Tsar's Men'.[7] Nobody could, or should, have been in any doubt: Putin was extending his grasp across all eleven time zones of the Russian Federation.

✦————✦

TV2 in the university city of Tomsk was one of the Siberian stations I spent a week with as a consultant in June 2002. In previous chapters I have quoted its editor-in-chief, Victor Muchnik. Now, coming up to date, is the time to recount the station's history in detail, because the rise and demise of TV2 exactly tracks Vladimir Putin's curtailing of democracy generally and media freedom specifically.

TV2 went on air in May 1991 during the last gasp of the Gorbachev era – one of the 600 or so startup stations which took advantage of the relaxed political climate of the time and which, like many of them, unashamedly filled its schedule with pirated Western movies. But, from its earliest days, TV2 stood out from the pack, becoming the model of what a regional television station should be: locally engaged, financially sound (Oligarch Mikhail Khodorkovsky had invested in its holding company, TMG), editorially independent and offering its viewers an alternative to the state-controlled network news beamed out of the capital. TV2's charter called for the station to provide viewers with 'truthful, complete and verifiable information'. Its symbol was a cat – not any cat, but Rudyard Kipling's 'Just So' cat, the one who 'walked by himself and all places were alike to him'.

Two things made TV2 different. First, its founder Arkady Maiofis was a former reporter for state television; a man who, unlike all the chancers and amateurs who jumped on the broadcasting bandwagon, knew how television worked, its technical nuts and organisational bolts. Second, Maiofis persuaded Victor Muchnik, a history professor still in his early forties, to come on board. Muchnik brought a unique perspective to the station. His academic knowledge of the past enabled him to see the big picture and spot the news stories that, in hindsight, would be seen as turning points. (Victor's wife, Victoria, joined him as the station's news editor and his sister, Yulia, as a presenter and producer.) Thus, TV2 became a regional station that afforded its viewers a national and, later, even international outlook. There were times when the viewers in Tomsk knew more about what was going on in Russia and beyond than any other viewers in the entire federation, its capital included. Arkady Maiofis and Victor Muchnik made a formidable duo.

The station's first scoop was the August Coup of 1991 when hardline political opponents of Mikhail Gorbachev held the president and his wife prisoner in their Crimean holiday home in an ultimately abortive attempt to restore old-style Soviet rule. Following the conspirators' playbook, the plotters took control of the state broadcasters (transmitting on a loop a performance of *Swan Lake*, as had been the practice when past Soviet leaders were on their deathbeds and a successor urgently sought), but it seemingly never occurred to them that an independent station out in the wilds of Siberia would have a camera crew in the capital and send pictures back to Tomsk courtesy of obliging Aeroflot pilots. The result: for three days, TV2's regional audience got a virtual running commentary on the drama as it unfolded.

After Yeltsin succeeded Gorbachev and Putin succeeded Yeltsin, the station maintained its maverick status, conducting interviews with both of Putin's high-profile political opponents, Boris Nemtsov and Alexei Navalny, at a time when state television was under orders to deny them the oxygen of publicity.

Maiofis and Muchnik knew the risks. In 2007 they received unofficial warnings that independent journalism had its limits and the one thing *off*-limits was any attack on Putin himself.

Undeterred, in late 2013, in a move even more likely to earn the president's displeasure, they sent a team to the Ukrainian capital, Kyiv, to report the first stirrings of popular discontent with the Russian-backed government of Viktor Yanukovych. The Maidan Revolution followed. Yanukovych fled to Moscow and Ukraine aligned itself with the West.

The messenger duly paid the price. When TV2's licence came up for renewal at the end of 2014, Russia's media regulator Roskomnadzor and the telecom operator RTRS effectively combined efforts to block the application. This was followed by the liquidation of other media outlets affiliated with TV2. Its last program went out on the last day of the year, New Year's Eve 2014 – followed by boss Arkady Maiofis' emigration to Israel. (One of the suspicions that allegedly prompted the Kremlin's action was that TV2 intended to launch a satellite channel, broadcasting its 'alternative' news and funded by Khodorkovsky who had been released from prison a year earlier. Muchnik dismisses the idea as 'a delusional fantasy of some FSB major'.)

Now under Victor Muchnik's leadership, the former TV station was reborn as a website, shedding all but fifteen of its 250 employees. During the COVID pandemic of 2020/22, it continued to break stories critical of the authorities that the mainstream media failed to cover.

The invasion of Ukraine in February 2022 gave Putin the perfect pretext to silence rogue media with the threat of jail for 'the public dissemination of knowingly false information' about Russia's armed forces. But for TV2, the game was already up. The licence-granting authority, Roskomnadzor, had once again stepped in – this time to shut down the TV2 website, the only platform still generating advertising revenue. Faced with the possibility of prison for both himself and his journalists, Muchnik felt he had no choice but to suspend operations. He and his wife Victoria left Tomsk and moved to Prague where, using the YouTube platform, they now chronicle the views of those whose lives have been impacted by Putin's 'special military operation'. They see no hope of returning to Russia unless there is a change of leadership. But, as Muchnik ruefully notes, cats – not just Kipling's 'Just So' cat – proverbially have nine lives.

The fate of TV2 was shared by countless more media organisations. John J. Sullivan, the US ambassador in Moscow from 2020 to 2022, saw the impact of Putin's clampdown at first hand: 'The widespread designations of independent media organizations and journalists as "foreign agents" . . . eventually drove almost all of them out of business or at least out of the country.'[8]

And, if the 'foreign agent' tactic didn't get them, the reporting restrictions imposed during the Ukraine war would. BBC Monitoring's assessment in March 2023 built on Sullivan's: 'Since the start of the invasion of Ukraine . . . nearly all independent media outlets in Russia have shut down, been forced to close, or have left the country to operate from exile.'

At the time of writing, Radio Free Europe/Radio Liberty (RFE/RL), which is funded by the U.S. Congress and in February 2024 was labelled not just a 'foreign agent' but an 'undesirable organisation', has felt it necessary to warn its Russian audience: 'If you comment, share, like, save or otherwise react to our content on any platform, you could be endangering yourself.' Scary stuff.

Even displaying a combination of colours – specifically, the blue and yellow of the Ukrainian flag – could get you into trouble. In April 2024, Antonida Smolina, a journalist in the Vologda Region, reported being visited by the police after she was denounced for posting online a photo of herself wearing a yellow jacket against a blue(ish) sky.[9]

No doubt the sun has been put on notice.

The Former Soviet Republics: Looking beyond Russia to the other fourteen Soviet republics, it is now clear that 'the triumph of Western values' was partial at best. In terms of the battle for media independence, we lost in those reborn republics that remained under autocratic rule, but there is reason for optimism in those facing West, such as Armenia, Moldova, Georgia, Ukraine (in Georgia's case, currently less so), as well as the Baltic states of Latvia, Lithuania and Estonia, which have joined the European Union (more later).

In many cases it comes down to leverage: the West's ability to make media freedom, or at least tolerance, a condition of financial aid, protection against a newly belligerent Russia or support in seeking membership of NATO and/or the EU. This partly explains why we have little or no leverage when dealing with those former Soviets that are resource-rich: Azerbaijan (oil and gas), Uzbekistan (oil, gas and gold), Kazakhstan (oil, gas and uranium) and of course Russia itself (oil, gas . . . and a lot of both).

It's not just their economic independence that has made these states impervious to external pressure. Internal politics have also played their part. Following the 1991 collapse, there was an optimistic assumption that Western values would spread like a benign virus through the former Soviet republics; that democracy would take root and, with it, media freedom. That is not what happened.

Looking back, it is remarkable how many of those leaders who had formerly implemented the old discredited communist ideology came to power or remained in power post-transition: Aleksandr Lukashenko in Belarus, Islam Karimov in Uzbekistan, Nursultan Nazarbayev in Kazakhstan, Askar Akayev in Kyrgyzstan. Or, after a break, returned to power: former Soviet Foreign Minister Eduard Shevardnadze to Georgia and former member of the Soviet Politburo Heydar Aliyev to Azerbaijan.

No less significant is that, to date, eight of the presidents of the fifteen former Soviets have rewritten – or, if now deceased, rewrote – their national constitutions to extend their terms in office, most notably Vladimir Putin himself. Meanwhile in Azerbaijan, the Aliyev family shows every sign of going one step further and establishing a ruling dynasty.

Perhaps it shouldn't have come as a surprise. Continuity of leadership was a comfort for those who had lived most of their lives – or, in the case of those under seventy-five, their *entire* lives – under the Soviet system. Continuity meant stability. At least there was someone in charge who knew how to operate the levers of power rather than an ideological ingenu, fresh from a crash course in London or Washington, flailing around in the control room. In truth, back in the 1990s, there were many who believed, and hoped, that democracy and capitalism would be short-lived. To a degree, history has proved them right.

But autocrats cannot be entirely blamed. From what I saw on the ground in the late 1990s and early 2000s, one of the principal reasons independent journalism struggled to take root in the crucial first decade of the post-communist era was that the economic environment couldn't sustain it. Capitalism, like democracy, was in some places barely understood, let alone implemented.[10] As one of the media consultants drafted in, I often felt that I was delivering an IKEA flat pack without the instruction sheet. At best, I was the Allen key; useful but not enough to build the wardrobe.

It's an old media aphorism but true: you cannot have editorial independence without first having financial independence. But for the hundreds of regional television stations, attaining that financial independence required a fully functioning media marketplace. And what applied to television stations applied no less to individual journalists.

Journalists may think of themselves as fulfilling a unique role in society, members of a profession rather than a craft or trade, but they are workers like any other. To survive, they need a demand for their 'product' and a minimum income. They don't have to have an employer, but it certainly helps. (At various times in my own career, I've been BBC staff, BBC contract and an independent documentary maker for both public service and commercial broadcasters.)

In the West, in those countries with functioning market economies, these criteria are broadly fulfilled. Demand and competition ensure that in the UK, the US and Australia, staff and contract jobs are available for journalists on all platforms, whether print, online, radio or television, in both the public and private sectors. Journalism is a hard profession to get into but, with persistence and a bit of luck, you can earn a living. Freelancers too. Not an easy existence but, with drive and talent, possible. And of course, with training, whether discrete or provided in-house by an employer.

But here's the rub: training is wasted unless it leads to meaningful employment. Over the period this book covers, many of us, broadcast consultants and trainers, would occasionally raise a delicate question: 'Why are we training people who cannot, in any meaningful sense, use what we're giving them?' Either because they didn't have the chance to put our training into practice; or because they weren't being paid a living wage. Or both. The ones we had most in mind were those working for small regional television stations, many of which treated their news staff like slave labour.

A male participant on one of my six-week courses in Azerbaijan personified the sort of young television journalist who was going to make a difference. Presenter, reporter, interviewer – Fuad was a natural. I duly gave him a glowing report at the end of the course and was gratified by his enthusiasm for the glittering career that we both believed lay ahead. Four months later, I got an email from Internews Azerbaijan to tell me that Fuad had left his TV station 'for economic reasons'. Worse, he had abandoned his career in television. Despite his obvious talent and a fluency in English, the station had been paying him thirty-five dollars a month. No matter how he cut it, he couldn't support his family. So when a local bank offered him *two hundred* dollars a month, he had taken it. Six weeks of USAID-funded training down the drain.

The Eastern Bloc and The Former Yugo-Republics: All the members of the Eastern Bloc – those satellite states formerly in the Soviet sphere – have been absorbed into the European Union: Bulgaria, the former Czechoslovakia (now the Czech Republic and

Slovakia), the former East Germany (since reunification, part of the Federal Republic of Germany), Hungary, Poland and Romania. They join the three Baltic republics already mentioned: Estonia, Latvia and Lithuania. Finally, two of the six former Yugo-republics – Slovenia and Croatia – have also become EU members.

Every one of these countries can now lay claim to media freedom, whether in terms of their governments recognising it or their journalists benefitting from it. Article 11 of the EU's Charter of Fundamental Rights requires that 'The freedom and pluralism of the media shall be respected'. It is further enshrined (in more detail) in Article 10 of the European Convention on Human Rights. Indeed, during the lengthy admission process that leads to EU membership, a guarantee of media freedom is regarded as a 'key indicator'.

But media freedom can be a nebulous concept, particularly in relation to national broadcasters.

All EU countries have them and, one way or another, they all need to be funded. Advertising revenue and income from the sale of programs can help but in most cases it's 'the state' that pays, even when it is euphemistically described as 'the public'. It's a fine – some would say, disingenuous – distinction. The money may come directly from the government's consolidated revenue fund or, more obliquely, as an earmarked percentage of income tax. Or indirectly, via a compulsory levy or licence fee processed through the machinery of the state. In this regard, it's worth repeating that even the BBC's much vaunted licence fee, which the corporation collects directly from the public, is a hypothecated tax that has to be periodically negotiated with the government of the day.

And the effect of this linkage? It would be naïve to think that the principle of not biting the hand that feeds you applies any less to public broadcasting than to every other area of human activity. Self-censorship, hard though it is to detect, can never be wholly discounted. Closely question any editor who says, 'We must choose our battles, and this is not one of them'.

Similarly, charters and conventions. Reassuringly carved in metaphorical stone though they may be, they are by nature declamatory rather than reflective of reality. What may look like an unequivocal principle on paper – 'the freedom and pluralism of the media shall be respected' – can turn out in practice to be a picnic for the bureaucrats and lawyers. Take as an example the issuing and revoking of broadcasting licences. Or look at the situation in Hungary (note: an EU member, though described by the European Parliament as an 'electoral autocracy'),[11] where premier Viktor Orban's government has ensured the supposedly public broadcaster supports his political party, Fidesz, while starving independent channels of advertising revenue or using Fidesz-friendly proxies to buy them out.[12]

In this context, it is worth noting the 2024 findings of the State Media Monitor organisation. Globally, it reports, 'the number of media outlets falling under government control continues to grow', while in the case of Europe, there has for the first time been 'a notable shift toward a state-controlled model'. It adds, 'The number of [European] media outlets . . . representing the form of absolute state-controlled media, has increased from 24 in 2023 to 31 in 2024'.

Despite these caveats, there is no question that for the former communist states, the EU guarantees are better than what went before. Democracy does make a difference. As the BBC has found over its hundred-year history, the best defence against government interference is public support and, when needed, public outcry with the implied threat of action, not on the barricades but at the ballot box.

At the time of writing, former communist states make up eleven of the current twenty-seven members of the European Union (not counting East Germany which in effect joined the EU when Germany was reunified in 1990). Impressive as that figure is, it doesn't tell the whole story when discussing media freedom. Membership of the EU provides umbrella protection but, at the regional level, association and cooperation with other broadcasters offer more consequential benefits.

Circom Regional, a broadcasters' organisation created in 1983 to promote 'the European idea' while strengthening the regional identities within it, now comprises 233 regional TV stations in the public service sector across 30 European countries. (Full disclosure: for five years, 2007–2011, I was lead trainer for the annual Circom Summer Academy in Nuremberg, funded by the Robert Bosch Foundation.)

A key part of Circom's role in supporting media freedom is journalist training, along with the exchange of knowledge and experience – journalistic, technical, financial, legal and managerial. In this respect, it's doing for Europe what Internews did for Russia and some of the other former Soviet republics. As a result, arguably its greatest contribution has been empowerment, bringing together those regional TV stations in Eastern Europe that for decades never knew editorial independence, with those in Western Europe that have long assumed it as a right.[13]

—————

If there is any final thought in these closing paragraphs, it is that, when it comes to promoting and protecting media freedom, there is no avoiding politics. Politics is both the problem and, potentially, the solution. On a balance of plusses and minuses, independent journalism has benefited from two tectonic shifts since the end of the Second World War: the collapse of one union, the Soviet, and the creation and expansion of another, the European. But the minus column cannot be ignored. The farther east you look, the darker the clouds, the fewer the rays of hope.

As catalysts of instant change, revolutions might reasonably be thought a likely source of media freedom. History suggests otherwise. Too often, those behind the revolution – happy to have used the media before – demand its subservience to 'the cause', once in power. There is no better example than the October Revolution itself.

Coming back to my own specialism. In those authoritarian countries where it is most needed, the training of journalists has been seen to carry the seeds of its own destruction: the more successful the training, the greater the repression. Look no further than the fate of Internews Russia. A healthy, functioning democracy recognises the need for independent media – the Fourth Estate – to monitor its performance, expose corruption, hold those in power to account and, crucially, inform the electorate. But you don't get all, or any, of that if you don't first have the democracy. You cannot start from a base of autocracy.

NOTES AND SNIPS

It's usual, certainly with academic works, to add exhaustive chapter notes citing sources. All rather dry and with strings of *ibids*. This is a little different. Apart from indicating sources where the text doesn't, it includes tangential thoughts and information which got squeezed out because they took the narrative down a cul-de-sac. *Ah, the warmed-up left-overs!* you'll be thinking. Not so. Rather, a selection of bon-bons to round off the meal. Compliments of the management.

Note re sources: Because internet URLs can be subject to loss, squatting, corruption and malware, I have sought instead to provide enough detail to enable the use of a search engine.

THE MEDIA LANDSCAPE

1   Although the *khrushchevki* played a crucial role in the development of Russian independent broadcasting, they are also associated with an appalling blunder by the Soviet central planners – which anyone who has visited Russia in June may recall less than fondly. Hoping to give the new housing estates an 'established' look, the planners ordered the planting of a cheap, fast-growing species of balsam poplar. Unfortunately, little attempt seems to have been made to distinguish between the male and female of the species. A pity, because, on reaching maturity, the female produces white, fluffy seed-bunches similar to cotton balls which, when not filling the air like a blizzard, settle in drifts and ankle-deep carpets. It's called 'pook' and is regarded as a curse – not just in Russia but across the former Soviet Union where the poplars were also planted. The good news

is that they are now coming to the end of their 70-year natural lives.

2   There's an intriguing parallel between what happened when Yeltsin unleashed capitalism in the early 1990s and the early 1920s when Lenin, to the despair of his older Bolshevik comrades, introduced the New Economic Policy and, with it, a significant element of free enterprise. The NEP created the so-called NEPmen, while 70 years on, the Yeltsin era saw the rise of the New Russians. Different times but the same phenomenon: a breed of suddenly enriched opportunists keen to flaunt their wealth. While the intention may have been to stimulate the economy, the effect was to highlight social inequality.

3   Valentin Yumashev, Boris Yeltsin's son-in-law and chief-of-staff, compared the times to an alcoholic binge: 'We were given so much freedom . . . we drank so much freedom, we were poisoned by it.' As quoted by Catherine Belton of the *Washington Post*.

4   I've been astonished in writing this book how often quotations from the Soviet era, the attributions of which I thought were set in stone, have turned out otherwise. 'Death solves all problems. No man, no problem' – so frequently credited to Stalin – is a case in point. The online consensus is that the phrase was actually coined by Anatoly Rybakov in his novel, *Children of the Arbat*, set in the 1930s during the lead-up to the Great Terror but published in the late 1980s under Gorbachev's *glasnost*. Rybakov put the words into the mouth of his fictional Stalin and was allegedly much amused when journalists attributed it to the man himself. There seem to be several reasons for such misattributions. First, so-called 'great men' (less so, 'great women') act as quote-magnets. Thus, any well-articulated observation – *what oft was thought but ne'er so well expressed,* as the poet Alexander Pope put it – ends up being attached to a historically significant figure; the rationale being, 'Whether he said it or not, it's the sort of thing he *would* have said'.

This is notably true of Lenin, Stalin and, no less, Churchill. The 'iron curtain' which Churchill famously referred to in his speech at Fulton, Missouri, in March 1946, and forever associated with him, was in fact a term used by British socialist Ethel Snowden in 1920 after a fact-finding tour of Russia. Earlier still, in 1918, the Russian author Vasily Rozanov had written, 'Creaking and squeaking, an iron curtain is being lowered over Russian history'.

ON THE ROAD

1   *New York Times*, 4 March 2002: 'In Siberia, Serious TV News Fights to Survive' by Sabrina Tavernise.

2   Radio Free Europe / Radio Liberty, 7 July 2000: 'Russia: Regional Television Faces Challenges' by Floriana Fossato.

INTO THE LION'S DEN

1   Quoted by Sidney and Beatrice Webb in *Soviet Communism: A New Civilisation*, published during the mid-1930s in various editions.

2   Television's support for Yeltsin's re-election involved not just favourable coverage, nor even the sort of manipulation practised by advertisers, but downright lies. When Yeltsin had a heart attack on 26 June, a week before the decisive run-off, the television people working for his campaign suppressed the news and announced he had a cold. The effect, when the truth emerged, was to discredit not only the media but the democratic process itself. We are still living with the consequences.

3   Source: David Hoffman, *Citizens Rising; Independent Journalism and the Spread of Democracy*, CUNY Journalism Press, 2013.

4   *The Times of London*, 11 September 1998: 'Television that Battles through the Chaos' by Michael Delahaye.

5   The video clip of Putin saying the words appears in the first part of the television documentary series, *Putin: A Russian Spy Story;* Rogan Productions for Channel 4, 2020.

6   *SLATE, News & Politics,* 9 April 2001: 'I Want My NTV!' by Anne Applebaum.

7   *Moscow Times* (republishing an interview conducted by Russian-language sister paper, *Vedomosti*), March 2000: 'Boris Berezovsky on Putin and Power'. Berezovsky was one of many who would feel the 'Putin backlash'. An oligarch and a member of the Yeltsin inner circle, he supported Putin after his suggestion of Igor Malashenko as 'heir apparent' failed to gain traction. He thought he had the man's measure but, as is often the case with Putin, it was the other way round. Once president, Putin moved to regain full state control of the ORT television channel of which Berezovsky was the main shareholder. Switching sides and now a targeted opponent of Putin, Berezovsky was granted political asylum in Britain, lost nearly all his reputed $3 billion fortune and in 2013 ended up hanging from a shower rail with a lethal ligature round his neck. The UK coroner recorded an open verdict, saying there was no proving beyond reasonable doubt whether Berezovsky took his own life or was unlawfully killed.

CREATING A MEDIA MARKET

1   Open Democracy website, 26 May 2016: 'Happy 25th birthday, TV-2' by Victor Muchnik.

THE 'C' WORD

1   BBC Radio 4, *Desert Island Discs,* 25 April 2003, quoted by comedian Rory Bremner.

2   Confession or, as we journalists prefer, clarification . . . So far

as I'm aware, George W. Bush has never publicly used the word 'truthiness'. It was the late-night TV host Stephen Colbert who jokingly attributed it to him – where it stuck.

3   BBC World Service, Azerbaijan Country Profile, 2002: *Viewpoints*.

ASK THE GOVERNOR

1   International Republican Institute Report on Georgia, February/ March 2009. Survey conducted nationwide by the Institute of Polling and Marketing for Baltic Surveys/Gallup. Sample: 1500. Response rate: 73%.

ALICE IN ABKHAZIA

1   With hindsight, I was selling myself short. I had forgotten that, if only in name and for barely two weeks, I *had* been a war correspondent – in early 1976 during what came to be called the 'Cod War' between the UK and Iceland. It was a centuries-old dispute over who could fish in Icelandic waters, which Iceland kept extending. In a classic David and Goliath showdown, it culminated in British trawlers being escorted by Royal Navy frigates while the Icelanders cut British nets, along with numerous ramming incidents on both sides. For the record, the Icelanders won. My enduring memory is sitting in my Reykjavik hotel room on the night of my arrival in the capital and phoning the Icelandic Foreign Ministry to arrange an interview with the minister. Late though it was, the phone picked up. I explained, supposedly to the night duty officer, the reason for my call. 'No problem,' the voice responded. 'What time do you want to interview me?'

THE UNPREDICTABILITY OF THE PAST

1   For small, impoverished towns that could boast a railway station

or at least a halt, there was a cheaper alternative to a statue: a plaque that read: 'Lenin changed trains here.'

2 President Putin's response re proposals to bury Lenin, addressing a gathering of 500 international journalists attending a Q&A conference, 17 July 2001. He repeated his view on 19 December 2019, at his annual press conference: 'It should be left as it is, at least as long as there are those . . . who link their lives . . . with that.' (TASS news agency translation)

3 Lenin's principle as characterized by his biographer, Victor Sebestyen, in *Lenin: The Man, the Dictator, and the Master of Terror*, published by Pantheon, Knopf Doubleday, 2017. A master of terror though Lenin undoubtedly was, he used it dispassionately, almost clinically, in the service of the Party; unlike Stalin who seems to have relished his ability to inflict it while keeping those around him in constant fear of falling out of favour. During the Great Terror, 1936 to 1938, Stalin would personally go through the lists of names submitted for execution, signing off his assent in red or blue crayon with a cursory 'za' ('approved') and his initials. One doesn't have to be a novelist to imagine how the pearl-handled penknife he used to sharpen the crayons would have become an object of terror in its own right.

KEEP ROLLING!

1 Dmitry Likhachev speaking in 1987.

2 Televised interview with Vitaly Mansky in the first part of the documentary series, *Putin: A Russian Spy Story*; Rogan Productions for Channel 4, 2020.

3 Acting President Putin's midnight broadcast. *New York Times*, 1 January 2000: 'Yeltsin Resigns: The Overview' by Celestine Bohlen.

4   There's an intriguing backstory to Yeltsin's immunity and how far, indeed whether, it extended to The Family. The reporting at the time, and for months after, was split. The *Irish Times* probably came closest to an answer. Acknowledging that Putin's decree was open to interpretation, it cited the exact wording: that Yeltsin would be immune from 'prosecution, arrest, bodily search and interrogation' and that, crucially, the immunity would extend to his 'place of residence, his offices if he continues to work, his vehicles, his means of communication, his baggage and his correspondence'. The fact that all members of the Yeltsin family lived at the same address, the *Irish Times* concluded, meant they were 'pretty safe'. But not totally. Speculation over the prosecution of some family members continued for another nine months until the Russian prosecutor's office announced it had closed a corruption investigation into whether Yeltsin and those close to him had received kickbacks from a Swiss company in exchange for construction contracts, including renovation of the Kremlin. It doesn't take a cynic to point out that it was in Putin's interests to keep the Damoclean sword dangling until he had consolidated his grip on the presidency.

THE GRIP TIGHTENS

1   U.S. Department of Justice Investigation into the Death of Mikhail Lesin, released 28 October 2016: Manner of Death Determined an Accident.

DINNER WITH ZAZA

1   One of the first British journalist-spies to work in post-tsarist Russia was the foreign correspondent Arthur Ransome who, unlikely as it may seem, went on to write the children's classic,

Swallows and Amazons. Covering the October 1917 Revolution, first for the *Daily News* and then for the *Manchester Guardian*, he got close to both Lenin and Trotsky, while reporting back to the British secret service. He got even closer to Trotsky's secretary – and later married her. More recently, the late novelist Frederick Forsyth admitted in his 2015 autobiography, *The Outsider*, and repeated in a follow-up interview for the *Guardian*, that he had sometimes helped MI6 – not as a spy exactly; more as an 'intelligence asset'. He did this when working as a freelance print reporter but never, he insisted, when working for the BBC: 'It was the Cold War ... A businessman might be approached, quite gently, with a courteous, "If you would be so kind to accept an envelope under your hotel door and bring it home . . ." So that was what I did. I ran errands.'

2   For details, see Georgia Media Landscape Assessment, 2021, commissioned by Europe Foundation and conducted by Toby Mendel, Executive Director of Centre for Law and Democracy. Published: Tbilisi 2022. More recently: see report by Georgia's Media Advocacy Coalition, released April 2025, covering Georgian Public Broadcaster's operations from 2017 to 2025.

THE TROUBLESHOOTER

1   *New York Times*, 4 March 2002: 'In Siberia, Serious TV News Fights to Survive' by Sabrina Tavernise.

2   Serendipitously, the six-year delivery time for a Morgan sportscar is echoed by a Soviet joke. Having saved up to buy a car, Ivan is told by the salesman that delivery will be in ten years. 'Morning or afternoon?' Ivan asks. 'What does it matter?' the salesman responds. 'Well,' says Ivan, 'I've got the plumber coming in the morning.'

US AND THEM

1 I was so struck by the Russian take on the television breakfast program that, back in the UK, I suggested to my producer colleague Jenny Clayton that it would make an excellent documentary – entertaining and informative, telling us much about the role of Russian television (this was 2000) while offering a window into the lives of 'real Russians'. Jenny bought into the idea and produced a compelling pitch to sell to commissioning editors. We proposed to base the documentary on the transmission of a single morning program, focusing on a handful of characters – not just the producer and his team but, importantly, some regular members of the audience (male, female, and from different socio-economic strata) to gain an insight into their daily concerns by recording them in their homes, along with their reactions, as the program was going out. When I floated the idea to a Siberian television station, they offered a barter arrangement: to provide their cameras and crews (under our editorial and directorial control) in return for the right to transmit the finished documentary - which would have cut the production cost by half. In the event, we failed to interest a single commissioning editor. Looking back at those turbulent times, I still think it was a lamentably missed opportunity.

2 Lenin, according to his biographer Victor Sebestyen (see above), deplored his compatriots' habit of turning up unannounced. When planning the revolution years earlier in London, he would sequester himself in the Reading Room of the British Museum, away from the 'squabbling émigrés who would pester me . . . in the Russian fashion at all hours'. When in Geneva, he and wife Nadya would enforce strict visiting hours, Tuesday and Thursday afternoons, to stop comrades dropping by whenever they pleased, day or night.

3   Official Kremlin translation of President Putin's televised address to the nation on 24 February 2022, the day Russia invaded Ukraine.

KNOWING ME . . . KNOWING YOU . . .

1   Slava Nikolaev, a reporter/producer who would later work for TV2 in Tomsk, remembers doing an interview in 1969 with the first man in the city to have acquired a pair of Levi's. Such was his celebrity status.

2   BBC website, 5 September 2015: 'Seva Novgorodsev: The DJ who "brought down the USSR"' by William Kremer, BBC World Service.

3   My visit to communist Bulgaria was the only occasion, to my knowledge, that I have been tailed by foreign government agents. At the time, early 1980s, you couldn't visit the country as an individual unless personally invited by a Bulgarian national. Pegasus Tours, then in London's Oxford Street, ingeniously got round this by persuading the manager of a hotel in the capital to invite me, though he made clear that the authorities would know. Disappointingly, my tail turned out to be a single agent. The poor man, having drawn the short straw (Suspect: ex-BBC reporter, allegedly researching novel), made no attempt to hide his activity as he tagged along behind me. It was like taking a reluctant dog for a walk. Wherever I stopped for lunch or dinner, he would sit a few tables away but in line of sight. Within days, we were raising fraternal glasses to each other. Le Carré, it wasn't.

OF ADJECTIVES AND ADVERBS

1   *Moscow Calling: Memoirs of a Foreign Correspondent* by Angus Roxburgh, published by Birlinn in 2017.

THE INCREDIBLE SHRINKING CAMERA CREW

1   Apart from the added workload and responsibility, the reporter who works alone has to contend with one other, unanticipated, downside. It's purely psychological: the need to maintain a distance between oneself and those one interviews, an essential buffer traditionally provided by the cameraman or the producer. One VJ (a video-journalist equipped with a camcorder and laptop) explained to me how often those she interviewed perforce became part of what previously would have been called 'the crew'. She instanced a land dispute when she had found herself having to give a farmer, one of the litigious parties, an on-camera grilling that quickly turned nasty – this, after he had driven her to the location and even helped carry some of her equipment across a boggy field. Such was his reaction when she switched to professional mode that she feared she would have to find her own way back to base.

A MONTH IN THE BALKANS

1   Centuries-old ethnic differences are not of course limited to the Balkans. In 2008, while working in Ireland as a consultant for TG4, the Irish-language television channel, I was shadowing a reporter and cameraman as they shot a story on the Aran Island of Inishmore off the coast of Galway. We needed a taxi to get to the far western side. The driver was noticeably reticent, even hostile. It was only when we came to settle the fare that the reason emerged. I pulled out a couple of euro notes but he refused to handle cash from a hated Brit whom he identified with Oliver Cromwell's merciless subjugation of the Irish in the 1650s. The same went for our cameraman Stuart who was only marginally less hated, being a 'Prod', a Protestant from the North, and so evoking memories of The Troubles as recently as four decades earlier. That left the

reporter Máire Treasa who fortunately was authentically Irish by any measure. But even she was suspect in our driver's eyes on account of being an off-islander from the mainland and so seemingly worthy of a third degree of hatred. It took Máire to point out that her grandmother had been Inishmore-born for him, finally, to accept our money. I was left wondering how exhausting it must be harbouring so much hatred on so many levels. It did, though, give me a better understanding of the various Balkan conflicts.

2   The nostalgia that one came across among the older generation in the former Yugoslavia – the so-called Titoists – was subtly different from that in Russia. What older Russians missed most keenly was the system that had given them a job, an apartment and free healthcare. For the former Yugoslavs, there was an added personal element: memories of the man who had forged their now dismembered multi-ethnic nation, Josip Broz Tito. There was a belated appreciation of the leader who, for all his despotism, had not only stood up to Stalin to ensure the country's postwar non-alignment but, incredibly, had for thirty-five years contained the centrifugal forces of nationalism among its component republics. Tito's likeness, still hanging on so many walls, was a bitter-sweet reminder of a time of peace and stability that perhaps had been taken too much for granted.

THE FÜHRER'S FURBISHER

1   Leni Riefenstahl interview with *Magdeburger Tageszeitung*, 12 December 1935, in specific reference to *Triumph of the Will*.

MY OBJECTIVITY OR YOURS?

1   The 'Osama bin Laden's mouthpiece' slur came about in part

because of a failure by the print media to understand how Arab leaders at the time, reputable and disreputable alike, responded when asked by a TV news outlet for an interview. Rather than submit to a Western-style cut-and-thrust exchange, they would demand the questions in advance and then give their answers in a succession of prepared statements. There would be no follow-up questions, effectively rendering the reporter irrelevant. In that respect, Bin Laden's preferred 'statement to camera' was more honest than a sham interview that brooked no challenge. John Miller, when a reporter for the American ABC channel, tells in *Esquire* magazine of 'interviewing' Bin Laden in Afghanistan in May 1998. Because he wasn't allowed a simultaneous translator (no need, an aide explained, because there'd be no follow-ups), he didn't understand a word of Bin Laden's answers during the hour-long interview. As a result, says Miller, when Bin Laden was threatening America with genocide, 'I'm nodding like an asshole'. I had a similar experience to Miller's when interviewing the Ayatollah Khomeini outside Paris in October 1978 before his return to Iran. His media handler had stipulated a maximum of three agreed questions. After I squeezed in a cheeky fourth which I knew Khomeini would want to answer ('What is your message to the British people?'), we were thrown out on to the street. Our biggest problem then was to find a wall with the same floral paper, against which we could record my 'cut-away' questions (necessary for editing when using a single camera pointing throughout at the interviewee). By sheer fluke, the producer spotted it out the back of the village baker's as we queued for some stuffed baguettes. The helpful proprietor then watched in bemusement as, sitting cross-legged on the cold, flour-dusted floor, I repeated my questions to thin air while the camera rolled.

2   Although I was aware of the BBC's part in the birth of Al Jazeera
    when I started working with the channel in early 2004, the details
    I relate here are mostly drawn from Hugh Miles' comprehensive
    history of the channel, *AL-JAZEERA, How Arab TV News
    Challenged the World*, published by Abacus in 2005; pages 30 to
    36 inclusive. Recommended reading for anyone who wants to
    understand not just Al Jazeera but the vital role of the broadcast
    media in the Middle East. As noted, Al Jazeera was regarded as a
    rogue network in its early days – and there were some among my
    Jewish friends who questioned my decision to work with it. (After
    I was asked by the Jewish community in Oxford to give a talk about
    my travels in the former Soviets, there was uproar when I mentioned
    in passing my work with Al Jazeera. One member of the audience
    complained they should have been given advance warning of my
    'background', likening my presence to that of a member of the
    IRA at a Protestant rally.) There was no denying that the original
    channel, Al Jazeera Arabic, took a Palestinian perspective on the
    Middle East but my view was simple: that if a serious, securely
    financed Arab television channel was prepared to put pride aside
    and admit that it needed help, it deserved a positive response. And,
    without exaggerating our contribution, I believe those of us – a
    dozen or more Thomson Foundation consultants – who answered
    the call succeeded in building on the liberal Western values of those
    BBC-trained journalists recruited by the station at its inception
    (as mentioned in the text). Our message was both aspirational
    and practical: that you will never earn the viewers' trust, let alone
    expand their number, unless you're prepared to show and tell them
    what they'd rather not see or hear. That is how, in the long run, you
    earn a reputation for accuracy and impartiality. The fact that AJ

management were receptive explains in large measure why the Al Jazeera English channel, launched in 2006, can now credibly claim to rival the BBC and CNN as a respected global broadcaster.

3   Martin Bell laid out his views in an article, published by Sage Journals in January 1998, entitled, 'The Truth is Our Currency'.

NEVER MIND THE QUALITY, FEEL THE BANDWIDTH

1   Most of what I write about *Provintsia* on this and the following two pages has been drawn from a report compiled by Internews Russia and Internews Network (USA) for its funders, covering the period June 2001 to July 2004.

HUMAN RIGHTS AND HORRIFIC WRONGS

1   A full transcript of Ambassador Murray's speech to Freedom House, Tashkent, on 17 October 2002, can be found on his website.

2   I got an explanation, of sorts, from *ex*-Ambassador Murray himself via an exchange of emails in July 2025. While admitting to difficulty recalling events more than twenty years on, he said the British Foreign Office, as part of its promotion of human rights, made funds available for HR training, although '*ambassadors were supposed to understand it as window dressing*'. It would therefore seem that, by tapping into a resource routinely available to all ambassadors, Murray sneaked in the training under the Foreign Office radar. That, I stress, is my interpretation.

3   Victor and Yulia Muchnik's powerful, personal response to the closure of Internews Russia was posted on the USAID website. Since, at the time of writing, USAID has been 'dismantled', it can no longer be viewed there – blocked not by the Kremlin but by the current United States administration.

4   For details of the ECtHR's ruling on Russia's foreign agent legislation, see its website, 22 October 2024, 'Judgment concerning the Russian Federation'. The relevant case is *Kobaliya and Others v. Russia*.

5   A video of Rosenberg's interview with Lukashenko can be seen on the BBC website, 20 November 2021: 'Belarus's Lukashenko tells BBC: We may have helped migrants into EU.'

6   Viktor Orban's threat to close down foreign-funded NGOs was reported by the Associated Press, 7 February 2025: 'Hungary's Orban says he will do away with pro-democracy and rights groups receiving U.S. aid.'

7   For FARA's requirements for registration and, specifically, the source of the quote, see press statement, 11 January 2016, released by the United States' Israeli embassy.

8   Source: Kremlin website: 'events/president/transcripts/24034', dated 10 February 2007.

9   A fact that, inexplicably, seems to have gone unnoticed is that Putin and Lenin assumed power as leaders of Russia at the same age, forty-seven. Given this, it's revealing to compare how each handled the 'inconvenience' of democracy. While Putin inherited democracy from Yeltsin, Lenin had cynically supported elections to 'a free parliament' before the Revolution, knowing he was never going to follow through. When, weeks after coming to power, his Bolshevik party polled barely a quarter of the votes in the promised elections, he ensured the subsequent opening session of the new parliament would be a shambles, bringing in his Red Guards to shut it down under the pretext of restoring order. His biographer, Victor Sebestyen, records: 'Russia's first freely elected parliament – the Constituent Assembly – survived for about twelve hours. There would not be another for nearly seventy-five

years.' As Lenin had calculated, the subsequent protests about the assembly's dissolution came mainly from intellectuals. The masses were largely indifferent, enabling him to claim he had respected the will of the people.

By contrast, there's nothing to suggest that Putin craved supreme power during his early career. Rather, it was handed to him, gift wrapped, by Yeltsin and his advisers. Not that he was reluctant to take it, but his strategy regarding democracy has been to bide his time and pick his moment, whether using his United Russia party to dominate the State Duma or the war in Ukraine to censor the media. For both Lenin and Putin, Western-style multi-party democracy would always be anathema. Lenin's answer was speedy abortion; Putin's, slow asphyxiation.

PRIME MINISTER, THAT IS JUST NOT TRUE!

1   A full transcript of the Paxman-Blair interview is on the BBC NEWS website: 'Transcript of Blair's Iraq interview', *Newsnight*, 6 February 2003. The interview itself is also on YouTube.

2   During Saakashvili's presidency, 2004–2013, ownership of Rustavi-2 changed hands an estimated (such is the opaqueness of some of the transactions) *twenty* times. For a brief but illuminating history of Rustavi-2 during this period, see the online article posted by Transparency International Georgia, dated 2 August 2013: 'The TV station of "victorious people": the story of Rustavi 2' by Ana Dabrundashvili.

3   Not only is the cameraman the true hero; he is also the Keeper of the Secrets. Any television reporter (this one included) who is tempted to publicly embroider a story for greater personal glory must reckon with the fact that there is one other person who will know where the porkies are buried. Back in the 1970s, a BBC

colleague was sent to South Africa to report for the program we both worked on. His habitual way of handling pressure was to wash down a couple of Valium tablets with a double whisky. It turned out to be a particularly stressful assignment and by the time he came to record a concluding piece-to-camera at Johannesburg Airport, it was clear he was far from performance ready. 'Not a problem,' he declared. 'All airports are the same. I'll be fine by the time we get to the stop-over at Nairobi.' As indeed he was. At the end of his perfectly executed piece farewelling South Africa, the cameraman slowly panned across the tarmac to the terminal building and the words, WELCOME TO KENYA. The picture editor who viewed the rushes back in London felt no obligation to respect any professional omertà and, to the hilarity of all, conducted multiple viewings. (I am aware, incidentally, of always talking about camera*men*. Of course there have long been camera*women* but during my entire decades-long career I have never worked with one. Regrettably.)

BLESSED ARE THE FILM-MAKERS

1 Eric Johnson's analysis, 'The Media in Tajikistan', appears in the official US Government transcript of a hearing about developments in Tajikistan before the subcommittee on Europe and the Middle East of the Committee on Foreign Affairs, House of Representatives, one hundred third congress, second session, 22 September 1994.

2 Nailya Babayeva's comments, among many others, appear in an illustrated publication produced by Conciliation Resources, London, titled: *A Handbook, Dialogue Through Film.* Downloadable from CR website and recommended.

THE LUXURY OF HINDSIGHT

1 When conducting human rights courses, I've found that one of the snippets that elicits most surprise is the fact that Alexander II emancipated the Russian serfs four years before the United States abolished slavery via the Thirteenth Amendment (1861 and 1865, respectively).

2 President Obama made his remarks on 25 March 2014 during a news conference following a nuclear security summit in The Hague.

3 President Obama made the comments at a news conference in the Oval Office, 9 August 2013.

4 Angus Roxburgh's article appeared in the *Moscow Times*, 27 December 2016.

5 Television address by President Vladimir Putin, 24 February 2022. Official Kremlin translation.

6 Yumashev's quote taken from the first part of the television documentary series, *Putin: A Russian Spy Story;* Rogan Productions for Channel 4, 2020.

7 Gubernatorial elections were restored in 2012 after the mass anti-government rallies in December 2011, the biggest since the fall of the USSR. Such, however, is the mechanism and the way it's been skewed to favour Putin's ruling United Russia party that the power to select candidates and get them elected still lies with the Kremlin.

8 Quote from *Midnight in Moscow*, by John J. Sullivan, published by Little, Brown US, November 2024.

9 See details of Smolina's case, along with others, in online report by BBC Monitoring's Russia Editor, Vitaly Shevchenko: 'Fined for yellow and blue shoes: How Russian laws smother dissent', 21 July 2024.

10   The financial turmoil of the Yeltsin era played its part. One television producer working in Siberia told me how, after the devaluation crisis of August 1998, he wasn't paid for a year. He and his family survived on porridge.

11   The European Parliament described Viktor Orban's Hungary as 'a hybrid regime of electoral autocracy, i.e. a constitutional system in which elections occur, but respect for democratic norms and standards is absent' in a motion passed overwhelmingly on 15 September 2022, blaming in part 'the lack of decisive EU action'.

12   See website of RSF, Reporters Without Borders, and its report on the state of Hungarian media, 2025: 'Prime Minister Viktor Orban has built a true media empire subject to his party's orders. While independent media outlets hold significant market positions, they are subject to political, economic, and regulatory pressures.'

13   By way of a footnote to this updated overview, I should mention the shock closure of Al Jazeera Balkans by its Qatari parent company in July 2025. Based in Sarajevo, the capital of Bosnia and Herzegovina, with regional centres in Belgrade, Zagreb and Skopje, AJB performed an exceptional trans-national public service that covered most of the former Yugoslavia. I conducted workshops for their Sarajevo staff in 2013 and 2018. What impressed me was not just their professionalism but the melding of one-time warring factions. I recall sitting in their newsroom and, looking around, marveling how Serbs, Croats and Bosnians, who only two decades earlier would have been killing each other, were now pooling their journalistic talents to produce arguably the best news service in the Balkans. It's hard to see how and by whom the hole left by AJB will be filled.

ACKNOWLEDGEMENTS

In a reverse of the norm, this book was more fraught in the conception than the birth. When I first started thinking about it in late 2021, my then London literary agent declared there was no longer a market for books about the former Soviet Union. Another UK agent to whom I sent a proposal responded with a publishing aphorism that 'books about journalism are read only by journalists'. So, both wings – the former Soviet Union and journalism – were shot off before the idea got off the ground.

My most heartfelt thanks therefore go to the book's three principal begetters. Roger Bolton, my one-time editor at the BBC and lifelong friend, was the one who, after I had bombarded him over two days in the spring of 2024 with *Tales of the Old Soviets*, urged that, in whatever form, they should be put on record for the benefit of future researchers. Eric Johnson, a colleague from my years working with Internews, was no less insistent that it was a story worth telling and was an invaluable moral support, as well as an unofficial editor, throughout the writing process. And, as much the midwife as a begetter, there was Michael Bollen, owner of Wakefield Press; one of that rare breed of publishers who, if he believes in a book, follows through and sends it out into the world.

Awards for exceptional endurance go to the 'peer reviewers' whom I pressed into devoting hours of their time to reading the entire 300-page manuscript and who, through their comments, suggestions and corrections, contributed so much to the book's final form. In alphabetical order (and in addition to those above) they are: Martin Bell, Dan Bolger, Karol Cioma, Jenny Clayton, David Fickling, Peter Fickling, Irakli Imnaishvili, Zurab Khrikadze, Robin Laurance, David Seymour, Andy Simpson, and Stephen Whittle. Many people double-checked my memory of events dating back more than two decades and, adding their own insights, corrected my mistakes and misinterpretations. The fact that more errors haven't slipped through is due entirely to them. Again in alphabetical order: Natia Abramia, Sally Broughton Micova, Tony Chapman, Jonathan Cohen, Larisa Malinova, Elena Merle-Beral, Glen Mulcahy, Nouneh Sarkissian, Alexey Simonov, Eugene Simonov, and Frank Smyth.

I am indebted to the staff of Internews for their exceptional support throughout my time in the former Soviets: in Armenia, Nouneh Sarkissian (again) and Dan Bolger (again); in Azerbaijan, Whit Mason; in Uzbekistan, Khalida Anarbaeva and Marika Olsen; in Georgia, Zurab Khrikadze (again) and Jano Zhvania. It is a cause of great sadness that those I worked with in the Moscow office of Internews Russia, the legendary Manana Aslamazian and the equally irreplaceable Persephone Miel are no longer with us.

My gratitude and respect are due to those courageous Russians who, after fighting for independent media, now find themselves in exile: Alexander Karpov, the former head of Afontovo TV, Krasnoyarsk, and Victor Muchnik, the former editor-in-chief of TV2, Tomsk. I hope I have done justice to the personal stories they shared with me when I was working with them and in our many subsequent email exchanges.

Working in no fewer than eight of the post-Soviet republics, I was reliant on a succession of interpreters, sometimes for a few hours, other times for weeks and even months. They weren't just my mouth and ears but, on many occasions after a punishing day, my brains too, while also having to act as my fixers. I am indebted to them all. Their names would take up an entire page but there are three with whom I spent most time and from whom, over many hours in planes, trains, majestic Chaikas and beat-up Ladas, I learnt more about life in both the Soviet and post-Soviet Union than from any history book. To Olga Missiri, Irina Rudakova and Oleg Dmitriev, I tender my warmest *spasibo bolshoe*.

Without Ian Masters, the former broadcasting controller of the Thomson Foundation, there would have been no book. It was Ian who, late one Saturday night and desperate to send someone to Siberia, thought to himself, Delahaye might be up to it . . . But for that call and his faith in me, I would have missed out on a wholly unexpected and endlessly engaging twenty-plus years as an international broadcast consultant. My gratitude also to the then director of the Thomson Foundation, the late Gareth Price, whose support I could always count on during what were often challenging times.

Roger Zubrinich, my excellent editor, was the man who found the nuggets among the dross and gave the book the shape I was too close to see. His expertise, patience and good humour made what is often a painful process almost a pleasure.

As always, my wife Anni is due the final and most personal thanks. Not only my first reader and critic ('You *really* want to say that?'), but the one who knew when to leave me alone, indulging my outrageous conceit that creative types produce most when they seem to do least. I plead guilty and will be forever grateful.

INDEX

Republica MOLDOVA
VIZA

NUMĂRUL / NAME
Tipul de viza / Type of visa
Numărul de intrari / Number of entries
Calitation / Localitea / Issued in

Серия: Б
АРЕСПУБЛИКА
АҐӘСНЫ
Гр. _____
Фамилия

REPUBLIC OF UZBEKISTAN

VISA No. 120125
TURI / TYPE   S-2
SAFARLAR SONI / FROM 04.01.2003   DAN / UNTIL 24.01.2003 GACHA
NUMBER OF ENTRIES   1 (one)
ISTIQOMAT MUDDATI / DURATION OF STAY   15   KUN / DAYS
BERILGAN JOYI / ISSUED IN   London
PASPORT RAQAMI   093065395   TARDO / ON 03.01.2003

ВИЗА

ปุปฉ - VISA   0001793   V<UZBDEL
09306539

ԱՆՁՆԱԳՐԻ ՀԱՄԱՐԸ / NUMBER OF PASSPORT   002859808
ԱԶԳԱՆՈՒՆ / SURNAME   DELAHAYE
ԱՆՈՒՆ / NAME   MICHAEL JOHN
ՎԻԶԱՅԻ ՏԵՍԱԿԸ / CATEGORY OF VISA
ԱՅՑԵԼՈՒ ՔԱՆԱԿԸ / NUMBER OF ENTRIES
ԿԵՑՈՒԹՅԱՆ ԺԱՄԿԵՏԸ / DURATION OF
ՏՐՎԱԾ Է / ISSUED ON   08/02/1
ՈՒԺՄԵՋ Է / VALID FROM
ՄԻՆՉԵՎ / UNTIL

КЫРГЫЗ РЕСПУБЛИКАСЫ
THE KYRGHYZ REPUBLIC
ВИЗА / VISA
КИРИП-ЧЫГУУ / ENTRY-EXIT
ДИПЛОМАТЫК / DIPLOMATIC
КЫЗМАТ / ЖӨНӨКӨЙ / OFFICIAL
ОРДИНАРЫ / ORDINARY
ТУРИСТТИК / TOURIZM
ТРАНЗИТ / TRANSIT

РОССИЙСКАЯ ФЕДЕРАЦИЯ
RUSSIAN FEDERATION

ОДНОКРАТНАЯ   01.05.02
ВЕЛИКОБРИТАНИЯ
ДЕЛАХАЙ МАЙКЛ ДЖОН/DELAHAY
06.04.1946   МУЖ   0398067/
КОММЕРЧЕСКАЯ   261
ООО БИЗНЕС ОКЕАН

АZӘRBAYCAN RESPUBLIKASI
18 07 98 6

Single
ENTRY
GOOD FOR
ACCOMPANIED BY
08.11.2000
17.11.200

ВИЗА

К № 3545911
ОБЫКНОВЕННАЯ
ВЪЕЗДНАЯ–ВЫЕЗДНАЯ
Гр. ВЕЛИКОБРИТАНИЯ
Фамилия ДЕЛАХАЙ
Имя, отчество (имена) МАЙКЛ ДЖОН
Дата рождения 060446   Пол МУЖ
С детьми до 16 лет ОДИН
Цель поездки КОММЕРЧЕСКАЯ
В учреждение ООО БИЗНЕС ОКЕАН
основание: 1М459153
В пункта
Действительна для въезда с 090600 ...19...г,
пребывания и въезда до 090900 ...19...г.
через пограничные пункты, открытые для пассажирского движения

ЧУМХУРИИ ТОҶИКИСТОН   REPUBLIC OF TAJIKISTAN
№ 01723
То ду хафта / Till two weeks
Номи хонаводагӣ / Surname   Делайхи Джон Майкл
Ракамипиносма / Passport No   002859808
Навъ / Type   обыкнобен
Вуруд - Хуруҷ / Exit - Вуруд / Entry
Таърихи интиҳо / Date of expiry   17 10 00

საქართველო
GEORGIA
პასპორტის ნომერი / NUMBER OF PASSPORT   002859808
გაცემის თარიღი / DATE OF ISSUE   18 03 99
მოქმედების ვადა / VALID UNTIL   19 06 99
მოგზაურობის მიზანი / PURPOSE OF TRAVEL   ...
ღირებულება / FEE   £19 00
ხელმოწერა / SIGNATURE
შენიშვნა / REMARKS
საქართველო
05-04-1999
GEORGIA

30 დღე VISA
№ 144618
ვიზის სახე / TYPE OF VISA   E-E×/ONE
კატეგორია / CATEGORY
ვადა / DURATION OF STAY   1
BUSINESS
19 03 99
27-03

Выдана 250500 ...19... г.
К паспорту № 002859808

В Ъ Е З Д

Wakefield Press is an independent publishing and
distribution company based in Adelaide, South Australia.
We love good stories and publish beautiful books.
To see our full range of books, please visit our website at
www.wakefieldpress.com.au
where all titles are available for purchase.
To keep up with our latest releases and news,
subscribe to the *Wakefield Weekly* at
https://mailchi.mp/wakefieldpress/subscribe

Find us!

Facebook: www.facebook.com/wakefield.press
Instagram: www.instagram.com/wakefieldpress